Levi's
STADIUM
Unsafe in Any Seat

Would You TRUST Your SAFETY at This Venue?

Levi's STADIUM

Unsafe in Any Seat

Would You TRUST Your SAFETY at This Venue?

FRED WEAVER

An Unauthorized Report Based on a True Story

MILL CITY PRESS

Mill City Press
2301 Lucien Way #415
Maitland, FL 32751
407.339.4217
www.millcitypress.net

For information about special discounts for bulk purchases, please contact Publisher at: Local Phone: 321-345-7724

Book design by Fred Weaver

Editors: Venkat Raman and Gail Ramberg

The Library of Congress has cataloged the printed edition as follows: Weaver, Fred (Fred L.)

Levi's Stadium – Unsafe in Any Seat / Fred Weaver. — First Edition. pages cm

The Internet references cited in this publication were valid as of August 2019. Given that URLs and web sites are in constant flux, the author cannot vouch for their current validity.

If you have comments, lawsuits, suggestions, or death threats, please send them to 650 Castro Street, Suite 120-211, Mountain View, CA 94041

Or email me at: Fred@unsafeinanyseat.com

LCCN: 2019-2019915180

Printed in the United States of America.

ISBN-13: 978-1-54565-909-0

Dedication

—∭—

This book is especially dedicated to:

All the teachers who are dealing with the additional threat of classroom shooters.

All the soldiers who globally put themselves in harm's way providing security for us.

All the police and law enforcement agencies worldwide who are dealing with not only local crime, but global threats hatching locally.

Fred Weaver - Author
Levi's Stadium - Unsafe in Any Seat

Table of Contents

—ɯ—

INTRODUCTION

'Reactive Only' Responses

—ɯ—

9/11

On September 11, 2001, the terrorist group al-Qaeda hijacked 4 American commercial airplanes:

- "The attacks on 9/11, were a series of four coordinated terrorist attacks by the Islamic terrorist group al-Qaeda against the United States on the morning of Tuesday, September 11, 2001. The attacks killed 2996 people and injured over 6000 others. Additional people died of 9/11-related cancer and respiratory diseases in the months and years following the attacks." (1)
- Three of the hijackers flew planes into the two towers of the World Trade Center, and the Pentagon.
- The fourth hijacked plane never reached its intended target and crashed down in a rural Pennsylvania field because the hijackers were overtaken by its crew and *passengers themselves*. The Flight 93 passengers made the ultimate sacrifice. Their heroic selflessness saved countless number of lives.

Elaine Scarry, Harvard University philosopher and author, discussed the following during a March 23, 2014 interview with Kenneth Baker, reporter for San Francisco Chronicle. "In a little book I wrote during the Bush Administration called "Who Defended the Country" I made the point that it was the citizens who brought down Flight 93, whereas the Pentagon couldn't defend itself even with a 55-minute lead time. That our defense has excluded the population is exactly wrong. The reason the population had to be quiet about these things, we were always told, is that we rely on our military to defend us 'in a matter of minutes.' Yet on Sept. 11, when it really was a matter of minutes, it was the people on Flight 93 who gathered information and acted." (2)

Hertz Equipment Rental Blast

On October 31, 2005, San Francisco, California, a blast from an illegal propane filling installation caused a three-alarm fire at the Hertz Equipment Rental facility on South Van Ness Street in San Francisco. This blaze involved 120 firefighters, destroyed a home, and rocketed exploding propane tanks into the surrounding three-city block area. Thankfully there were no fatalities or injuries. I had previously warned the Hertz Equipment Rental staff about this location, and other illegal fueling installations of theirs I was investigating in the San Francisco Bay Area. Unfortunately, they ignored my warning. (*"Blaze ignites propane tanks, sets off explosions."* https://www.sfgate.com/bayarea/article/Blaze-ignites-propane-tanks-sets-off-explosions-2575224.php (3)

2014 Levi's Stadium Near-fatal Assault

On October 5, 2014, at Levi's Stadium in Santa Clara California, minutes after the start of a San Francisco 49er's home game vs the Kansas City Chiefs, a 49er's season ticket holder was brutally beaten by two gang members in a men's room. The beating victim suffered a coma, brain damage, and partial paralysis. None of the Santa Clara Police Department nor any of the visiting law enforcement officers assigned that afternoon witnessed the incident, nor were any of the law enforcement officers positioned to take action. Other 49ers fans had to bring the tragic event to law enforcement's attention for the two assailants to be captured and taken into custody. (*Kiran Patel and Amish Patel v. San Francisco Forty Niners, et al.*, Santa Clara County Superior Court Case no. 115CV286138, (2015) (4)

Stanford Sexual Assault

On January 18, 2015, in Palo Alto, California, a Stanford University student athlete, Brock Allen Turner, sexually penetrated and attempted to rape an intoxicated and unconscious 22-year-old woman. It was only because of two Stanford international students from Sweden, who caught Turner while he attempted to flee the scene as they approached, resulting in the two apprehending and restraining Turner until police arrived to take Turner into custody. (*People v. Brock Allen Turner,* Santa Clara County Superior Court Case no. B1577162, (2015) (5)

Artist Collective Fire

On December 2, 2016, in Oakland, California, a fire broke out in an 'artist collective' warehouse, known as Ghost Ship. A total of 36 people were killed in the fire, the deadliest in the history of Oakland. Multiple factors contributed to these completely preventable deaths, including negligence by the City of Oakland's own Building Inspectors, Police, Fire, and Planning Departments. Police and Fire officials warned that the warehouse was a fire hazard but did not follow through on enforcing the codes already in place. The City of Oakland's Planning Director revealed that the building had not been inspected for three decades. (*IN RE Ghost Ship Fire Litigation*, Alameda County Superior Case no. RG16843631 (2017) (6)

Second Levi's Stadium Near-fatal Assault

On October 7, 2018 following a San Francisco 49ers vs Arizona Cardinals game, a man punched another fan causing great bodily harm including brain damage and the victim becoming comatose. Again, none of the Santa Clara Police Department nor any of the law enforcement officers assigned that day witnessed the incident, nor were any law enforcement positioned to take action. Police asked for the public's help to call with any information. (*The State of California v Gonzales, David Aguilera*, Santa Clara County Superior Court Case No. C1802883, (2018).

November 1, 2018 - Levi's Stadium Assault

On November 1, 2018 at Levi's Stadium in Santa Clara, California, the San Francisco 49ers hosted the Oakland Raiders on a nationally televised Thursday Night Football game. During the beginning of the 3rd Quarter, a savage assault took place between two 49er's fans in the lower level section 119 seats just yards from the field. As the assailant involved in the fight slowly walked up the stairs to the mezzanine, NO ONE at Levi's Stadium took any action, including NFL field security personnel who simply watched the fight in the stands without calling any security or law enforcement. There were over 400 combined and documented, Santa Clara Police Department and visiting law enforcement officers assigned that night. Yet as the assailant slowly tried to escape, not one of those 'sworn to protect and serve' was even aware of the brutal beating incident until a single visiting Oakland Raider's fan put himself in harm's way to contain, restrain and bring the assailant to arrest and custody. (7)

Reactive Only

In each of the above cases the respective authorities were only 'reactive' in their responses to the incidents. In five of the above incidents, it was individuals who took control of the situation, while authorities were either late, non-responsive or were guilty of gross negligence in their duties to 'protect and serve.'

CHAPTER 1

The Lonely Chase

—ɷ—

"If things get any worse, I am going to have to ask you to stop helping me."

The rivalry between the San Francisco 49ers and the Oakland Raiders has existed for years with both teams based in the San Francisco Bay Area. The rivalry known as the "Battle of the Bay" intensified since both teams met during a preseason game back on August 20, 2011.

In previous litigation, after the infamous August 20, 2011, 49ers-Raiders game, according to two lawsuits filed in San Francisco Superior Court, the San Francisco 49ers failed to "pro-actively create an environment that was free from fighting...and gang activity." Statements were taken from San Francisco 49er Hall of Fame quarterback Joe Montana mentioning the team advising 49ers players to keep their families at home during Raiders games because of safety concerns. "Tell your families to sit this one out and watch it on TV," Montana recalled Coach Bill Walsh saying in an interview, "It just wasn't that safe to be around." (8)

Fast forward to the 49ers-Raiders game on November 1, 2018 which was a high profile game for many reasons; it was a nationally televised Thursday Night Football home game for the San Francisco 49ers, it would be the last "Battle of the Bay" contest played against the rival Oakland Raiders, who recently decided to move their team to Las Vegas, Nevada.

San Francisco 49ers and the Oakland Raiders games are notoriously sold out events with the stands filled to capacity and at 68,500, Levi's Stadium has the 16th largest of 31 total NFL stadiums seating capacity in the National Football League. According to *Pro Football Reference*, for that night on November 1, 2018, there were 69,592 in total attendance, including credentialled national and local new media.

In the weeks prior to the game, there were published print and news media reports by the 49ers and the Santa Clara Police Department of 'stepped up' (9)(10) security during the game at Levi's Stadium.

On typical game days, according to an October 26, 2017 *ESPN* video interview with NFL Chief of Security Cathy Lanier, "Local police are the lead agency for every game throughout the season. A typical game requires at least 10 different agencies, from the FBI to private security." (11)

The Santa Clara Police Department (SCPD) has stated that for a typical NFL game, eighty officers are assigned to work at Levi's Stadium.

SCPD Captain Tony Parker would later confirm in a November 10, 2018 phone conversation with me, "there were well in excess of 400 (four hundred) law enforcement officers working the game," the night of November 1, 2018.

––––––––––

On November 1, 2018, I attended the San Francisco 49ers nationally televised Thursday Night Football game at Levi's Stadium against longtime rivals Oakland Raiders along with my daughter.

I am a season ticket holding Oakland Raiders fan who travelled to Levi's Stadium for the game and my daughter and I were dressed in black and silver Raiders gear.

The game began at 5:20 P.M. and the tickets we purchased were located on the visitor's side of Levi's Stadium.

Before the halftime break, the 49ers score was a lead of 17 - 3 over the Oakland Raiders, yet 49ers fans were viciously attacking *other* 49ers fans.

At two minutes into the start of the third quarter of the game, after returning from the main concourse food court, we noticed a savage and brutal fight starting below us, between two San Francisco 49ers fans in lower field section 119.

San Francisco 49ers fan Vincent Crain was being brutally attacked by another San Francisco 49ers fan, Steve Gonzales Guardado. We had a clear view of the attack since we were sitting in upper middle of section 221.

During this attack, we witnessed the assailant punching the victim with repeated strikes to the head that caused the victim to fall over backwards, helpless as both of his feet were caught between the seat uprights. Crain' head struck the ground and Guardado continued the brutal attack by punching him several more times in the head.

Alarmingly, dozens of fans and on-field NFL security wearing yellow and red vests, watched this savage attack for almost two minutes without anyone taking any action against the assailant or to assist the victim. NFL Field Security, and Santa Clara police officers and all other law enforcement officers, and security staff failed to respond and or intervene in the attack.

During the brutal attack on Crain, no law enforcement officers, or security were present anywhere near lower section 119. None of those responsible who swore to 'Protect and Serve' as law enforcement and security were anywhere in the vicinity of where Crain was attacked. In fact, no 49er security, SCPD or any other law enforcement officers were present *anywhere* on the eastern side of Levi's Stadium. There was no security staff or law enforcement staff to observe or to diffuse the situation or stop the assault on Crain. That means there was also no one available to ensure the safety of other fans attending the game, seated near the victim Crain.

Since no law enforcement or security staff were visible anywhere in the stadium, I sensed something was horribly wrong. I decided to intervene and rushed down the steps to intercept the assailant as he slowly left the scene of the attack. He ascended the lower level seat stairs upwards toward the shared main concourse mezzanine, in his attempt to escape.

I worked my way down from my seat in the upper section and intercepted Guardado at the top of the section 119 stairs. This was a shared connection to the main concourse. There was a woman on the main concourse, in black 'security' attire, and I was yelling very loudly at the top of my lungs for this security member to call police and or backup. She was trying to work some sort of clicking device, as I continued screaming for her to get backup or help. As the assailant and his smaller companion wearing a dark #80 San Francisco 49ers jersey started walking across the main concourse, I intercepted and confronted Guardado and told him to stop. The security woman then got in front of me and begged me not to hurt either of the two 49ers fans. The assailant and his companion continued to walk toward the outer perimeter of the main concourse, counterclockwise northward toward the stairs leading to Levi's Stadium northeast exit gate 'F'.

As I was closely following the assailant Guardado, on the outer mezzanine and just before descending the Levi's Stadium northeast exit gate 'F' stairs, I briefly encountered a Santa Clara Police Department officer, positioned counterclockwise to the stairs less than 20 yards away. I yelled at the top of my lungs at him, "Give me some fucking help and arrest this guy, he just beat up and severely hurt another 49ers fan!" The officer looked directly at me, noticed I was limping, and also saw that I was wearing a black Oakland Raiders jersey. He literally, and physically turned his back on me. I was limping due to excruciating pain having to chase the assailant Guardado three quarters of the length of the stadium in attempt to keep him from hurting any other attendees. (The pain in my hip was from 'bone on bone' loss of cartilage over the last few years, for which I underwent pre-scheduled surgery exactly fifteen days later for a full right hip replacement.)

My daughter and I continued to closely follow the assailant, and when he and I reached the northeast stairway, his smaller companion, grabbed me and tried to keep me from following them. My daughter and I continued following Guardado and his companion down the stairs, while yelling loudly for help, and I was finally recognized, and heard by a 'visiting' (the officer's words) uniformed California Highway Patrol (CHP) officer, who was just outside the exit gate 'F' close to the light rail train tracks.

I screamed, "Look at his fucking hands. He just beat the hell out of another 49ers fan!" The CHP officer grabbed Guardado, and a couple of Santa Clara Police Department officers finally surrounded the assailant and his companion. The officers handcuffed him as he glared and mouthed something at me. My daughter and I then gave individual accounts to one of the arresting SCPD officers.

It took over five minutes from our initial observation of the assailant's attack on the victim until Guardado escaped the area and reached the main concourse.

It took approximately another 10-15 minutes while I took the actions discussed above that finally led to the arrest of Guardado by the SCPD.

In total, there was a 15-20 minute period of time, as documented in the four separate Police Reports I obtained, (12)(13)

(14)(15) when no law enforcement officers or backup security were visible, posted, operating, managing, controlling, maintaining, inspecting or surveilling the entire east side of the San Francisco 49ers' home stadium, known as "Levi's Stadium."

However, as documented in a local *KNBR* news report and video, several on-field NFL field security personnel watched this savage attack between these two people for almost two minutes without taking any action in any way. They didn't call ahead for law enforcement or other security to act as backup, and they didn't make any attempt to assist the victim. (16)

The next morning, November 2, 2018, I drove to the City of Santa Clara Police Department with additional information and backup to assist with the previous evening's arrest of the assailant. I was met by three SCPD officers and spoke to the officers through the glass while standing in the lobby side. I provided copies through the glass of our seating tickets along with a marked-up Levi's Stadium overall seating diagram from the November 1, 2018 game, detailing the area from where we observed the vicious attack.

That same morning, I also travelled to the City of Santa Clara's administrative offices with additional information and backup hoping to assist and discuss the events of the previous evening, with City of Santa Clara Attorney Brian Doyle. I was met by two city administrative clerks, and I spoke to them over the counter. I requested a meeting with the mayor and city attorney regarding the incident I witnessed. I was told by the clerks that the mayor and city attorney were not available.

What I didn't realize on that morning, was that while I was trying to help resolve the incident, the City of Santa Clara Police Department would be filing false police reports to cover up my involvement regarding the incident and attack the night before.

You are about to read the chain of events leading to the 'cascading failure' resulting in the dangerously inadequate security at Levi's Stadium.

CHAPTER 2

How Media Shapes Policy

—ᴍ—

Rachel Carson

" **R**achel Carson's 1962 publication of her book *Silent Spring* helped launch the environmental movement and spurred a nation to question its role in altering the environment through chemical means.

Silent Spring (17) awakened a nation to the detrimental health and environmental consequences of DDT (dichloro-diphenyl-tri-chloro-ethane). The title for *Silent Spring* came from the book's apocalyptic vision of the long-term ecosystem destruction caused by indiscriminate spraying.

The book became pivotal in shaping policy on toxic chemicals because (this) environmental event had both a real-world impact and mass media appeal. The media attention garnered by Rachel Carson's book led to national awareness and concern for the toxics issue involved. Consequently, policy makers developed environmental toxics policies to respond to the public's heightened concern.

Silent Spring warned mainstream America about the dangers of DDT, a persistent, toxic chemical that would threaten public health and the environment for years to come. The book outlined

8

how DDT disrupts the natural ecological balance by accumu-
lating in the food chain and harming non-target organisms such
as birds, fish, and perhaps even humans." (18)

DDT became the pesticide of choice for agriculture after its
first mass use in World War II. (19) Following the 1945 approval
of DDT for civilian use, farmers frequently applied the chemical,
already known to be toxic, throughout the country (20) Over the
next thirty years, approximately 1.35 billion pounds of DDT was
used domestically. (19)

As early as the mid-1940's, scientists began warning people
about the possible effects of DDT. (19) Not until, *Silent Spring*,
however, did the general public become aware of the risk. *Silent
Spring* had an immediate and profound impact on public opinion
regarding DDT.

"One of *Silent Spring's* lasting effects is that it brought into
the consciousness of the public and the government the notion
that no chemical should be assumed "safe." Carson's book helped
shape toxics policy because the potential health effects of DDT
addressed in *Silent Spring* left people questioning the safety of
the environment around them. It had a real-world impact because
at the time of *Silent Spring's* publication few people were immune
from coming in contact with the DDT-tainted environment. The
chemical industry vehemently opposed *Silent Spring*, spending
more than $250,000 ($2.1 million in 2019 dollars) in a publicity
campaign against Carson and her book. The subsequent debate
and media attention surrounding the book further fueled the public's awareness of the potential environmental and health problems DDT created. This convergence of factors helped ignite the
environmental movement, shape toxics policy, and led to EPA's
banning of DDT." (18)

Ralph Nader

Paralleling Rachel Carson's warning, Ralph Nader cautioned the public about automobile safety issues. He is acknowledged as the man most responsible for alerting the nation to the need for more comprehensive auto safety laws.

"Ralph decided that auto safety was of interest to him when some friends of his had been victimized by unsafe cars."(21) "Frederick Condon was a Harvard Law School classmate of mine and at age 28 with a wife and four children, he was driving home from work in New Hampshire one evening and the car rolled, there were no seatbelts in those days, he was half in half out on the road and he became a paraplegic," recounted Ralph. "And on his own as a freelance journalist Ralph wrote an article for *The Nation Magazine* in 1959 about designed-in dangers of automobiles, a totally novel topic at the time." (21)

"In the '50's, Ford Motor Company put a 'safety package' on the road, in 1955 and 1956. It had a lap belt, a padded dashboard, a padded sun-visor, these were all optional equipment. That safety package was extremely popular. But then General Motors got infuriated and called up Henry Ford II and said, "If you don't get rid of that package, we're going to undercut you and put you out of business!" Henry Ford II decided they would drop the safety package. It wasn't that safety didn't sell, they couldn't supply enough safety belts for this, it was that the program had been cut off by the auto executives" (21)

"Behind it all was they didn't want the Federal regulators telling them how to build the car in terms of safety," Ralph Nader noted.

"There were people that were being needlessly burned and killed in vehicle crashes. Ralph Nader said, "No, this is something that is preventable." People knew that automobile accidents had been occurring for decades. What they didn't know was this was a systemic issue." (21)

Then in 1965, Ralph Nader published *Unsafe at Any Speed* (22), "which became an immediate bestseller but also prompted a vicious backlash from General Motors (GM) who attempted to discredit Nader by tapping his phone in an attempt to uncover salacious information. When that failed, they hired prostitutes in an attempt to catch him in a compromising situation. Nader, by then working as an unpaid consultant to United States Senator Abraham Ribicoff, reported to the Senator that he suspected he was being followed." (23) Nader received calls at odd hours of the night. Two private detectives tailing Ralph approached several of his friends and asking multiple sources if Nader smoked pot and if he was gay.

After Nader's book *Unsafe at Any Speed* was published, and just before he was to testify before Congress about auto safety, the big three automobile companies were contacted and asked about the surveillance on Ralph. Ford Motor said, "it's not us.". Chrysler was called and said, "It's not us." But, at the Congressional hearings, under questioning by Senator Abraham Ribicoff and Attorney General Robert Kennedy, General Motors CEO James Roche, when placed under oath, admitted that GM had ordered an investigation on Ralph Nader in an attempt to obtain dirt and besmirch Ralph Nader's character. (24) Ribicoff then allied with consumer advocate Ralph Nader in creating the Motor Vehicle Highway Safety Act of 1966, which created the National Highway Traffic Safety Administration. The agency was responsible for many new safety standards on cars. (24)

Erin Brockovich

Years later, a seemingly unconventional event may be included with these other policy-shaping events namely the movie *Erin Brockovich*. (25) Based on a true story, *Erin Brockovich* dealt with how one company contaminated a small Californian desert town's water supply with chromium 6. (25)

At first glance some may question whether a movie could have any legitimate effect on toxics policy. Change, however, can and does come through alternative vessels. Many parallels can be drawn between the impact of *Erin Brockovich* on toxics policy and the other policy-shaping events. (25)

As with *Silent Spring,* the environmental phenomenon depicted in the movie *Erin Brockovich* inspired fear and concern in the public psyche. The story began in Hinkley, California, a town of roughly 3,500 residents, located 120 miles northeast of Los Angeles. (26) Hinkley is also home to a natural gas compressor station belonging to Pacific Gas & Electric Company (PG&E), a Californian utility that is an affiliate of one of the world's largest energy companies. (27) In the 1980's, residents of this small San Bernardino County town began complaining that PG&E's compressor station had polluted their drinking water supply with chromium 6. (27)

PG&E built the Hinkley compressor station in 1952 as part of a pipeline system that brings natural gas into PG&E's service territory. (28) The natural gas flows through a pipeline from the Texas Panhandle to California and then throughout much of the state, fueling heating systems and power plants. (27) As the natural gas moves through the pipeline friction causes the gas to lose pressure. (29) Compressor stations like the one in Hinkley force the gas back up to a higher pressure to facilitate transmission. (29) During this process oil and water cool the gas compressor. (29) To prevent rust from corroding the cooling PG&E uses a corrosion inhibitor. (30)

Chromium 6 is one of the cheapest and most efficient commercially available corrosion inhibitors and was used by PG&E in their compressor stations. (30) Unfortunately, chromium 6 is also a highly toxic and a suspected carcinogen. (30) PG&E used chromium 6 as its corrosion inhibitor. (26) PG&E disposed 370 million gallons of chromium-tainted water into open, unlined ponds around Hinkley from 1952 to 1966. (31)

In 1987, during an environmental assessment, PG&E discovered that the chromium had migrated into Hinkley's groundwater supply, contaminating ten private drinking wells with chromium 6 concentrations exceeding the state standard. (32) Some Hinkley residents claim that PG&E knew of the chromium 6 contamination as early as 1965 but told no one. (33)

This book

The title for my book, *Levi's Stadium - Unsafe in Any Seat* is a variation of the title of Ralph Nader's book, *Unsafe at Any Speed*. My book is intended to be a different type of warning to mainstream America about the dangers of stadium security resulting from multiple recent near-fatal assaults on fans at Levi's Stadium, plus a recent vicious beating and attack on a fan I personally witnessed while attending an NFL football game there on November 1, 2018. Levi's Stadium in Santa Clara, California is home of the San Francisco 49ers, which has now become the most dangerous venue to attend in North America. And similar to the publication of Rachel Carson's *Silent Spring* and Ralph Nader's *Unsafe at Any Speed,* even before this book was published there had been a coordinated effort to keep me from bringing this dangerous lack of security at Levi's Stadium to the attention of the general public.

I was warned by more than one attorney about the publishing risks of *Levi's Stadium - Unsafe in Any Seat*. I was told by publishing the book, I may incur significant liability arising from Levi's Stadium, the NFL and maybe other's allegations of "trademark infringement" and "defamation", among other claims.

Trademark infringement is likely to be alleged because the cover of the book prominently features the Levi's Stadium name, which may be judged to cause "consumer confusion" about the source of the book. The provocative nature of the book coupled with the financial size and power of the San Francisco 49ers and the NFL makes it likely that I could be sued for a litany of reasons. The book includes literary portraits of, and observations about, Levi's Stadium, the San Francisco 49ers owners and corporate officers, the NFL personnel, and each of their attorneys. Defamation could be alleged because these portraits and observations may be judged to be false statements that injure the reputation of San Francisco 49ers, the NFL or its agents. In addition to the above causes of action, I was told I may also be liable for other causes of action, including but not limited to, invasion of privacy torts, business torts, and punitive damage claims.

Due to the size of the National Football League (revenue for 2018 currently total approximately $8.1 billion), my book could potentially cause significant damage to the NFL's reputation, financial status, and future. The San Francisco 49ers may also allege that I could cause them tens of millions of dollars in damages. The attorneys giving advice also wanted me to understand that if, or more likely, when, the San Francisco 49ers and NFL sue me regarding my book, they may be able to physically stop publication prior to the resolution of the lawsuit through a "preliminary injunction," which, if granted, could stop publication immediately pending the outcome of the trial. Finally, I was told to consider the risk involved in publishing my book, remembering that San Francisco 49ers and especially the NFL have significant resources. When the San Francisco 49ers and NFL choose to sue me, they have millions of dollars to spend on lawyers' fees and costs.

After listening to all of the above concerns, I would ask the San Francisco 49ers and NFL to total up all the costs and let me know what value they come up with. And then I would ask the San Francisco 49ers and NFL, "What is the cost of a human life?"

And to my readers, I made the decision to publish the book that you are now about to read. The first human life lost at Levi's Stadium will finally expose the 'cost' of Levi's Stadium's dangerously inadequate security.

I hope this book serves as yet another warning and wake up call.

CHAPTER 3

A Quietly Escalating Issue for the NFL

—⁓—

D ue to ongoing dangerously inadequate security at Levi's Stadium, a recent pair of personal injury attacks resulted in comas. In the case of a 49ers season ticket holder Kiran Patel, this resulted in brain surgery and partial paralysis.

A Chicago Tribune October 28, 2016 article states, "Officials at NFL headquarters dispute that games are unsafe or any perception that stadiums are anything but family-friendly. Behind the scenes, however, the league puts a high priority on controlling fan behavior and identifying possible trouble spots. Certain venues seem to be hotbeds for police activity, particularly in parking lots, where oversight is not regulated by the league office and where alcohol consumption goes largely unmonitored." "If you are concerned about bringing your family to a game, then that is an issue," said Amy Trask, a former executive with the Raiders who has served on the NFL's security committee. "It's not just an issue for one team, it's an issue for all 32 teams. The teams know this. The league knows this." (34)

With all of the recent world-wide violence, terrorism, random attacks, school shootings, and hate crimes, one of the last places you might expect injury or near-fatal attacks would be an NFL game or music concert. The NFL has confirmed women now makeup 45 percent of the fan base. It is important for women to understand, they are just as likely to become innocent victims of vicious and violent attacks at these stadiums.

At any stadium, there is an assumption of security by the attending sports fans or concert goers. However, that security may be insufficient or non-existent, putting a visiting fan at increased risk of violence during attendance at one of these venues. And due to the lack of security at Levi's Stadium, visiting fans and patrons are literally 'taking their life in their own hands', and should make an informed decision about whether to invest so much money to attend games and other events with such an increased risk of harm.

Prior to the near-fatal attack on Kiran Patel that resulted in a coma, brain surgery and partial paralysis, all of the 49ers entities, the City of Santa Clara and the Santa Clara Stadium Authority had specific knowledge of reports of more than 500 recent prior assaults and fights, all of which were criminal acts, over the recent previous three years at San Francisco 49ers home games. And yet the NFL tries to avoid any discussion of the quietly escalating issue of fan and gang violence at Levi's Stadium and other teams' stadiums as well.

One of the reasons is that NFL signed a $1.5 billion-dollar deal with beer maker Anheuser-Busch InBev, which will allow Bud Light to stay on as NFL's official beer sponsor through the 2021-2022 season as part of a new deal with the league that gives Anheuser-Busch InBev expanded marketing rights. We are trying to help them sell beer and the way they can do that is to leverage the NFL to the most avid fans in sports," said Renie Anderson, the NFL's senior VP of Sponsorship and Partnership Management, in an interview. "Bud Light can still only use the team logos if it has an individual sponsorship deal with the teams. The brand has such deals with 28 of the 32 NFL teams." (35)

Court filed depositions in personal injury lawsuits expose a conflicting view of the NFL benefits of their billion-dollar beer sponsorship. Even though every NFL team greatly benefits financially from its Anheuser-Busch InBev sponsorship, "It's a challenge for the entire NFL right now, the amount of drinking that happens in stadiums," stated ex-Santa Clara Police Sergeant Ray Carreira during his deposition in the civil lawsuit involving the alcohol-induced near-fatal beating of Kiran Patel. (36)

"It's rough out there," said Bill Smith, a Bay Area attorney who, on behalf of the man who suffered a brain injury in an assault at Levi's Stadium in 2014, has sued the 49ers. "It's alcohol and bravado, and when you add gang activity, which we have, it's a deadly combination." (34)

CHAPTER 4

"Jerry...remember Jerry? It's a lawsuit about Jerry"

—⚏—

"Life is tough. Life is tougher if you are stupid"
- Iconic western film actor, John Wayne

NFL Football Commissioner Roger Goodell said, "It is our responsibility to meet the standards of the NFL, and to make sure people who attend Super Bowl or any of our events have a positive experience." (Roger Goodell deposition statement in the Class Action lawsuit, *Steve Simms, et al., vs. Jerral "Jerry" Wayne Jones, National Football League, et al., 3:11-cv-00248-M, 2011, Dallas*) (37)

"Public officials have a duty of responsible administration that consists of three elements. It requires that officials articulate reflectively the policies and principles that govern their work. It demands that they monitor the activities of peers and subordinates to induce compliance with these policies and principles. And finally, the duty mandates frequent reassessment of these policies and principles in light of the officials' own experience and that of comparable institutions." (*2016 The Duty of Responsible Administration and the Problem of Police Accountability*) (38)

"Principles...of *comparable institutions*."

Quite a while ago someone else had a similar concept and legal use for 'comparable institutions.'

Louis Brandeis, a Supreme Court Justice from 1916 to 1939, achieved recognition by submitting a case brief, later called the "Brandeis Brief", which relied on expert testimony from people in other professions to support his case, similar to present day cross-industry innovation, thereby setting a new precedent in evidence presentation. The Brandeis Brief is still regarded as a pioneering attempt in combining law and social science.

"In 1907, Florence Kelley and Josephine Goldmark hired Louis D. Brandeis to represent the state of Oregon in (*Muller v. Oregon, 208 US 412, 1907*), a case before the US Supreme Court that involved the constitutionality of limiting hours for female laundry workers. To support his argument that overwork was inimical to the workers' health, Brandeis with the help of Goldmark, his sister-in-law, compiled a number of statistics from medical and sociological journals and listed citations to the articles in his brief. The brief was significant in that it was the first one submitted to the Supreme Court that relied primarily on extra-legal data to prove its argument. Not only did the brief help Brandeis win the case but it also became a legal landmark in its own right. Briefs that cited non-legal data quickly became commonplace and became known as "Brandeis briefs." However, the brief for Muller v. Oregon is the original Brandeis Brief." (39)

Brandeis also held that government officials be subjected to the same rules of conduct that are commands to the citizen.

Principles...of comparable institutions. This is exactly what Supreme Court Justice Brandeis achieved recognition for over one hundred and ten years ago, and is now called, 'cross-industry innovation.' Applying cross-industry innovation to safety and security at football stadiums and concert venues, one could think about the automotive industry. And think about protective caps and seals on consumer goods. Maybe think about the airline industry? And one might even consider thinking about amusement parks. All comparable institutions? All potential candidates for 'cross-industry innovation'?

NFL Commissioner Roger Goodell unwittingly utilized a 'cross-industry innovation' when faced with a public relations predicament. When Dallas Cowboys owner Jerry Jones made a chaotic attempt to install unsafe and unsecure temporary seating just to break a Super Bowl attendance record, Roger and the National Football League brought in the Walt Disney amusement park folks to help with the public relations aftermath.

On February 6, 2011, the Super Bowl XLV (forty-five) was held in Dallas, Texas hosted by the Dallas Cowboys at their AT&T home Stadium. Ten days prior, the press reported that an additional 13,000 temporary seats were installed to accommodate Dallas Cowboys owner Jerry Jones's goal of a record-setting game day crowd of 150,000. Installation of the temporary seats was not completed prior to game time. The Dallas inspectional authorities wouldn't allow Jerry Jones's hastily put together seating to be used due to safety and security concerns.

Both the NFL and Jerry Jones knew about the seating crisis since January 30th, one week prior to the most important NFL football game event of the year. Approximately 2,800 total fans were affected, and their seats were not available. The NFL and AT&T Stadium decided not to allow the affected fans to enter the stadium. Instead, they were placed in a fenced-in holding area with no restrooms.

According to subsequently filed class action lawsuits, in addition to numerous fans who specifically purchased tickets to Super Bowl XLV, this episode would affect hundreds of the Dallas Cowboys' best season ticket holders known as the 'Founders' of Cowboys Stadium who also had trouble. Each of the 'Founders' paid at least $100,000 per seat for a personal seat license at Cowboys Stadium, which the Cowboys and Defendant Jerry Jones represented would entitle them to the "best sightlines in the stadium" and the right to purchase a ticket to Super Bowl XLV at face value. Most of the 'Founders' fans arrived at the stadium on that Sunday to discover that Jones and the Cowboys had assigned them to seats with obstructed views and temporary folding chairs, which had been installed in an effort to meet Jones' goal of breaking the attendance record. In addition, almost all of these seats lacked any reasonable view of the stadium's prized "video board," which Defendant Jerry Jones and the Cowboys routinely claim is one of the most unique and best features of Cowboys Stadium.

Additionally, over 2,400 of these ticket holders, were unreasonably delayed, relocated or completely displaced from their seats, which were deemed unsafe and unusable. For example, approximately 864 ticket holders arrived at the February 6, 2011 Super Bowl game and, after being identified through a scanning process, were told that there were problems with their assigned seats at Cowboys Stadium and that personnel were looking for different seats in which to relocate them. Ultimately, these individuals were provided with different seats than they had anticipated--seats which were inferior in location and/or quality than the ones that these ticket holders had previously purchased and/or acquired.

Furthermore, a subset of this group comprising approximately 400 ticket holders were completely displaced from their seats in the end zone at Super Bowl XLV as a result of the incomplete installation of temporary bleachers, which were deemed unsafe and unusable. Accordingly, these approximately 400 ticket holders were denied seats to the game altogether and were forced to watch the game on monitors in the Miller Lite Club, where they had no view of the field whatsoever.

The following are highlight questions and answers taken verbatim from NFL Commissioner Roger Goodell's Deposition in the related Class Action Complaint.

August 9, 2013 - VIDEOTAPED DEPOSITION OF ROGER GOODELL (40)

CIVIL ACTION Case No. 3:11-CV-00248 M
Consolidated with Case No. 3:11-CV-00345 M

Attorney for Plaintiffs – All questions (Q.)

Roger Goodell – National Football League (NFL) Commissioner – All Answers (A.)

Q.   "Why was it determined that you needed to bring in Disney to instruct the NFL on how to deal with its fans? Did you need Disney to come in and tell you that in general you shouldn't put your fans in a fenced-in area when the seats aren't available?"

A.   "Disney has some very positive things about dealing with their customers. We wanted to implement that in the NFL."

Q.   "It's your responsibility as the leader of the NFL, the CFO if you will, to ensure that various tasks that are important to the league are in fact getting done...right?"

A.   "It is my responsibility at the end of the day."

Q.   Are you aware of the fact that thousands of NFL fans who appeared for the Super Bowl, Super Bowl 45, and discovered that their seats were not available, are you aware that they were put in a fenced area outside of the stadium for a lengthy period of time? Do you think Mr. Suovitz (NFL Head of Events) made the right decision when he decided not to allow the fans whose seats were not available to enter the stadium, and instead to put them in a fenced-in holding area with no bathrooms?

A.   "I can't speculate on that."

Q.   "Have you caused anyone to lose their jobs over the failures in connection with Super Bowl 45 temporary seats?"

A.   "No. I have not."

Q.   "Have you ever seen a single document that described in any way what went wrong and what needs to occur to make sure it never happens again? A report as to what went wrong in connection with Super Bowl 45 and the temporary seating issues, have you seen a report or not?"

A.   "I don't know about document...what we have to do is make sure they don't happen again, so we make changes to our procedures."

Q.   "Why is it that you never contacted Jerry Jones before kickoff and impress upon the fact that if these seats were not installed properly, that the (NFL) 'shield' was going to be tarnished and it was going to be an embarrassment to the league? You do recall having a number of communications in the days leading up to the game and on the day of the game relating to the Super Bowl attendance record, correct?"

A.   "With who?"

Q.   "With Jerry Jones."

A.   "I don't recall having it on the day of the game, but I did have discussions with him about that, yes."

Q.   "Mr. Jones expressed to you on a number of occasions prior to the game that he was intent on breaking the Super Bowl attendance record; is that true?"

A.   "I don't know if I would characterize it that way. I know he said that publicly, that he would like to have more people at the stadium than any other prior Super Bowl."

Q.   "We've already agreed that leading up to the Super Bowl, Mr. Jones was not bashful about making it known that he wanted to break the attendance record of Super Bowl 45. My question is, did you ever attempt to dissuade Mr. Jones from breaking the Super Bowl record in connection with Super Bowl 45?"

A.   "Mr. Jones at that point didn't have much control over the attendance. The number of people
in the stadium were going to be the number of
people in the stadium. We had credentials (personnel including the media and league and team
officials). Whether they were counted or not, that
was going to be clearly stated -- that was my position – including the people outside – is that we
needed to announce those as separate numbers."

("Jerry Jones wanted to announce one big number
and not explain it."- Deposition Exhibit 160)

Q.   "When JJ called about the attendance, meaning
Jerry Jones, did you happen to say to him: Hey,
Jerry I appreciate you calling me about attendance, but we've got bigger fishes to fry here. We
got fans that are coming to the Super Bowl, our
biggest event of the year, that aren't going to have
any seats."

A.   "As I said earlier to you, I don't even remember
if I spoke to him about this issue."

Q.   (Deposition Exhibit 161), is an, "NFL statement on
options to be offered to fans without seats at Super
Bowl 45, for immediate release. Commissioner
Goodell has initiated a complete review of the
matter, including all seating and stadium entrance
issues to determine where the breakdowns
occurred, period. Did I read that correctly?"

A.   "Yes."

Q. "During your communications with the 32 owners in the days and weeks following Super Bowl 45, did any of those owners' express anger to you about what had happened with the temporary seat issues at Super Bowl 45"

A. "They were not happy that we had let our fans down."

Q. "Well, I'm assuming you communicate with a number of them on a fairly regular basis. Is that an accurate assumption?"

A. "Fairly regular basis, yes"

Q. "Okay. They're like a board of directors, and you're similar to a CEO. Is that a fair characterization?"

A. "It's a broad general characterization, but yes"

Q. Did any owner, Mr. Goodell, ever express to you that Mr. Jones's attempts at breaking the Super Bowl attendance record has left the league with a black eye or otherwise tarnished the 'shield'?"

A. "I don't recall that."

Q. "Do you think that Mr. Jones's interest in breaking the Super Bowl attendance record contributed to the temporary seat issues that we've been discussing here today?"

A. "I do not."

In the complaint, attorney for the plaintiffs argued that the Cowboys and the NFL "engaged in a failed and reckless attempt to maximize revenue and attendance at Super Bowl XLV and, in the process, betrayed the trust of many of its most loyal fans."

In 2015, the plaintiffs prevailed against the National Football League after a two-week jury trial in Federal District Court in Dallas, Texas after obtaining a court order requiring Dallas Cowboys owner Jerry Jones to attend trial and be cross-examined.

On the most important NFL football game of the year, with a seating crisis known for over a week, NFL Commissioner Roger Goodell didn't even talk with Dallas Cowboys owner Jerry Jones on the day of the Super Bowl which Jerry Jones was hosting. Roger Goodell stated on public record, "I don't even remember if I spoke to him about this issue."

The NFL spent more than $20 million in attorney's fees connected to these Super Bowl XLV cases.

The day after the Super Bowl, Dallas Cowboys owner Jerry Jones described the issue as a seating "error."

To this day, NFL Commissioner Roger Goodell has never published a complete review of the matter, including all seating issues to determine where the breakdowns occurred in order to keep it from happening again.

Goodell and the NFL didn't realize at the time that they were possibly on to something about cross-industry innovation, by utilizing an outside industry such as Disney to help smooth over the public relations aftermath of Jerry Jones's seating publicity stunt. Unfortunately, and although unwittingly, this is one of the last known documented attempts by the NFL to benefit from any 'lessons learned' outside their own cloistered and protected orbit.

CHAPTER 5

"Honey you really knock me out"

—⟋⟍⟍—

"Smile, you're on Candid Camera!"

The following is an abtract from the January 8, 2015, Robert S. Mueller "Report to the National Football League of an Independent Investigation into the Ray Rice Incident." (41), Attorney Robert Mueller was brought in to investigate the NFL's mishandling of the incident. The entire report can be found at: https://www.nytimes.com/interactive/2015/01/08/sports/football/document-robert-s-mueller-iiis-report-on-ray-rice-domestic-violence-case.html

———

Report to the National Football League of an Independent Investigation into the Ray Rice Incident (Abstract)

EXECUTIVE SUMMARY

In the early morning hours of Saturday, February 15, 2014, the Atlantic City Police Department responded to a report of an incident in an elevator at the Revel Casino Hotel in Atlantic City, New Jersey. Less than an hour later, the officers arrested Raymell Rice, then a Baltimore Ravens football player, and his then-fiancée Janay Palmer. Rice and Palmer were released that morning, each having been served with a complaint-summons to appear in the Atlantic City Municipal Court. Rice's complaint- summons charged him with assault "by attempting to cause bodily injury to J. Palmer, specifically by striking her with his hand, rendering her unconscious, at the Revel Casino."

Six weeks later, on March 27, the charge against Rice escalated to an indictment for felony aggravated assault against Palmer. That same day, prosecutors announced that charges against Palmer had been dismissed.

In May, Rice pleaded not guilty and applied for the New Jersey Pretrial Intervention program, which affords "opportunities for alternatives to the traditional criminal justice process of ordinary prosecution." On May 20, a New Jersey Superior Court judge approved and signed the pretrial intervention order, which postponed the criminal proceedings for one year, with the charges to be dismissed if Rice complies with the terms of the order.

On June 16, Commissioner Roger Goodell of the National Football League met with Rice, Palmer (who had by that time become Rice's wife), and others to discuss the incident and potential discipline of Rice under the League's then-existing Personal Conduct Policy.

Following that meeting, Goodell informed Rice by letter on July 23 that he was "suspended without pay for the Ravens' first two regular season games ... [and] fined an additional $58,824."

Then, on September 8, TMZ released the in-elevator video, and the public saw for the first-time footage of Rice striking Palmer at the Revel on February 15. That same day, the Ravens terminated Rice's contract and the League suspended Rice indefinitely. Both the Ravens and the League stated that they had not seen the video before its public release.

"We have identified the investigative steps that the League took in the wake of the Rice incident, steps that reflect the League's longstanding practice of deferring to law enforcement—a practice that can foster an environment in which it is less important to understand precisely what a player did than to understand how and when the criminal justice system addresses the event. In this case, that deference led to deficiencies in the League's collection and analysis of information during its investigation. We conclude that there was substantial information about the incident that should have put the League on notice of a need to undertake a more thorough investigation to obtain available evidence of precisely what occurred inside the elevator. Had the League done so, it may have uncovered additional information about the incident, possibly including the in-elevator video prior to its public release." (Page 3)

The League's investigation was limited, but it possessed substantial information suggesting a serious event

31

had occurred inside the elevator that the League should have further investigated. (Page 6)

That information did not provide the graphic detail that the in-elevator video depicted, but it should have put the League on notice that a serious assault had occurred and that it should conduct a more substantial independent investigation. (Page 6)

Our investigation identified a number of investigative steps that the League did not take to acquire additional information about what occurred inside the elevator. (Page 7)

But the League might well have received that information through more persistent and thorough communication with ACPD (Atlantic City Police Dept.) (Page 7)

Thus, had the League undertaken a more substantial investigation, it may have gathered available information about the incident, possibly including the in-elevator video prior to its public release. (Page 7)

Summary of Recommendations

Our findings demonstrate the weaknesses inherent in the League's longstanding practice of deferring to the criminal justice system with respect to the investigation of facts and the imposition of discipline under the Personal Conduct Policy. (Page 8)

The League has begun to address this fundamental issue in its revised Personal Conduct Policy, announced on December 10, 2014. Importantly, in the future, the League will conduct independent investigations in appropriate cases. We recommend that the League consider additional steps (Page 9):

- Expand the Security Department by adding supervisory resources;
- Adopt investigative guidelines for its investigations;
- Enhance its policies to assure information sharing between clubs and the League

B. Relevant League Policies and Procedures

It is important to understand the League's then-existing Personal Conduct Policy and its approach to investigations. (Page 11)

The then-existing Personal Conduct Policy governed all persons associated with the NFL. (Page 11)

Under the standard of conduct, "discipline may be imposed" in several circumstances, including, for example, "criminal offenses including, but not limited to, those involving: the use or threat of violence; Other examples of impermissible conduct included "conduct that imposes inherent danger to the safety and well-being of another person" and "conduct that undermines or puts at risk the integrity and reputation of the NFL, NFL clubs, or NFL players." (Page 11)

The League adopted a new Personal Conduct Policy on December 10, 2014. (42) (Appendix # 1)

With respect to repeat offenders, the Commissioner may impose discipline on an enhanced and/or expedited basis. In such cases, the timing and nature of the discipline will be determined by the Commissioner based on several factors including but not limited to: the severity of the initial charge and later charge; the facts underlying the later charge; the length of time between the initial offense and later charge.

Our longstanding policy in matters like this – where there is a criminal investigation being directed by law enforcement and prosecutors – is to cooperate with law enforcement and take no action to interfere with the criminal justice system. (Page 43)

- The League has long-standing relationships with law-enforcement authorities, which are extremely important to the League in the areas of stadium and event security. (Page 53)
- Finally, deference to law-enforcement officials is a byproduct of the fact that senior management in League Security has traditionally been made up of former law-enforcement officials. (Page 53)

We recommend that the League make clear that the information-sharing obligation, including for the clubs, is an ongoing one. (Page 65)

In the wake of yet another public relations nightmare, "the NFL named Cathy Lanier its Senior Vice President of Security in 2016 following Robert Mueller's investigation into the league's mishandling of the Ray Rice case." (43) Cathy Lanier was previously the Chief of Police for Washington D.C. (44)

Four years after the Ray Rice incident, another ugly assault involved Kansas City Chiefs star running back Kareem Hunt. In a hotel surveillance video, Kareem Hunt is shown knocking over and kicking a woman while she was laying on the ground. Once again, the video was released by TMZ. In both domestic violence assault cases the NFL was unable to obtain the videos before each of the videos was released by the news source, TMZ.

In 2014, Ray Rice knocked his then-fiancée, Janay Palmer, in an elevator—and the NFL said it had not heard of a video that was eventually found by TMZ. The league only reacted sternly once those horrific images from that elevator surfaced. But what happened with Rice was supposed to change everything. At least, that's what we were told. But now we have Hunt's actions of February 2018, and, again, a league with enormous financial and investigative resources was outhustled by TMZ. What we do know is the NFL utilizes a private army full of ex-cops, FBI agents and former investigators. And yet TMZ could get this tape but a billion-dollar league couldn't? "We again as a league look like amateurs on this issue," one NFC team executive told *Bleacher Report*.

"But it is totally fair to wonder if the NFL didn't want to find a video. The league's history has lost it the benefit of the doubt on that." (45)

In a December 10, 2018 interview NFL's new Senior Vice President of Security, Cathy Lanier stated, "We knew that there's video that we had to get our hands on to get the real story." (43)

Just over a month before Cathy Lanier made that statement in her December 10, 2018 interview, a different type of assault incident had occurred, at Levi's Stadium, which I witnessed. This time, the NFL and Cathy Lanier had possession and complete control of all the video of the assault they needed. However, the NFL, Cathy Lanier, the San Francisco 49ers, and the City of Santa Clara Police knew about, and made sure these videos—potentially damaging to each of their reputations—would *never* surface.

CHAPTER 6

Levi's Stadium Security -
"How do you work
this thing?"

—ɯ—

"There was more to this than meets the eye," - from the
southern rock group 38 Special song, "Teacher, Teacher"

In a December 11, 2015 ICMA online article, City of Santa
Clara Police Chief Mike Sellers states that, "Santa Clara Police
Department has one of the smallest law enforcement agencies
in the country to protect an NFL stadium." (46) And according
to the Santa Clara Police Officer's Association website as of
March 2019, it has 144 dedicated sworn members. The Santa
Clara Police Dept. hires additional law enforcement officers on
49ers game days from nearby communities including Sunnyvale,
and also pulls from the Santa Clara County Sheriff's Dept. and
the California Highway Patrol. Police Chief Michael Sellers continues, "In turn, this model has also strengthened relationships
between the Santa Clara Police Department (SCPD) and federal,
state, and local law enforcement jurisdictions." (46)

During an October 26, 2017 interview with *ESPNW.com*
NFL Security Chief, Cathy Lanier says, "The local police (Santa

Clara Police Department) are the lead agency for every game throughout the season. A typical game requires at least 10 different agencies, from the FBI to private security." (47) According to the SCPD, 80 police and law enforcement officers are assigned to a typical San Francisco 49er's home game. As referenced on the Levi's Stadium website, "Levi's Stadium has an extensive security plan in place that utilizes both private security and the Santa Clara Police Department personnel." The 'private' security currently utilized by Levi's Stadium is Landmark Event Staffing Services. On November 10, 2018, I had a phone with Santa Clara Police Captain Tony Parker where he confirmed, "the Santa Clara Police Department have 'tactical command' for 49ers' game-day security at Levi's Stadium."

Levi's Stadium is the third newest stadium in the National Football League. The San Francisco 49ers, the Santa Clara Police Department and multiple news and vendor sources have claimed Levi's Stadium cameras and security system to be 'high tech' and 'state of the art.' An October 26, 2016 *American Security Today* article states Levi's Stadium made a "unanimous decision to opt for Genetec 'Security Center' the unified security platform which combines video surveillance, access control... and other business systems in one intuitive solution." (48)

According to Lou Pezzola, Director of Security Systems (for Levi's Stadium), "Security Center was a great security platform for all aspects of our environment, but unification was the most significant advantage for our team because we can carry out every task in a single platform."

Levi's Stadium also, "selected Veracity's COLDSTORE due to its high reliability and large capacity, which allowed the stadium to economically store video archives for longer periods of time." According to Veracity's website, their Surveillance Storage System product COLDSTORE "is a network attached Sequential Array designed specifically for today's video surveillance systems which need very high capacity storage for megapixel IP cameras and/or long archive periods. Designed from the ground up for IP video surveillance, this sequential storage system achieves the following unique features: Massive 2101:B capacity using around 60 watts - a 90% power saving versus RAID; Very high disk reliability even using the lowest cost disk drives available; No data loss on disk failure, with no rebuild required, and simple disk hot-swap; Sequential filing system (SFS™) uses hard disks sequentially for easy location of data." (49)

Lou Pezzola continues in the *American Security Today* article, "Security Center has been instrumental in helping our team identify suspects and monitor their whereabouts through the stadium, which ultimately (leads) to arrests and prosecution."

Alarmingly, however, even though Levi's Stadium spent millions of dollars on installing a high capacity, high reliability, sequential video surveillance and storage security system, the Santa Clara Police Department does not implement, know how to use, are not trained on, or benefit from this high technology 'real time cameras' and security system. As a first line of defense, the Santa Clara Police Dept does not utilize the highly sophisticated installed security system at all. Instead of using this camera and security system, the Santa Clara Police Department defaults to relying on 'unreliable' delayed social media uploads and posts.

During a 2017 deposition in the Kiran Patel near-fatal assault case, the defendant Santa Clara Police Dept. admitted to analyzing social media posts instead of utilizing Levi's Stadium's high technology cameras and security system. In his police report filed November 1, 2018 by Santa Clara Police Dept. Staff Sergeant Alex Torke (50), Officer Torke reports he was working detail at Levi's Stadium as an investigator and relied on a video posted to Instagram involving the victim being severely beaten by assailant later identified as Steve Guardado. And as defendants in other recent personal injury court cases, the City of Santa

Clara Police admit in multiple court filed depositions and their own police reports of relying on social media including Twitter and Facebook postings.

Maybe this explains the comment made by Lou Pezzola Director of Security Systems for Levi's Stadium, "Due to the complexity of our system, it is best served by the folks that know the system better than us." (48)

However, depending upon who the 'voice' is that day for the Santa Clara Police Dept., there are sometimes different communications about the Levi's Stadium camera and security system. Sometimes they say the system is far too complex to use, and other times they say it's great. Like this quote, "To identify the person and apprehend them is just fantastic work, and it's the type of luck we have continuously have at the stadium, given the stadium's technology, and the security personnel," said Capt. Wahid Kazem, spokesperson for the Santa Clara Police Department, (in reference to assailant Steve Guardado). (51)

It is quite interesting that police spokesman Capt. Wahid Kazem speaks so highly about a security system the City Santa Clara Police Department did not even use on November 1, 2018.

CHAPTER 7

Two times Zero equals Zero

—⚭—

"All animals are equal, but some animals are more equal than others." A proclamation by the pigs who control the government in the novel *Animal Farm*, by George Orwell. (52)

The misuse, misunderstanding, and ineptness of utilizing Levi's Stadium's multi-million dollar installed security system wasn't the Santa Clara Police Department's only struggle. Even before the opening of Levi's Stadium on July 17, 2014, they were dealing with their own issues unrelated to their incompetence of providing security at the stadium.

Moneeb, Ikram and Ikram v City of Santa Clara, Mike Sellers, et al., **United States District Court (ND CA 2015), Case no. 5:15-cv-01987-NC** (53)

According to a civil lawsuit filed October 19, 2015, on February 10, 2014, three Santa Clara police officers wrongfully entered and illegally searched the home of Mohammad Moneeb and Mohammad Ikram. Mr. Moneeb and Ikram just happened to be law enforcement officers of the United States Department of

Homeland Security. The police officers had no warrant to enter the home, no consent, and no legal justification to do either. The SCPD demanded information about a $300 camera.

Family members of Mohammad Moneeb and Mohammad Ikram protested and recorded the wrongful conduct during the illegal entry and unreasonable search of their property. Moneeb subsequently visited the SCPD station to request a police report regarding the February 10, 2014 incident and complained about the conduct of Police Sergeant Henry, Officer Peter Stephens, and Officer D. Bell.

In retaliation for Moneeb's complaints, SCPD Detective Sergeant Ray Carreira, (now Global Security Manager for Facebook), Sergeant Henry, Officer Bell, and Officer Stephens then wrongfully procured a search warrant by judicial deception to illegally search Mohammad Moneeb's, home for the camera. The search warrant was unlawful and lacked probable cause. It was also based on deliberate false statements made by Detective Sergeant Ray Carreira to the judicial officer who issued the warrant. "They did not inform the court that the Plaintiff is a federal law enforcement officer who had never threatened anyone, particularly any Santa Clara officers." (54)

On March 27, 2014, SCPD Officers Carreira, Bell, Stephens and thirteen other officers then entered and unreasonably searched Moneeb's residence for the second time. The raiding SCPD officers arrested, detained, assaulted, battered, and used excessive force against Moneeb and Ikram, the other resident of the home. The police officers had no objective, reasonable information that Moneeb and Ikram posed any danger or threat whatsoever. Sergeant Ray Carreira and the raiding SCPD officers arrived in a convoy comprised of unmarked police vehicles, marked police vehicles, motorcycles, a helicopter and other vehicles. Some of the police officers wore battle dress uniforms, and carried assault rifles and other long guns, as well as bringing police dogs.

Moneeb and Ikram were in their car, when the SCPD officers struck their vehicle as they arrived, and then removed Mr. Moneeb and Ikram from the car. Although Moneeb posed no threat to anyone, obeyed the officer's orders and was totally compliant the entire time, the raiding police officers held him at gunpoint and took him forcefully to the pavement. The police forced him onto his stomach, where several of the officers, including Detective Ray Carreira, roughly restrained him using a "figure-4" control on his legs, as well as a control on his arms and shoulders, which caused Moneeb excruciating pain. One of the police officers also forcefully pressed his knees on Moneeb's head. At no time did Moneeb resist. Police then handcuffed Moneeb and placed him in a police vehicle.

Without a legal and justifiable warrant or probable cause, the SCPD arrested and took Moneeb to the Santa Clara County jail where he was booked and held in custody until the next day.

Additionally, Mohammad Ikram posed no threat to anybody, obeyed the police orders and was completely compliant the entire time. The Santa Clara police officers held Ikram at gunpoint and ordered him to sit on the pavement in front of his driveway. At no time did he resist. After seizing him, the police officers handcuffed Ikram very tightly, photographed him and forced him to sit on hard ground for approximately 3 and one-half hours while the City of Santa Clara police ransacked their home.

The city of Santa Clara police used a battering ram to break down the front door of Moneeb and Ikram's house, despite the fact that Moneeb and Ikram were being held in their front yard and were available to provide a key. The police destroyed various items during the raid. This included squeezing out and emptying entire tubes of toothpaste and deodorant and ransacking the laundry room. The raiding police officers threw a copy of the Koran and other religious writings on the floor, leaving them strewn about for Moneeb and Ikram to find when they were eventually able to re-enter their home.

The city of Santa Clara police caused Moneeb to be maliciously prosecuted by providing false information to prosecutors and withholding and concealing information. Despite the SCPD lack of probable cause to do so, the sixteen Santa Clara police officers caused Mohammad Moneeb to be prosecuted for violation of receiving stolen property. Moneeb did not qualify for a public defender and was forced to hire a criminal defense attorney at a significant cost to him and his family. The criminal charges were resolved on December 18, 2014, when the Superior Court of the State of California for the County of Santa Clara dismissed all charges against Mohammad Moneeb in the interests of justice.

Mohammad Moneeb and Mohammad Ikram were deprived of the following clearly established and well-settled constitutional rights protected by the First, Fourth, and Fourteenth Amendments to the U.S. Constitution.

   a. The right to be free from unreasonable searches and seizures as secured by the Fourth Amendment to the U.S. Constitution;

   b. The right to be free from excessive and unreasonable force in the course of arrest or detention as secured by the Fourth Amendment to the U.S. Constitution;

   c. The rights to be freed from malicious prosecution as secured by the Fourth Amendment, and to petition the government through the courts for redress of civil rights violations and to exercise rights including speech and expression, without retaliation, malicious prosecution, or denial of equal protection of law as secured by the First and Fourteenth Amendments to the U.S. Constitution; and

d. The rights to Equal Protection of the Laws as secured by the Fourteenth Amendment to the U.S. Constitution.

These unconstitutional actions were pursuant to the following customs, policies, practices and procedures of the Santa Clara Police Department and the city of Santa Clara, which were directed, encouraged, allowed, and ratified by Santa Clara Police Chief Mike Sellers, and other policy making officers for the Santa Clara police department.

The Santa Clara mayor and councilmembers had direct knowledge of the facts of this incident. The policy makers for the SCPD were and are aware of a pattern of conduct and injury caused by their law enforcement officers but failed to discipline the culpable law enforcement officers. Those policy makers also failed to institute new police procedures and policy within the SCPD.

In 2016, the city of Santa Clara paid out a $500,000 settlement to the Moneeb and Ikram families for multiple illegal searches of their home by the SCPD. None of the City of Santa Clara police officers or Chief of Police Mike Sellers were ever disciplined for their actions in this incident.

Danielle Harmon v. City of Santa Clara, City of Santa Clara Police Chief Mike Sellers, et al., **United Stated District Court (ND CA 2016) Case no. 5:16-cv-04228-EJD (55)**

According to another civil lawsuit filed July 27, 2016, five Santa Clara police officers once again wrongfully entered and illegally searched the home of a resident, without a search warrant.

On April 12, 2016, at about 5:00 p.m., at 1450 Emory Street, San Jose, California, at the request and initiation of Santa Clara Police Officer Mark Shimada, Detective Sergeant Gregory Hill, Officer Mitchell Barry, Officer Peter Stephens, and Officer Greg Deger, wrongfully entered and searched the home of Danielle

Harmon. The SCPD Officers demanded to know the whereabouts of Danielle's fifteen-year-old daughter, Jazmyne, who the officers stated they were coming to arrest for a possible crime that had happened at Jazmyne's school on April 4, 2016. These officers had no warrant to arrest Jazmyne or anyone else in Harmon's home. The officers had no warrant to enter the Harmon's home, no consent, and no legal justification to do so. Danielle Harmon had committed no crimes and behaved peacefully and lawfully throughout the incident. SCPD Officer Hill kicked in Harmon's door, illegally forcing their into the home, and then the five Santa Clara police officers illegally searched it.

In the course of this illegal entry, and Danielle Harmon's protest of it, Officer Barry, assisted by Officer Hill and Stephens, grabbed Danielle and very forcefully threw her through her doorway, slamming her into a rock and mortar outcropping on her porch, and shattered both the rock and Danielle's left leg. Danielle Harmon never threatened the officers, and the officers had no justification to use any force against her.

The sequence of events started on April 4, 2016, when Danielle and her daughter Jazmyne, spoke with SCPD Officer Shimada regarding a fire that happened at Santa Clara High School earlier that day. Officer Shimada later reported that he lacked probable cause to arrest Jazmyne at that time, and that he had no intention to detain or arrest Jazmyne. Several minutes into the conversation, he began to accuse Jazmyne of setting the fire. Danielle Harmon immediately stopped the conversation asserting her daughter's right to counsel and right to remain silent. She told Officer Shimada that he could not speak to Jazmyne without an attorney present. Danielle and her daughter left the meeting.

The next day, April 5, 2016, based on a rumor at school that there was a warrant for Jazmyne's arrest, Danielle Harmon called the SCPD and was told that there was no warrant for her arrest.

Later that day, April 5, 2016, Danielle was driving near Santa Clara Central Park looking for Jazmyne when she noticed a police car driven by Officer Shimada. He appeared to be following her. Danielle pulled into a 7-Eleven parking spot and turned off her car's engine. Officer Shimada and another officer pulled up behind her car to block her from leaving. He then knocked on her car's window. Danielle did not feel free to leave as he was blocking her car. Officer Shimada had detained Danielle Harmon without any legal cause. She exited her vehicle and Officer Shimada asked her if she had called him. She informed him she had not called. He then demanded to know where her daughter was. She informed him that she did not know where Jazmyne was. He informed her in an angry tone that if he saw Jazmyne, he would arrest her. Danielle Harmon informed him that she and her daughter had obtained counsel and he could not talk to Jazmyne without counsel present.

Over the next several days, Officer Shimada had a number of conversations with Jazmyne's attorney, Brendan Barrett, concerning the SCPD investigation of the fire. On April 6, 2016, Barrett met with Officer Shimada at the SCPD, and informed him that the SCPD did not have probable cause to arrest Jazmyne, and therefore, Jazmyne would not surrender to the authorities at that time.

According to court documents, Officer Shimada then went on personal vacation from April 7 until April 12, 2016. Neither Shimada, nor any other police officer or member of the SCPD or other law enforcement authority ever made any effort whatsoever to secure an arrest warrant for Jazmyne at any time.

On April 12, 2016, Officer Shimada falsely told Santa Clara Police Officer Hill, the leader of the SCPD's tactical "Special Enforcement Team" (SET), that Danielle Harmon was uncooperative, adversarial, and confrontational. He requested that Officer Hill and his SET arrest Danielle's daughter in her home, without a warrant. The violations of Danielle Harmon's rights and Danielle's injuries were initiated and set in motion by the conduct of Officer Shimada.

The decision of officers Shimada, Hill, Barry, Stephens, and Deger, to immediately arrest Danielle's daughter in Harmon's home without a warrant and to do so forcefully should Danielle Harmon continue to assert her and her daughter's constitutional rights, was in retaliation for Danielle Harmon's previous assertion of her and her daughter's constitutional rights that Officer Shimada and his fellow police officers chose to construe as "uncooperative, adversarial, and confrontational." These rights include the right to counsel, the right to remain silent, and the rights to be free from unreasonable entry of her home and unreasonable seizure of her daughter without probable cause and a lawful warrant.

At approximately 5:00 p.m., on April 12, 2016, SCPD officers Hill, Barry, Stephens, and Deger arrived in plain clothes, in unmarked cars, at Danielle Harmon's home. Upon Officer Shimada's request and initiation, the other police officers, acting as the SCPD Special Enforcement Team, intended to arrest Jazmyne in her home without a warrant. Danielle was in her front yard when she noticed several large young men in street clothes walking up the street from a neighbor's house. Not realizing they were police officers, she entered her home and shut the door.

Officers Hill, Barry, Stephens, and Deger, arrived at the home moments later and began to pound on Harmon's door demanding to be let in. Danielle told Officer Hill that she wanted to see a warrant. Officer Hill replied that they did not have a warrant. Danielle informed him, "then you are not coming into my house." Officer Hill then said that, "you either let us in or we break down the door." Officer Deger, started to go around the side of the house to the backyard, at which point Danielle yelled through the closed window that there was a gate to the backyard, and he did not have her permission to enter.

While she was on the phone with her daughter's attorney, Danielle Harmon informed Officer Hill that her attorney advised her that he could not enter the house without a warrant. Officer Hill replied, "Tell him it's fresh pursuit", which the attorney heard him say because the phone was on speaker phone. The SET leader, Officer Hill, later wrote in his police report that he along with the other Santa Clara police officers knowingly broke down the door, forcefully entered the home, and arrested Danielle's daughter without a warrant, because they concluded that they were in "fresh pursuit" from the school incident that happened over eight days earlier, and during the investigation of which, the lead investigator, Officer Shimada, had gone on a five day vacation.

Officer Hill next told Danielle to step back because he was going to kick the door down. When he did so, Danielle put her hand up and pushed the door away so that it would not hit her. Once inside, officers Hill and Barry grabbed her by the shoulders, assisted by Officer Stephens and threw her in a flipping motion from the kitchen over the threshold of the kitchen door, smashing her ankle into a stone pillar, and breaking both her leg and the stone pillar. Danielle immediately felt extreme pain, and told the officers "you broke my leg, it's broken." Officers Barry and Stephens handcuffed her when she was on the ground crying out in pain. One of the officers told her to calm down, but once he looked at her ankle, he could see that it was obviously twisted and severely fractured. Officer Barry stayed near her, searched her pockets and read a piece of mail she had in her pocket at which point Danielle asked him why he was reading her mail.

Although Danielle Harmon posed no safety threat, while the officers went into her home, she was handcuffed with her arms behind her back and was in extreme pain. She was held in custody, handcuffed, for several minutes. The Santa Clara police officers found Jazmyne, upstairs taking a shower, and arrested her without a warrant. Officer Hill later reported that Danielle was released at the scene. She was then transported by ambulance to a hospital.

Acting as integral participants, each with fundamental involvement in the violations of Danielle Harmon's rights described herein, officers unlawfully entered Harmon's residence, damaged and/or destroyed her personal property, and unlawfully searched her property without a warrant or other legal cause. The Santa Clara police officers subjected Danielle to wrongful seizure and arrest without reasonable suspicion or probable cause. The officers also subjected Danielle to the use of excessive force in the absence of any immediate threat, the absence of any objectively reasonable information that she had committed any crime, and in the absence of any unlawful resistance by Danielle. There was no need to use any force against Danielle Harmon under these circumstances.

At all times during Danielle Harmon's contact with the officers, she behaved peacefully and lawfully. She never possessed or displayed any weapon, nor did she threaten anyone in any way. Further, she never resisted a lawful order and never attempted to escape (although she was never wanted for any crime).

The force used by the Santa Clara police officers Hill, Barry, and Stephens against Danielle was at a very high level, caused very severe injuries, and was unjustified and objectively unreasonable under the circumstances.

The officer's entry, search of the home, and seizure of Danielle's person and property were unreasonably executed and were unlawful from the start. The City of Santa Clara police officers kicked down the front door of the house. The officers unreasonably destroyed property during the entry and search. This included breaking a stone pillar on the porch with Harmon's leg.

Santa Clara's City Attorney, Brian Doyle said, "...there was no dispute that the plaintiff sustained a broken ankle in the course of the entry to the plaintiff's home without a warrant." (56)

Danielle Harmon required medical treatment for her injuries the police officers caused, including multiple surgeries, and she incurred those medical bills. Once again similar to the illegal search of Mohammad Moneeb's home, none of the Santa Clara police officers or Chief of Police Mike Sellers were ever disciplined for their actions in this incident.

"Our officers' actions were fully within the law and in accordance with accepted police practices," said Chief Mike Sellers in a prepared statement. (57)

Less than five months later, after unconstitutionally kicking down the second of two residents' front doors without a warrant, the Santa Clara Police Officers Association wrote a September 2, 2016 letter to the San Francisco 49ers and its CEO Jed York. The SCPOA summarize their letter at the end by stating, "The men and women of the Santa Clara Police Officers Association are sworn to protect the rights of ALL people in the United States, a duty we take very seriously." (58)

CHAPTER 8

September 2, 2016 - SCPOA letter to Jed York

—ɯ—

T he attached letter below was sent by the Santa Clara Police Officers Association to Jed York of the San Francisco 49ers regarding their quarterback Colin Kaepernick.

Santa Clara Police Officer's Association

P.O. Box 223
Santa Clara, CA 95052
Phone: (408) 243-COPS
"Courage – Honor – Commitment"

Mr. Jed York   September 2, 2016
San Francisco 49ers
4949 Marie P. DeBartolo Way
Santa Clara, CA 95054

Mr. York,

The members of the Santa Clara Police Officers' Association (SCPOA) have a long history of working with the San Francisco 49ers organization. This relationship was greatly expanded with the construction of Levi's stadium. Our officers and 49er employees have worked incredibly well together to create a safe and enjoyable environment for guests and employees. This partnership has made Levi's stadium the premier sports venue in the world as evident in the extremely successful Super Bowl 50 operation.

Unfortunately, some recent actions by a 49ers employee have threatened our harmonious working relationship. On August 26, 2016, prior to the start of the 49er pre-season football game at Levi's stadium, on duty 49er employee Colin Kaepernick made the decision to exercise his right of free expression and not stand to honor the National Anthem. This expression caught the attention of the media. Following the game, your employee explained to the media that his actions were an attempt to get public attention to the oppression of African Americans and minorities in the United States by police officers. Your employee then insinuated that police officers are being placed on paid leave for murdering minorities. This statement is obviously insulting, inaccurate and completely unsupported by any facts.

On August 28, 2016, at 49er training facility in Santa Clara, Mr. Kaepernick again made the allegation that police officers are getting paid to murder people. Your employee further insulted all law enforcement officers in America by stating, "There is police brutality. People of color have been targeted by police." Mr. Kaepernick then made inaccurate and untrue statements about the level of training that is required to be a police officer.

On August 31, 2016, it was learned by the members of the SCPOA that the 49er organization has been allowing Mr. Kaepernick to wear exposed socks with the image of a pig wearing a police hat during practices at the training camp in Santa Clara. Photos of Mr. Kaepernick wearing these socks with the derogatory image have been broadcast nationally.

Our membership acknowledges that police officers are human and are not perfect. However, blanket statements that police officers in general, murder minorities is completely false and insulting to the dedicated men and women in law enforcement agencies across America.

These intentional acts and inflammatory statements by Mr. Kaepernick are insulting to the members of the SCPOA. It is apparent, that the 49ers organization is aware of Mr. Kaepernick's actions. These actions have occurred while Mr. Kaepernick was acting as an employee of the 49ers and at 49er facilities in Santa Clara. The 49ers organization has taken no action to stop or prevent Mr. Kaepernick from continuing to make inaccurate, incorrect and inflammatory statements against police officers, which include members of the Santa Clara Police Officers

September 2, 2016 - SCPOA letter to Jed York

Association. Furthermore, your organization has made no statement disagreeing with Mr. Kaepernick's accusations. It is the unanimous opinion of the SCPOA that the 49ers organization has failed to address your employee's inappropriate workplace behavior. The board of directors of the Santa Clara Police Officers Association has a duty to protect its members and work to make all of their working environments free of harassing behavior. SCPOA members have worked thousands of hours at Levi's stadium, 49er training camp and headquarters protecting guests, players and fellow employees. Our officers voluntarily agree to work these assignments. If the 49ers organization fails to take action to stop this type of inappropriate workplace behavior, it could result in police officers choosing not to work at your facilities. Please contact us as soon as possible with the corrective actions your organization intends on implementing.

The men and women of the Santa Clara Police Officers Association are sworn to protect the rights of ALL people in the United States, a duty we take very seriously. Our members, however, have the right to do their job in an environment free of unjustified and insulting attacks from employees of your organization.

SCPOA Board of Directors

Cc: Rajeev Batra
    Chief Mike Sellers

CHAPTER 9

Colin Kaepernick

—ɯ—

"... Just as every cop is a criminal....," from "Sympathy for the Devil," Rolling Stones 'concert staple' song. (60)

In April 2016, without a warrant, the Santa Clara police kicked down a door of a San Jose resident injuring and breaking the resident's ankle. The resident was later paid a $6.7 million-dollar federal lawsuit settlement. Santa Clara Police Chief Mike Sellers insisted his officers acted responsibly.

Also, in 2016, the city of Santa Clara paid out a $500,000 settlement to a family for multiple illegal searches of their home, again without a warrant, by the police department. However, the social media giant Facebook took no issue with SCPD Detective Sergeant Ray Carreira's illegal police behavior and later hired him as their Global Security Event Manager.

Ironically, and during this same period of questionable police activity by the department, in a September 2, 2016 letter from the Santa Clara Police Officers' Association to the San Francisco 49ers CEO Jed York, (61) (Appendix # 2) the police officers threatened not to work at Levi's Stadium because of the 49ers quarterback Colin Kaepernick's not standing during the National Anthem, and because of the socks he wore.

During this same time, and only thirty miles away, a concurrent Oakland Police scandal underscored just one of the reasons and importance of Colin Kaepernick's protest. Beginning in 2015, over thirty law enforcement officers from four separate agencies had sex with a 19-year old Hispanic teen prostitute. Four of these law enforcement officers had sex with the young woman before she turned eighteen. At least a dozen Oakland California cops were terminated as a result of this sexual misconduct scandal, including tipping off the young prostitute about upcoming 'sting operations', both of which were clear abuses of their authority.

In a September 8, 2016 *News One* article, civil rights attorney John Burris said, "You can't have this kind of widespread misconduct and not have some supervisors know something about it." He continued, "When you have officers conducting misconduct while on the job and engaging in criminal activity, it's very difficult for the citizens in the community to have trust and faith in the department notwithstanding all the other issues." (62)

News One host Roland Martin said the scandal in Oakland was an example of what San Francisco 49ers QB Colin Kaepernick was protesting. Amazingly enough, after the news of the sex scandal broke, no other law enforcement officials have come out to condemn the actions of the officers involved in this massive scandal. Martin asked, "Where are all these police associations, the Fraternal Order of Police, issuing the statements of condemnation of these officers? (62)

Sadly, Roland Martin brings up a very troubling point.

The SCPD filed false police reports in connection with each of the two illegal unwarranted searches. They also violated each of the two parties' Fourth Amendment Constitutional rights with their unlawful search of the two residents' homes without any legal search warrant, but with full support of Santa Clara Police Chief Mike Sellers.

Colin Kaepernick was only exercising his First Amendment Constitutional right of free speech by kneeling in demonstration and protest of these types of police misconduct, including excessive force and brutality, yet the Santa Clara Police Officers Association wrote a letter to the San Francisco 49ers condemning Colin Kaepernick for his actions.

But only Colin Kaepernick and the two injured parties who filed lawsuits, condemned the actions by the SCPD.

In fact, after the scandals involving Santa Clara Police Chief Mike Sellers' approval of his Santa Clara police officers kicking down and injuring a citizen and two illegal searches of residents' homes without a warrant, there is not one documented resignation, public protest or denouncing, condemnation, or taking any stand against these illegal police activities from the Police Officers Association or any of its members. Additionally, there has not been one Santa Clara police officer who was terminated or disciplined for any of these actions.

In a statement obtained by *People Magazine* on Saturday, September 3rd, 2016, Santa Clara Police Chief Michael Sellers commented on the letter released by the association. "Many of us in the law enforcement community have been saddened and angered by Kaepernick's words and actions," Sellers wrote. "As distasteful as his actions are, these actions are protected by the Constitution. Police officers are here to protect the rights of every person, even if we disagree with their position." Sellers said his community's safety must be prioritized over disagreement with Kaepernick's statements and actions.

"I will urge the POA leadership to put the safety of our citizens first," he wrote. "I will work with both sides to find a solution. I will ensure we continue to provide a safe environment at Levi's Stadium." (63)

However, during the previous two years, Santa Clara Police Chief Michael Sellers, on two separate occasions, sent police officers who kicked down doors of Santa Clara and San Jose citizens without legal search warrants. As 'distasteful' as *those* police actions were, those citizens whose rights were violated were also protected by the Constitution from unlawful search and entry.

Chief Mike Sellers later told San Jose Mercury News in a statement, and documented in Danielle Harmon's court filings, "Our officers' actions were fully within the law and in accordance with accepted police practices." (64)

As one of the only elected police chiefs in California, during his 2016 election campaign, Chief Michael Sellers number one of his 'Top 3 Priorities' was, "Maintain an open dialog with community members." (65)

But after an upcoming November 1, 2018 vicious assault incident at Levi's Stadium, he would not be commenting, or speaking at all. Because if he did, Chief Michael J. Sellers, whose entire law enforcement career has been spent with the City of Santa Clara would be at risk of watching that career come to an end.

CHAPTER 10

Kiran Patel

—ᴍ—

On Sunday October 5th, 2014, the visiting Kansas City Chiefs game against the 49ers held at the new Levi's Stadium was the fifth game into the season including two pre-season games. Becoming familiar with their new football field wasn't an issue for the San Francisco 49ers. After all, the size of the field is consistent across the league, and the number of all NFL football team players is constant. Additionally, the 49ers, like all other NFL teams, travel during half of their regular season schedule to eight other teams' stadiums and getting to be familiar with various football fields is just part of their adjustment in professional football.

Unfortunately, the same cannot be said about the Santa Clara Police Department. The SCPD have only one stadium, Levi's Stadium, to become familiar with. And the SCPD only have to manage security at one NFL stadium. But unlike the NFL football teams, the Santa Clara Police do not have the same size law enforcement 'team' as other major cities hosting NFL stadiums. In fact, with 144 sworn officers, according to SCPD Police Chief Mike Sellers's own words, "the city of Santa Clara has one of the smallest law enforcement agencies in the country to protect an NFL stadium." (66)

Levi's Stadium on 49ers game day is a 'finite', 'static' structure. It is not a 'dynamic' structure. It is finite in that there are a fixed number of seats, fixed amount of seat aisles and stairways, and fixed and finite areas of inner and outer mezzanine areas. This finite seating situation never changes on 49ers game day. The Levi's Stadium seating layout does change, however, for certain other uses including concert type venues where some seating is placed on the non-game day football field. Examples of these non-game day seating arrangements would be the on-field seating arrangements for the recent Taylor Swift and Coldplay music concerts, and on-field seating accommodations for the recent concert stop by the Rolling Stones.

On October 5, 2014, the SCPD was still getting acquainted with the layout of Levi's Stadium and was unfamiliar with and had no training with the new multi-million-dollar camera and security system. But the SCPD was well aware of the known local gang members. Unfortunately, Kiran Patel had *no* awareness of what he was about to endure.

It was also on October 5, 2014, when Kiran Patel as a 49er season ticket holder, patron and invitee on the premises of Levi's Stadium, attended the Kansas City Chiefs game being hosted by the San Francisco 49ers. Unbeknownst to Kiran Patel, the game would be attended that same day by brothers, Dario Robollero and Amador Robollero, who were also patrons and invitees on the premises of Levi's Stadium. Entering Levi's Stadium, the Robollero brothers, members of a well-known local gang, were visibly intoxicated and wore and displayed gang clothing.

Less than five minutes after entering Levi's Stadium, Kiran Patel was lying unconscious in a coma on a men's room floor after being viciously attacked and savagely beaten by the Robollero brothers.

While trying to recover from the coma, resulting brain surgery and partial paralysis, Patel through his attorney, filed a Complaint for Damages against the San Francisco 49ers entities. (67) In his complaint, his Causes of Action included Negligence, Lack of Security and Kiran being unaware of the Dangerous Condition of Public Property on behalf of the San Francisco 49ers entities.

The San Francisco 49ers entities hired attorneys, and as part of their defense, viewed the situation differently and asserted that Kiran Patel was fully aware of these conditions. In their First Amended Answer to Kiran's complaint, San Francisco 49ers entities' Fourth Affirmative Defense, claimed the following: "At the time and place of the incident alleged in Plaintiff's Complaint, Plaintiffs (Kiran Patel and his cousin) knew of the dangers and risks to their undertaking, but nevertheless, freely and voluntarily exposed themselves to all risks of harm incidental thereto, and therefore assumed all such risks of harm."

Kiran Patel probably wasn't aware of the dangers or risks asserted by the San Francisco 49ers entities. And what he actually knew may never be known. The coma and resulting brain surgery, from the near-fatal assault which Kiran endured, can tend to have a lifetime effect on one's memory.

But the SCPD were certainly well aware of and 'knew the dangers and risks' at Levi's Stadium. Or at least they should have known if they performed any due diligence before their new relationship with the San Francisco 49ers. They should have known the 49ers brought with them a history of fighting and attacks at games. If there was any doubt, in what the SCPD knew, they were officially updated of the dangers and risks during the personal injury trial of Kiran Patel. Several other people also responsible for safety and security the Levi's Stadium patrons, were previously aware of the fights, attacks, gangs, and criminal history at recent 49ers games.

Court documents pertaining to Patel's personal injury lawsuit reveal that all of the San Francisco 49ers entities, the City of Santa Clara and the Santa Clara Stadium Authority did have specific knowledge of reports of more than 500 assaults and fights at recent San Francisco 49ers home games prior to this.

Due to the dangerously inadequate security at Levi's Stadium, Kiran Patel was severely injured and lay on the men's room floor in a coma. None of the SCPD nor any of the visiting law enforcement officers assigned that afternoon witnessed the incident, nor were any law enforcement positioned to take action. It was only due to the actions of other 49ers fans who brought the tragic event to law enforcement's attention, that the two assailants were captured and taken into custody.

Since no law enforcement was anywhere near the area or witnessed the near-fatal beating themselves, the SCPD needed some help with their investigation. "Santa Clara police were asking for more witnesses to come forward following a brutal fistfight earlier this month inside a crowded restroom at Levi's Stadium that left one victim paralyzed," according to a police spokesman, Lt. Kurt Clarke. Police were looking for "additional witnesses to step forward in this case," he said. In a statement of probable cause to support the charges against the brothers, Santa Clara police Sgt. Ray Carreira wrote that he interviewed four witnesses to the fight, included two who were described as initially "reluctant" to talk about what they saw. Santa Clara police were requesting those who witnessed the assaults to contact Carreira, Sgt. Tony Parker or the anonymous tip line." (68)

The SCPD had been fully aware of gang activity at San Francisco 49ers home games but the SCPD was unaware of a curious trend of fights *between* 49ers fans. The SCPD were unable to discover and understand the reason for the trend of 'infighting' amongst 49ers fans because the SCPD was only focused on making arrests after an incident. They were not patrolling or providing any strategic placement of police officers to observe the crowd fan base during the game in effort to immediately diffuse any trouble.

Even with all the recent frequency of fighting, history and specific knowledge of reports of more than 500 prior assaults and fights at recent San Francisco 49ers home games, the SCPD seemed to be unaware to this growing trend of 'infighting.'

If the SCPD were to fully investigate the 49er-fan 'infighting' versus just being reactive, they might have discovered the following: There were mainly three reasons witnesses were "reluctant to talk about what they saw." The first reason which wasn't as likely, was the witnesses' knowledge and unwillingness to help out a police department who recently kicked down people's doors and illegally searched their homes without a warrant, on two different occasions. The second reason would be the repercussions of ratting out other Levi's Stadium assailants. And the third and more realistic reason witnesses were reluctant to talk is quite alarming. As mentioned by personal injury attorneys, and my interviews with other law enforcement, *"the witnesses themselves may have been in on it."*

CHAPTER 11

"And the Award goes to..."

—ᴍ—

S omehow, on June 7, 2017, the San Francisco 49ers were notified that Levi's Stadium had been selected as the 2017 NFL Facility of Merit by the National Football League for Spectator Sports Safety and Security.

According to the June 7, 2017 article on Levi's Stadium's own website, "The San Francisco 49ers were notified on Wednesday, that Levi's Stadium has been selected as the 2017 NFL Facility of Merit by the National Football League and the National Center for Spectator Sports Safety and Security (NCS4). This award, selected by each professional league and the NCS4, recognizes a facility that has performed above and beyond normal operations to demonstrate an innovative approach to enhancing safety and security." (69)

"The challenge of securing venues in this day and age requires stadium operators to utilize advanced technology and all available resources to ensure total collaboration between security forces," said Cathy Lanier, NFL Senior Vice President of Security. "Jim and his team are successfully leveraging the benefits of a state-of-the-art building to create a model partnership between a stadium manager and its law enforcement partners. Innovation is the key to our success in the future."

"We sincerely appreciate this recognition because it comes from our peers and truly celebrates the outstanding law enforcement partners we work with to secure all people and events at Levi's Stadium," said Jim Mercurio, 49ers Vice President, Stadium Operations & General Manager of Levi's Stadium. "We take pride in our ability to bring together local, state and federal personnel to work in collaboration with private sector partners to test and evaluate some of the most cutting edge and emerging technologies to keep our venue safe and secure." (69)

Two months prior to this mutual admiration society hugging of each other over this superb accolade, in a deposition, ex-Lieutenant with SCPD Ray Carreira (now Global Security Event Manager at Facebook) was discussing using anything but "cutting edge and emerging technologies." Ray Carreira gave testimony during his deposition in the Kiran Patel case. During his deposition, Ray discussed his capabilities with analyzing social media posts and receiving a 'first Tweet' while Kiran Patel was lying in a coma on a Levi's Stadium bathroom floor. Ray did not make any mention of receiving any 'video down-links' from Levi's Stadium's own in-house security system, which Cathy Lanier so highly touted in the article when she claimed, "Jim (Mercurio) and his team are successfully leveraging the benefits of a state-of-the-art building (Levi's Stadium)" (69)

Nonetheless, the Levi's Stadium website proudly boasts, "The National Football League has made a great decision in awarding the San Francisco 49ers organization their annual Safety and Security Facility of Merit Award."

In his own March 13, 2017 deposition for the Kiran Patel personal injury lawsuit, James Mercurio, Vice President of Stadium Operations and General Manager for Levi's Stadium, was asked if he knew in detail the staff directive (officer's beat) of SCPD throughout the facility. James Mercurio answered, "I do not." (70) Yet less than three months later, James Mercurio was appointed to the NFL Stadium Security Directors Committee, a new group responsible for updating security policies across the league. (71)

CHAPTER 12

Levi's Stadium Incident - November 1, 2018 - Part 2

—ɯ—

"I wouldn't advertise what you are looking for, incriminating records have a way of disappearing when people smell trouble" UCLA Professor Dr. Brian Frankel to Erin Brockovich (72)

Starting November 5, 2018, I initiated email correspondence with SCPD officers, Chief of Police Mike Sellers and City Attorney Brian Doyle, but not before I had temporarily suspended my VC Development Group website. On the afternoon of November 6th, City Attorney Brian Doyle checked my LinkedIn profile. I purposely kept a simple and vague Facebook page with minimal detail about my company VC Development Group's goings-on.

On November 8, 2018, I received a phone call from ex-Oakland Chief of Police Howard Jordan, who informed me that he was calling on behalf of City of Santa Clara City Attorney Brian Doyle. Jordan explained he was a security consultant to the City of Santa Clara. I found it unusual that an outside 'consultant' for the city would be reaching out to me regarding the November 1st incident. I had a twenty-five-minute conversation with Howard Jordan, during which I had completely forgotten about his previous involvement and work history with another city employee, the City Manager, Deanna Santana. As chief of police, Jordan shared a past professional relationship with her at the City of Oakland when she was also an employee there.

November 15, 2018

Once again, I travelled to the City of Santa Clara's administrative offices with additional information and requested a meeting with its mayor and city attorney regarding the incident at the November 1, 2018 game. I was told again by the city administrative clerks that the mayor and city attorney were not available. I left my business card stapled to handwritten note for City Attorney Brian Doyle.

Friday, November 16, 2018

The day after my second trip to the City of Santa Clara, I checked in for my prescheduled surgery for a complete right hip replacement.

November 26, 2018

Ten days later while recuperating from surgery, I prepared and sent individual letters via UPS Overnight to the City of Santa Clara Mayor Gillmor with individual certified copies to each of the city councilmembers with extensive narrative and backup including all email correspondence previously sent and received between myself, the City of Santa Clara City Attorney Brian Doyle and the SCPD.

November 28, 2018

Two days later, I received a letter from the City of Santa Clara acknowledging receipt of my November 26, 2018 letter stating, "Your letter will be distributed to the Mayor and Councilmembers, as well as the City Manager's Office, for their review."

November 28, 2018 would also be the day that City of Santa Clara Mayor Lisa Gillmor and the councilmembers ceased any further communication with me.

"City manager, I thought to myself." I reread the November 28, 2018 letter from the City letting it sink in, and then realized, I hadn't copied the city manager who wasn't even on my radar. I had individually copied only the mayor and each of the councilmembers. I wasn't even aware of who the city manager was until I doubled back to the City of Santa Clara website (73) and I saw that the City of Santa Clara had recently hired Deanna Santana as their new city manager.

I still hadn't made the connection of where I had encountered Deanna Santana's name before, and then it hit me. Deanna Santana had previously worked at both the City of San Jose and also the City of Oakland. During Santana's tenure at both cities, I had also been involved in hundreds of dealings with each of these two cities while managing entitlements and processing plan check reviews for projects with some of the world's largest companies. I vaguely remembered seeing Deanna Santana's name on some of each of those city's documents. But what I remembered most was Deanna Santana's involvement while she was with the City of Oakland and her chaotic and almost deadly mishandling of the Occupy Oakland incident. I also remembered Deanna Santana's apparent coverup attempt of police misconduct, and her other illicit activities at both the City of Oakland and City of San Jose while she was serving on each of their staffs.

With a little research, I refreshed my memory even more with the following recent history from media and court documented sources I found. The documents and lawsuits showed a clear pattern and progression of questionably illegal actions taken throughout Deanna Santana's public service career. And these documents also exposed Deanna Santana's reoccurring efforts to suppress reports of police misconduct and other evidence:

City of San Jose - Deputy City Manager - May 1999 - August 2011

In 2006, as Deputy City Manager for the City of San Jose, Deanna Santana attempted to launder reports about police misconduct including illegal searches and excessive force. According to an *East Bay Express* news article entitled, "Deanna Santana Tried to Alter Damning Report," dated September 19, 2012, "There is also evidence that this is not the first time that Santana appears to have attempted to dilute critical analysis of police actions. Deanna Santana was instructed by the San Jose City Council to analyze a report by Independent Police Auditor, Barbara Attard, highlighting San Jose PD's practice of downgrading Internal Affairs complaints against officers. Instead, Santana hired Macias Consulting Group, claiming auditor Attard had used "incorrect units." In response, Attard submitted a sharp rebuttal to the San Jose City Council that all but accused Santana and Macias of going out of the way to deflect attention away from the problem at hand." (74)

Subsequently, "None of the twelve cases cited by the police auditor were ever investigated."

City of Oakland - City Administrator - August 2011 - March 2014

As the second most powerful city official in Oakland at the time, Deanna Santana as City Administrator of City of Oakland, attempted to launder the 'Frazier Report' about police misconduct and falsifying reports. The Frazier Report was commissioned in response to the aftermath of an October 25, 2011 City of Oakland Police response to Occupy Oakland, the response to which Deanna Santana herself authorized in her capacity as City Administrator. The Frazier Report stated, "In the wake of these events serious concerns were raised by both City Officials and the community at large concerning use of unreasonable force, overall police performance, and OPD's ability to manage future events in an acceptable manner." (*Independent Investigation Occupy Oakland Response October 25, 2011 (Frazier Report), Frazier Group LLC - June 14, 2012*) (75). In the same *East Bay Express* article mentioned above, civil rights attorney Jim Chanin, who helped prepare the Frazier Report, battled with Santana and refused to send a Word copy of the unissued Frazier Report to Santana for her own editing. "A May 11 email from Frazier to Santana's email account at City Hall offered a glimpse into their argument about how much of the Frazier report's damning findings would become public." (74)

Deanna Santana was also the central figure named in a whistleblower lawsuit after Santana fired Oakland's Director of Employee Relations, Daryelle Preston. The lawsuit stated Deanna Santana pressured Preston to lie on multiple occasions and falsify reports. Plaintiff Preston reported that Fire Chief Teresa Deloach Reed engaged in a violation of Oakland City Ordinance when Reed repeatedly directly negotiated and signed tentative agreements ("TA's") with Firefighters Local 55 without Ms. Preston present as Employee Relations Director or City Council authorization. By law, Ms. Preston must have obtained approval from the City Council for Reed to sign the contract. Santana assisted Reed in attempting to conceal Reed's unlawful negotiation and signature of TAs, and Santana retaliated against Ms. Preston when she reported Reed's acts to Santana and the City Attorney of Oakland. Defendant Santana responded to plaintiff Preston's reports to her regarding these violations of law, and to plaintiff's refusal to obey illegal orders, by (Santana) carrying out a series of adverse actions culminating in plaintiff Preston's termination. A jury agreed with Preston, awarding her $613,302 in damages. (*Daryelle Lawanna Preston v. City of Oakland; Deanna Santana, et al., RG14-717585, 2014, Alameda County*) (76) (77)

It should also be noted, that during Deanna Santana's tenure at the City of Oakland, she had administrative oversight and was the 'boss' of the Building, Police, Fire and Planning Departments. On December 2, 2016, in Oakland, California, a fire broke out in an 'artist collective' warehouse, known as Ghost Ship. A total of 36 people were killed in the fire, the deadliest in the history of Oakland. Multiple factors contributed to these completely preventable deaths, including negligence by the City of Oakland's own Building Inspectors, Police, Fire, and Planning Departments. Police and Fire officials warned that the warehouse was a fire hazard but did not follow through on enforcing the codes already in place. The City of Oakland's Planning Director revealed that the building had not been inspected for three decades.

(*IN RE Ghost Ship Fire Litigation Master Complaint, RG16843631, 2017, Alameda County*) (78)

As reported in a December 7, 2016 *East Bay Express* article, "Oakland Firefighters Say Their Department Is So Badly Managed, Ghost Ship Warehouse Wasn't Even in Its Inspection Database." "When firefighters attempted to pull records for Ghost Ship from their own fire-prevention bureau's files, they discovered nothing. "It's not even in the system, one firefighter said." (79) (80) (81)

Deanna Santana was City Administrator during this period of negligence when Building, Police, Fire and Planning Departments, under Santana's management, were not enforcing the codes nor maintaining accurate files, which, if enforced under Santana's watch, would ultimately have saved 36 innocent lives.

City of Santa Clara - City Manager - October 2017 to Present

Deanna Santana in her current position as City Manager for Santa Clara is again in charge of the Police Department in addition to being Executive Director of the City of Santa Clara Stadium Authority, which involves Santana overseeing contracts related to Levi's Stadium and the San Francisco 49ers.

And since 'old habits die hard', in a recent article from *The Silicon Valley Voice*, "Santa Clara Subject of State Pension Investigation," dated October 12, 2018, (82) Deanna Santana's actions were the reason the City of Santa Clara was the subject of a State Pension Fraud investigation by CalPERS. A letter signed by Deanna Santana was revised and backdated for employment of an Assistant City Manager to her.

———————

The November 28, 2018 response letter I received from the City of Santa Clara confirmed Deanna Santana received a copy of my November 26 letter regarding Levi's Stadium security concerns. With her history of questionable illegal past dealings while at the City of San Jose and City of Oakland, Deanna Santana was now also the perfect candidate to work with the Santa Clara Police Department, the San Francisco 49ers, and the NFL to ensure my 'damning findings' about the dangerously inadequate security at Levi's Stadium would not become public.

CHAPTER 13

Levi's Stadium Incident - November 1, 2018 - Part 3

—ɯ—

"Now you see it, now you don't"

December 3, 2018

I investigated further and started to see a disturbing pattern. I found that there were various other incidents, including two recent near-death beatings at Levi's Stadium, arising as a result of lack of security since 2014 that put the City of Santa Clara, the 49ers, and the Santa Clara Police Department (SCPD) on notice of such a dangerous and unsafe condition both inside the stadium and in the parking lot. The City of Santa Clara, the 49ers and the SCPD also had prior knowledge that known members of gangs and other criminals actively used the occasion of San Francisco 49ers games to meet, plan and carry out criminal activity, and that these security and safety concerns have been accelerating both prior to and after the 2014 opening of Levi's Stadium.

a. As discussed in Chapter 10, on October 4, 2014, San Francisco 49ers season ticket holder Kiran Patel was viciously attacked by two drunken gang members, and suffered a coma, brain damage, and partial paralysis. (*Kiran Patel and Amish Patel v. San Francisco Forty Niners, et al.,* Santa Clara County Superior Court Case no. 115CV286138, (2015). (83)

b. In September 2015, after a Monday night game, a group of San Francisco 49ers fans punched and kicked a man wearing a Minnesota Vikings jersey.

c. On October 7, 2018 following a San Francisco 49ers vs Arizona Cardinals game, a man punched another fan causing great bodily harm including brain damage and the victim becoming comatose. (*The State of California v Gonzales, David Aguilera*, Santa Clara County Superior Court Case No. C1802883, (2018). (84)

d. Prior to the October 4, 2014 Kiran Patel beating, but later revealed in his subsequent personal injury lawsuit, court documents show all of the 49er entities, and the City of Santa Clara had specific knowledge of reports of more than 500 recent prior assaults and fights at San Francisco 49ers home games. (*Kiran Patel and Amish Patel v. San Francisco Forty Niners, et al.,* Santa Clara County Superior Court Case no. 115CV286138, (2015).

During the personal injury trial for the vicious attack and beating of Kiran Patel, the defense and contention of the 49er entities, and the city in court documents was, "Notifying the public about the lack of security would discourage use of the property and would also serve to invite violent attacks."

Once I found out about the Kiran Patel near-fatal attack, I immediately went to the Santa Clara County Courthouse on December 3, 2018 to review Kiran's personal injury complaint file. After filling out a request form, the court file clerk handed me four folders including the entire case file. The total file was over five and one-half inches thick. I did a quick review and tagged twenty-five pages with post-it notes for immediate copies to take with me, and then told the file clerk I wanted copies of the entire file and to put a rush on it.

While Patel's personal injury case file was being copied, I contacted and scheduled a call with his attorney, William B. Smith (Bill) of Abramson Smith Waldsmith, LLP. Six days and over $600 hundred dollars later, I received a call from the courthouse that the complete personal injury case file was copied and ready for me to pick up.

I separated out and organized the Kiran Patel case file into four binders. Then I read the entire case file and waited for the scheduled call with the attorney who handled the Kiran Patel personal injury case.

A week later, during my phone discussion with Attorney Smith, he initially stated he would not be able to discuss any settlement issues regarding his client Kiran. I assured him, I was not expecting him to disclose the injury settlement, and that I wanted to let him know there was another vicious attack that I witnessed on November 1 at Levi's Stadium. I also told him that I had reviewed Patel's file at the courthouse and had in fact also copied the entire case file for a full review.

Smith mentioned several issues at Levi's Stadium, before telling me one other very important thing before we ended our phone conversation. It was after a comment regarding his client, when it became clear there may be a conspiracy to conceal information about the vicious attack I witnessed on November 1. There would also be attempts by others to falsify reports, hide, bury, and make any incriminating records disappear.

CHAPTER 14

"Who's in Charge Here?"

—⚏—

"But I thought you were handling this?"

Unfortunately, such a storied and well-respected football team as the San Francisco 49ers has been made to suffer due to recent turmoil and publicly aired and documented political infighting between the SCPD, the City of Santa Clara, the Santa Clara Stadium Authority who operates Levi's Stadium, and the team's own 49ers management group. A recent grand jury investigation exposed this toxic environment and relationship between all of the parties responsible for security at Levi's Stadium.

This toxic environment combined with the already deteriorated morale and existing corruption within the Santa Clara Police Department created a perfect storm. These findings helped to explain the chaos involving those responsible for providing security management at Levi's Stadium, the chaos of which exposed sports fans, including season ticket holders, and other patrons of Levi's Stadium to extreme danger and recent near-death experiences.

"A significant problem, particularly in some locations, is that there is disagreement among the league, teams and local enforcement on who is ultimately responsible for fan safety." (85) Even

77

without the toxic political and corrupt environment, this is especially true at Levi's Stadium.

An outside audit found mismanagement by the 49ers in failing to provide timely security budgets over multiple years to adequately manage security. This resulted in the Stadium Authority having to "guess at" adequate security staffing needs.

An August 21, 2017 audit report was part of the August 24, 2017, City of Santa Clara Agenda Report. The audit report included a, *"Comprehensive Audit of Stadium Authority Finances,"* prepared by Harvey M. Rose Associates, LLC. Included in the August 21, 2017 audit Conclusions and Findings, finding 1.D contains, "The Stadium Lease requires that the Operation and Maintenance Plan Prepared by ManCo (Forty Niners Stadium Management Company) and submitted to the Stadium Authority include an annual Public Safety Budget. At approximately $5.7 million in FY 2015-16, public safety costs are one of the Stadium's largest expenses, but a budget for these costs were not submitted to the Stadium Authority in total or approved by the Board for the two years within the scope of this audit." (86)

The outside audit found that due to the unwillingness of the 49ers to provide security budgets for two years, law enforcement officers and security forces headcount at Levi's Stadium were ineffectively managed, endangering the safety of fans attending San Francisco 49ers home games. It was during this non-budgeted period affecting security on October 4, 2014, when San Francisco 49ers season ticket holder Kiran Patel was viciously attacked by two drunken members of a well-known gang, and Kiran Patel suffered a coma, brain damage, and partial paralysis.

CHAPTER 15

"Tale of the Tape"

—ϡ—

"Look Who's *Not* Talking Now"

"I look at every attack that takes place everywhere," NFL Security Chief, Cathy Lanier says in her October 26, 2017 interview with *ESPN*. "If we have video, or if we have other evidence that would sustain that more likely than not that the conduct occurred, then we can go forward." Cathy Lanier laughs when asked about critics who claim the NFL would hide video that could hurt a player or team's image. "It's so the opposite," she says. "The extraordinary efforts that we go through trying to determine if an allegation is true or not, it really is extraordinary."

Lanier continued, "On typical game days, local police are the lead agency for every game throughout the season. A typical game requires at least 10 different agencies, from the FBI to private security." (87)

In a return phone call conversation with me on the morning of Saturday, November 10, 2018 Captain Tony Parker was proud to boast and confirm that the SCPD had 'tactical command' for 49ers' game day security at Levi's Stadium.

Captain Parker, called me two days after my phone conversation with ex-Oakland Police Chief Howard Jordan. Captain

Parker confirmed he and other Santa Clara police officers studied in depth and completed their review of 'the November 1st incident' from Levi's Stadium security tapes, and the video capture of which, was available from the 800 installed cameras at Levi's Stadium.

I had previously stopped into the police station, on the morning of November 2 to fill out a Request for Police Report. During discussion then, multiple phone calls later that week, and email communications with the SCPD, I described in detail how easily I should be identified from anyone's review of that night's security tapes of 'the incident'. I told them to look for, a 6'-1", 270 lb., 61-year-old, grey haired, devout Oakland Raiders fan, wearing a number 75, Howie Long 'throwback' game jersey, with silver letters on black.

Later in that same November 10, 2018 phone discussion, Captain Parker confirmed that he and other police officers were able to positively identify me in the Levi's Stadium security tapes from the incident.

In an email follow up to the phone call, I copied Police Chief Mike Sellers, the Officer Captain Steve Buress who finally arrested assailant Steve Guardado, and City of Santa Clara Attorney Brian Doyle. I was clear in my direction to all of them that bottom line, I wanted to be involved and would to my satisfaction, receive a full and transparent review of how the security lapse occurred. I wanted to see actual footage of the Levi's Stadium security tapes to determine a complete understanding of what went wrong, and how this complete lack of security at Levi's Stadium could be avoided in the future.

Soon after the SCPD completed their review of the November 1, 2018 incident captured in the Levi's Stadium security tapes, and my follow up email to the SCPD documenting my call with Captain Tony Parker, that phone call on November 10 with Captain Parker was the last communication from anyone with the SCPD.

During investigation of Kiran Patel's savage beating, the Santa Clara Police were urging more witnesses to come forward. (88) But witnesses to the Kiran Patel near-death beating attack didn't want to talk. And similarly, in the vicious attack I witnessed on November 1st, neither the victim nor the assailant wanted to talk. And as a police officer, the Police Captain Parker was involved with both incidents.

As an interesting irony, it was now Captain Tony Parker and Police Chief Mike Seller's turn to be "reluctant to talk about what they saw," in the tapes.

Police Chief Sellers and Captain Parker had 'gone dark' on me, and for good reason, in light of what information and evidence from the November 1 incident the police feared would now be exposed.

CHAPTER 16

"November 26, 2018 Letter to City Hall

—૱—

In addition to serving on the City Council, the Mayor and Council Members also serve as Board Members of the Santa Clara Stadium Authority which owns Levi's Stadium. After the City Attorney Brian Doyle and the Santa Clara Police Department 'went dark' on me and ceased any further communication, I sent the attached letter below to the Mayor and City Councilmembers requesting their help. (89)

Mayor Lisa M. Gillmor

City of Santa Clara
1500 Warburton Avenue
Santa Clara, CA 95050

Monday, November 26, 2018 Sent via UPS Overnight

RE: Thursday, November 1st, 2018, Raiders at 49'ers Night Game - 49er fans savage assault

Dear Mayor Gillmor,

My daughter and I attended the above November 1ˢᵗ, 2018 Thursday Night Game. We were sitting in Upper Section 221 near the stairway, and during the beginning of the 3ʳᵈ Quarter, unfortunately, we witnessed a savage assault below us in Lower Section119, between two (2) San Francisco 49'ers fans.

Please reference the attached link from *KNBR*, second video on the link.
http://www.knbr.com/2018/11/01/fights-break-out-in-stands-during-49ers-raiders-game/

As observed in the video link of the fight, there were at least four (4) field personnel including two (2) wearing yellow jackets, and two (2) wearing red. None of these Personnel took any action to 'call ahead' or stop this fight. As two (2) of the individuals involved in the fight were slowly walking up the stairs to the shared mezzanine, and since no one else at Levi's Stadium was taking any action, I worked my way down to intercept them. There was a woman on the shared mezzanine, in Security attire, and I was yelling at the top of my lungs for her to call police and or backup. The Security woman was trying to work some sort of device, as I continued screaming for her to get backup or help. As the assailant in a red shirt and his smaller accomplice were walking across the mezzanine, I confronted the red shirt assailant and told him to stop. The assailant continued to walk toward the outer perimeter of the mezzanine deck, counterclockwise Northward toward the Exit Stairs. As my daughter and I continued to follow the two individuals, and when we reached the stairs the smaller of the two individuals wearing a dark # 80 SF 49'ers jersey, grabbed me and tried to keep me from following the assailant wearing the red shirt. I continued following both individuals down the stairs, while yelling for help, and finally convinced a 'visiting' (his words) uniformed California Highway Patrolman who was just outside the gate close to the light rail train tracks. The CHP officer grabbed the assailant wearing the red shirt, and a couple of Santa Clara Police Officers then surrounded the two individuals, and I first, and then my daughter second, gave individual accounts to one of the arresting officers.

It is my understanding there were over 400 (four hundred) combined Santa Clara Police Dept. and visiting Law Enforcement Officers, yet it took me an Oakland Raiders fan, to act solely, and insert myself and be the only line of defense in bringing the red shirted assailant to restraint and arrest.

The next day I immediately went to the Santa Clara Police Dept. to provide further information on our exact seating in addition to requesting a copy of the Police Report. As per the attachments and emails, I have visited the City of Santa Clara twice recently, along with email and verbal requests for information from the Santa Clara Police Dept., and personally delivering a hand-written note for the City Attorney.

Since Saturday, November 10th, the Santa Clara Police Dept. and City Attorney Brian Doyle have 'gone dark' on me, without any further responses.

So, Mayor Gillmor and City Council Members, I am requesting your help, for an immediate meeting this week before another Levi's Stadium event or venue of any type takes place, which quite literally could be a matter of life or death, due to the lax and non-existent Security and Law Enforcement at this Levi's Stadium venue.

Please contact me, and I will immediately schedule myself to everyone's availability.

Thank You.

Sincerely,

Fred Weaver

VC Development Group
650 Castro Street, Suite 120-211
Mountain View, CA 94041
fred@vcdevelopmentgroup.com

w/ Attachments

Cc:
Council Members:
Debi Davis
Patrick Kolstad
Patricia Mahan
Teresa O'Neill
Kathy Watanabe

CHAPTER 17

"November 28, 2018 City of Santa Clara Response

—⁓—

City of
Santa Clara
The Center of What's Possible

Mayor

Lisa M. Gillmor

Council Members

Debi Davis
Patrick Kolstad
Patricia M. Mahan
Teresa O'Neill
Kathy Watanabe

November 28, 2018

Fred Weaver
650 Castro Street, Suite 120-211
Mountain View, CA 94041

Dear Mr. Weaver:

Your letter regarding the Raiders at 49ers Night Game on November 1, 2018 was received on November 27, 2018. Your letter will be distributed to the Mayor and Councilmembers, as well as the City Manager's Office, for their review.

Sincerely,

Jose Armas
Office Records Specialist
Mayor and Council Offices

City of
Santa Clara
The Center of What's Possible

Mayor and Council Offices
1500 Warburton Avenue
Santa Clara, CA 95050

U.S. POSTAGE PITNEY BOWES

ZIP 95050 $ 000.47
02 4W
0000738788 NOV 29 2016

Fred Weaver
650 Castro Street, Suite 120-211
Mountain View, CA 94041

9404182093 C079

CHAPTER 18

"Every Picture Tells a Story"

—ɯ—

"It's like déjà vu all over again."
Baseball coach, manager, and player, Yogi Berra.

After receiving the City of Santa Clara's November 28, 2018 response letter, I assumed there would not be additional follow-up from them on my security concerns at Levi's Stadium, so I increased my research. And the more I researched, the more I uncovered. And then the research turned into a full investigation.

San Francisco 49ers home game vs the Seattle Seahawks

On December 16, 2018, exactly one month to the day after my right hip replacement, I had recuperated enough, and was able to walk again and decided to return to Levi's Stadium for the sole purpose of inspecting and reviewing security coverage. That San Francisco 49ers home game at Levi's Stadium was against the Seattle Seahawks. Rather than sit my assigned seat, I walked and surveyed the entire Levi's Stadium during the first half of the football game and took 630 separate photographs of the SCPD, other law enforcement officers and other security personnel mostly standing around, bunched up in groups, tucked away in warm areas, not providing any strategic placement or zone coverage, and not observing the crowd fan base. I did not see any law enforcement or security personnel patrolling any of Levi's Stadium fan seating sections or any of Levi's Stadium main entry and exit gates.

I also took pictures of all of the security cameras, and the location of each from the point I first intercepted the assailant Steve Guardado during the incident. I surveyed and photographed every camera from the lower section stairs connecting to the shared mezzanine, continuing counterclockwise around the outside perimeter of the stadium, down the stairway to northeast exit gate 'F' until my meeting point with the arresting officers.

A review of the Kiran Patel personal injury lawsuit revealed that all of the San Francisco 49er entities, the City of Santa Clara, and the NFL had specific prior knowledge of reports of more than 500 recent prior assaults and fights at San Francisco 49ers home games. And there were various other recent incidents each of them was very well aware of, including gross misconduct and criminal activity by the Santa Clara Police Department including the two 2016 warrant-less and illegal kicking down of doors, illegal searches, and injury to each of those residents.

After all the documented issues, not a single police officer was terminated or disciplined for any of these illegal actions and misconduct. The Santa Clara Police Department fostered a culture of impunity to such behavior.

I was beginning to think no one would respond or care enough to do anything about the dangerously inadequate security at Levi's Stadium, which I first experienced on November 1, 2018 and then personally witnessed again during my return visit on December 16, 2018.

To the City of Santa Clara Police Department, their handling of security at the stadium was just an afterthought. It was now completely apparent; the SCPD were no longer accountable to anyone and for some time now had simply 'gone rogue.' After reviewing all the pictures I took at Levi's Stadium that December day documenting the lack of security, I realized the only way I would get anyone's attention, was to file a lawsuit.

CHAPTER 19

"There's a New Sheriff in Town"

—◊◊◊—

"Few police administrators show much interest in 'planning' the deployment of their manpower and equipment." James Q. Wilson, political and social scientist, wrote in *Varieties of Police Behavior* (91)

"...Many Law Enforcement Agencies have no idea what their role is...on a daily basis...much less during another attack. Stadiums...are just a few examples of potential targets...creat(ing) a sense that no one is safe." Cathy Lanier, NFL Senior Vice President of Security, wrote the above words that were included in her 2005 graduate school thesis. (92)

Those are two disturbing findings from two very important people: James Q. Wilson, and Cathy Lanier respectively.
"James Quinn Wilson (May 27, 1931 – March 2, 2012) was an American academic, political and social scientist, and an authority on public administration. He gained national attention for a 1982 article introducing the broken windows theory in *The Atlantic*.

In 2003, he was awarded the Presidential Medal of Freedom by US President George W. Bush. The broken windows theory is a criminological theory that states that visible signs of crime, anti-social behavior, and civil disorder create an urban environment that encourages further crime and disorder, including serious crimes. The theory suggests that policing methods that target minor crimes such as vandalism, public drinking, and fare evasion help to create an atmosphere of order and lawfulness, thereby preventing more serious crimes.

The theory was introduced in a 1982 article by social scientists James Q. Wilson and George L. Kelling. It was further popularized in the 1990s by New York City police commissioner William Bratton and Mayor Rudy Giuliani, whose policing policies were influenced by the theory." (93)

The second person mentioned above, Cathy Lanier is the new NFL Senior Vice President of Security.

During my research, I found several articles about, and interviews with Cathy Lanier. A 2017, *ESPN* interview, "From teen mother to NFL security chief, Cathy Lanier's rise through the law enforcement ranks," (94) details that "she became the city's (Washington D.C.) first female chief of police in 2006. Throughout it all, she kept going to school, including stints at Johns Hopkins University and Harvard's Kennedy School of Government, until she had two master's degrees in national security."

As part of that same video interview, Cathy Lanier was asked, "What were you told when you walked in the door that they really wanted you to prioritize?" (94) And at these moments in the video interview, Cathy Lanier responds (with video segment milestones):

- She was hired by the NFL, "to reinvigorate and modernize the way we do security" - 2:03

- "Now you are looking at your private security, are they posted in the right places? - 2:49
- "We are as prepared as we can be. We go to great lengths to make sure that our venues are safe - 3:49

Additionally, during my research, I found a thesis Cathy Lanier wrote in 2005, *Preventing Terror Attacks in the Homeland: A New Mission for State and Local Police.* (92) I saved it and printed out a copy, which I extensively marked up and underlined. And then I read it again and realized something. If one was to 'cross out' or filter her thesis, like I did, eliminating just the references to 'terror' and 'terrorists', Cathy's 'abbreviated' thesis was actually, as abstracted, a good basis and instruction on stadium security! Without taking anything out of context, other than terror and terrorist references, here is my abbreviated version of her 2005 thesis:

Cathy Lanier's 2005 Thesis - *Preventing Terror Attacks in the Homeland: A New Mission for State and Local Police* (Abstract with page references)

- "Drilling down to the lowest local level to include businesses, industry and the private sector, the formation of the network expands our detection and prevention capabilities well beyond our current level." (Page v)
- "What if police chiefs had been asked how much time they had invested in training their officers to recognize potential indicators..." (Page 3)

B. DEFINING THE STRATEGIC ISSUES: CONFUSION REMAINS

- "This is a disturbing mindset in light of what we have learned about the obvious indicators that were missed in the weeks and months leading up to the...attacks" (Page 6)
- "...Stadiums...are just a few examples of potential targets...creat(ing) a sense that no one is safe" (Page 6)
- "One only needs to pay attention to the attacks that continue to take place around the world to realize that soft targets are becoming increasingly attractive" (Page 7)
- "...Many Law Enforcement Agencies have no idea what their role is...on a daily basis...much less during another attack." This is a disturbing mindset in light of what we have learned about the obvious indicators that were missed in the weeks and months leading up to the...attacks. One only needs to pay attention to the attacks that continue to take place around the world to realize that soft targets are becoming increasingly attractive. Stadiums...are just a few examples of potential targets...creat(ing) a sense that no one is safe" (Page 9)

C. METHODOLOGY

- "The motivation for this research was to identify problems and propose solutions to some of the many issues faced by local law enforcement..." (Page 10

- "It forces us to realize...one only has to look at the most recent attacks." (Page 15)
- "An effective strategy must redefine traditional roles and capabilities of our local police officers to establish multiple layers of prevention through detection and deterrence at all levels." (Page 17)
- "We must concentrate on reducing our vulnerabilities at the local level." (Page 17)

III. EMPHASIZING PREVENTION

A. IDENTIFYING INDICATORS

- "It may be a local business or particular industry that notices something that is out of the ordinary." (Page 19)
- "Like with crime prevention, the more realistic view of...prevention should be considered "law enforcements" best efforts to minimize the possibility of an attack occurring." (Page 19)

B. STRATEGIC AND TACTICAL PREVENTION

- "Deterrence is more tactically focused and will be used to secure specific locations or events based on an analysis of risk and potential consequences. Increasing physical security measures and the visibility of police officers around potential (attackers) forces the (attackers) to change their behavior and sends a message that the risk of failure is greater than their commitment to a specific target." (Page 20)

- "This concept, suggested by Davis and Jenkins in 2002, encompasses deterrence through an increased risk of failure." Paul Davis and Brian Jenkins, *Deterrence and Influence in Counterterrorism* (Santa Monica, CA: RAND, 2002. (95)
- "Therefore, law enforcement officials must now strategically rethink public security procedures and practices in order to maximize the full potential of their resources at certain locations and during certain events." (Page 21)
- "The role for local law enforcement becomes more defined allowing individual agencies to focus prevention and deterrence efforts on areas and activities that are most likely to occur within their jurisdiction. However, strategic coordination between agencies must still be clarified." (Page 24, 25)

D. OPPORTUNITIES MISSED

- "...Strategic coordination between agencies must still be clarified." (Page 25)
- "...Potential indicators may have been detected by state and local law enforcement had they realized and known what to look for. Although we now have the benefit of hindsight, one must wonder if any of these attacks could have been prevented had state and local police officers had a better understanding of their role in prevention." (Page 25)
- "...There were many opportunities for intervention by law enforcement, and private security in

the weeks and months leading up to all of these attacks." (Page 25)

- "The value added by using these additional "eyes and ears" as a force multiplier far surpass any effort that could be accomplished by…Law Enforcement agents." (Page 31)
- "This fact reinforces our need to expand our detection capabilities by ensuring that every police officer in the United States fully understands their role and is engaged in our national efforts to prevent future attacks." (Page 31)

1. National Level: National vs. Local Priorities

- "…Information sharing is important because people want to feel they are informed of potential threats so they can act to protect themselves." (Page 35)
- "…It leaves us in the dangerous position that no one is focusing on prevention at the local level which ignores the "lessons learned" (Page 35)

B. CONSIDERATIONS

- "Operational plans developed…cannot be too complex or lengthy, making them impossible to digest otherwise they will sit on a shelf and not be used." (Page 37)
- "Due to strong traditional nature of policing, change has always been slow and difficult for law enforcement organizations. Historically change has only been excepted when the organization

or society itself faces a significant threat or crisis." (Page 39)

- "In the simplest terms...local law enforcement is sworn to protect...against attacks of random, unsuspecting civilians." (Page 40)
- "The law enforcement community as a whole must incorporate...prevention in their missions, goals, objectives, training, performance evaluations and all other elements that define the culture and activities of their organizations." (Page 40) Mathew Scheider and Robert Chapman, "Community Policing and Terrorism," April 2003, (96) http://www.homelandsecurity.org/journal/articles/scheider-Chapman.html , July, 2005.

VI. THE ROAD MAP

- "...We must undergo some significant changes. Ideally, the structure should be built from the ground up..." (Page 43)
- "...The key to success will be to gather, report and share critical information in all directions. This then must be formalized through the development of standards, polices, and practices." (Page 46)

3. Intelligence for Prevention and Planning

- "In terms of prevention, intelligence is based on gaining or developing information...that can be used to apprehend offenders, harden targets and design strategies to reduce or eliminate threats." (Page 47), David Carter, *"Law Enforcement Intelligence: A Guide for State, Local and Tribal*

Law Enforcement Agencies," (U.S. Department of Justice, Office of Community Oriented Policing Services, 2003) (Page 46) (97).

- "Intelligence shared with local law enforcement must also be used strategically for planning and resource allocation. This aspect of intelligence will provide information to decision makers about the emerging threats for the purpose of developing response strategies and reallocating resources to accomplish effective prevention." (Page 48), David Carter, Law Enforcement Intelligence.

VII. Conclusions

- "The process begins by clarifying the role of the...agencies when it comes to preventing future attacks. It must be clear who will be held accountable for what in terms of preparedness and activities. Local law enforcement leaders must understand that they will be held accountable for ensuring that their agencies are fully engaged in preventing future attacks, not just responding to them." (Page 53)
- "Performance measures must be created (and) immediate implementation focus should be on suburban and rural agencies which currently lack the necessary skills and conduits to engage in an effective prevention strategy." (Page 60)

Again, based on the abbreviated version of her thesis, see if you agree that this abtract of Cathy Lanier's original 2005 Thesis is still fundamentally a good basis and instruction for designing security, and would also apply to stadium security?

Cathy Lanier also assisted with authoring the new <u>NFL Statement - Public Policy,</u> (Appendix # 1) which highlights and documents:

1. "The safety of our fans, stadium personnel, and teams at all NFL games is our priority, and security at our games is robust."
2. "The NFL and team security departments work closely with stadium operation personnel and federal, state, and local law enforcement to provide a safe experience for the more than 17 million fans who annually attend NFL games. The NFL and its teams continually evaluate and improve our comprehensive security plan."

I was also encouraged to find a September 13, 2018 'white paper' report, by Cathy Lanier which she wrote to the United States Senate, titled, "*Evolving Threats to the Homeland.*" (98)

In her report, Cathy Lanier states, "Club security officials and I work closely with local law enforcement officials, federal authorities, stadium owners, and many others to provide a safe and secure environment for our fans to enjoy the games. To help the clubs in this difficult environment, the NFL has developed and published best practices and standards for responding to... incidents. These best practices...are incorporated into our overall best practices for stadium security..."

While it's nice that Cathy Lanier and the NFL boast about 'best practices' for comprehensive stadium security, there isn't one team claiming to have ever seen them. "Casey Nice, an assistant sheriff in California's Alameda County, is in charge of overseeing the game-day security operation at all Raiders games at

Oakland Coliseum. Nice said he's in occasional contact with the NFL league office, and he attends the league's security seminar each year. But he has not received a list of the NFL's "best practices." (99)

Nonetheless, after extensively reviewing all the information I researched about Cathy Lanier, I felt she might be the last resort, and I was hoping someone in her capacity would care about the dangerously inadequate security I witnessed and experienced at Levi's Stadium.

Since I found comfort in the fact that she was a career police officer, on January 7, 2019, I called the National Football League offices in New York, and left a voicemail for her, after being unable to get any cooperation or even a further response from the SCPD.

It wasn't very long after I left the voicemail for Cathy Lanier, when I found a concerning *Washington Post* news article, "Former police chief's focus in new NFL gig is protecting the league's image." (100) In the article dated February 1, 2017, it mentions, "but there is a fundamental difference between protecting the public and protecting a corporate brand – the NFL or, to insiders, 'the Shield.' In this context, Lanier's charge isn't simply to keep fans safe. It's also to protect the league's image. For all its popularity, the NFL has an image problem that some believe is cutting into unrivaled hold on U.S. sports fans. The roots of that image problem are complex and lie, in large part, in the league's delayed response to the dangers..."

Unfortunately, after reviewing all the good things I found about her, I realized after reading the above article, that in her 'dual' protection role, I would *never* be hearing back from Cathy Lanier.

CHAPTER 20

"Out of Sequence"

—⟋⟍—

"Waiting to Exhale"

An older attorney friend of mine, Frank Nolan, used to be the lawyer handling Internal Affairs for the City of Chicago Police Department. Frank told me several stories about some of the inner workings and his dealings with some of the dysfunction while he was there, along with wayward officers he had to help investigate and also help discipline. One of the disciplinary measures included the use of prominent landmarks which still exist…in the middle of Lake Michigan. Chicago's water supply comes from Lake Michigan and "the water cribs are structures built to house and protect offshore water intakes used to supply the City of Chicago with drinking water." (101)

These 'water cribs' were "round chunky stone towers" structures built to house offshore water intakes and "are the only visible portion of the century-old tunnels that carry drinking water to city taps." (102)

When Chicago police officers were involved in violations including drunk driving or domestic abuse, depending upon the severity of the infraction, as a form of punishment the offending officers would be sent to one of these 'intakes' which served as a private 'Alcatraz'. This was one of the most hated forms of discipline by the police department. "They would be confined to one of these water cribs for a week or more, to either 'dry out' or 'cool off'…isolation and water have a way of doing that," as my friend explained.

Over time, Frank told me dozens of other stories and also gave me a lot of free advice. I will never forget one of the things he told me, "Everyone talks. Everyone eventually talks." The "everyone" Frank was referring to were criminals and corrupt individuals and his comment basically alluded to people wanting to get things off their chest, confess, brag, or just hear the sound of their own voice. It was just a matter of time, and some folks "talked' earlier than others. Those that like to hear the sound of their own voice talked the most.

Billy Langenstein, Director, Investigations & Security Services for the NFL was one of the latter.

Another friend of mine, an ex-California State Highway Patrol Captain, named 'Cliff' always smiled when he told me stories about his questioning of criminal suspects. Cliff said he always enjoyed waiting for the suspect to do a "big exhale." Cliff would go on to explain, "At that point, you start to get the truth out of the suspect, because they know they are in deep for their offense." He also said timing would be different for each suspect, some would "exhale" earlier, some later, but the result was usually the same. The "big exhale" was the point in the interrogation when you started getting the truth in the suspect's story.

To my surprise, the day immediately after I left a voicemail for Cathy Lanier, I received a phone call from Billy Langenstein, introducing himself as Director, Investigations & Security Services for the NFL. At the moment of receiving his call, I was actually in a very noisy environment, and asked Billy to repeat himself. I found a flat surface and opened my laptop. I kept the initial part of our conversation going, using the excuse of the noise behind me until I could get fully situated. Then I said, "Billy, sorry about that. You caught me on a job site." I was actually at Westfield Mall in San Jose, but I was able to find a quiet area where I could type notes to record our conversation.

Billy restarted the conversation again:

Billy: "Mr. Weaver, I am responding on behalf of Cathy Lanier, whom you left a voicemail regarding reviewing an incident at Levi's Stadium."

Me: "Billy, tell me again, you work with Cathy Lanier, what is your title?" "And I appreciate your call."

Billy: "To start with, why did you take the action you took?"

Me: "You mean my letter to the City of Santa Clara?"

Billy: "No, why did you put yourself in harm's way during that altercation at Levi's Stadium?"

Me: "I was concerned the assailant might try to hurt someone else while he snuck out. If you look at other fight and assault videos taken at Levi's Stadium, assailants continue to punch and attack others as they are trying to exit, and I was trying to keep them from injuring anyone else."

Billy: "Did you try to reach 49ers Security?"

Me: "I reached out to City of Santa Clara Attorney Brian Doyle but to no avail, but I now have contact information for Jim Mercurio (49ers

Vice President, Stadium Operations & General Manager) and others."

I also mentioned to Langenstein, that I made two trips to City Hall, and included City Attorney Brian Doyle on several emails, but he would not respond to me. During my second trip there, I even left a handwritten note stapled to my business card. But Attorney Doyle's only form of communication was checking out my LinkedIn profile, which I realized after I received an 'alert'.

During that call I discussed with him multiple concerns regarding Levi's Stadium security concerns and related issues pertaining to the SCPD. We briefly talked about:

- Emails sent to Chief of Police Mike Sellers, and City Attorney Brian Doyle
- Two visits to City Hall in unsuccessful attempts to see City Attorney Brian Doyle and the mayor
- UPS over-night copies of my letter sent to the mayor and council members who also serve as the 'Stadium Authority'
- Chief Mike Sellers's approval and public endorsement in interviews with the media of his police officers 'kicking down doors' of two residents' homes without legal search warrants
- Langenstein's awareness of the Kiran Patel personal injury case (and "Yes" Billy said he was aware)
- Visiting the county office and to review and copy Patel's complete personal injury case file
- Talking to Kiran Patel's personal injury attorney, William Smith

Billy Langenstein voiced several other interesting things, and it was towards the end of our phone conversation, I also mentioned that I returned a few games later to take pictures and I have 630 separate photographs of officers hiding, bunched up in groups, no zone coverage, no law enforcement patrolling fan seating areas, and main entry and exit points with no law enforcement whatsoever.

Langenstein asked, "What prompted you as an Oakland Raider's fan to return to the 49ers Levi's Stadium and take all those pictures?" I told him, there is a dangerous pattern here and it is concerning when someone from the community is trying to help and offer solutions to security concerns and no one seems to care. I told him I couldn't believe that, with over 400 law enforcement personnel assigned to work at the game on November 1 not one officer was visible or assisted with my restraint and control of the assailant in a highly visible seating section within full view across from all the major network cameras. I mentioned that I went back to Levi's Stadium to see if perhaps the lack of security situation was a 'one off' but my revisit on December 16th and my review of security that afternoon confirmed the pattern. My first-hand experience was captured and documented in the pictures I took.

Before ending the phone call, I told Billy Langenstein, no matter what, "we are going to review the security tapes of the November 1, 2018 incident together." And I also told Langenstein, "The Levi's Stadium tape footage should show even more than what was captured and shown on the local news. One broadcast I viewed several times and just like what I witnessed first-hand, showed at least five NFL 'on-field' security personnel in yellow and red vests doing nothing at all to help." Immediately after that comment, Langenstein took the longest pause of our conversation. And then he did a "big exhale."

Billy Langenstein's final comment to me before ending the phone call was, "Please don't refer to, or forward any items communicated or discussed during our call today." Langenstein said he would contact the 49ers, look into the investigation, and get back to me, and we then ended our phone conversation.

While I was reviewing the notes I typed during the phone call, the two most important items were during the middle of our discussion when I asked about Kiran Patel, and also when Langenstein "exhaled." I purposely asked Billy if he, Cathy Lanier and Roger Goodell had knowledge of Patel's injuries and personal injury lawsuit, and unwittingly he then gave 'a tell'. He said, "Yes," and Langenstein mentioned that the NFL uses LexisNexis (103) and that the City of Santa Clara's Attorney Brian Doyle in his capacity, most likely has a subscription to LexisNexis as well. This 'reveal' by Langenstein would explain why the City of Santa Clara, Brian Doyle, and the SCPD would 'go dark' and cease all further communication with me. Because now the City Manager Deanna Santana, Mayor Lisa Gillmor, City Attorney Brian Doyle, and the SCPD probably knew exactly whom they were dealing with. All they had to do was research the name Fred Weaver.

Later that night, I received an email from Billy Langenstein (104) which I had requested during our call. He thanked me for my time on the phone earlier that day, and that he would follow up with the 49ers on the active investigation I referenced. Langenstein also requested the six hundred-plus photos I mentioned taking during the second game I attended.

It's quite possible that right after his sending that email, Billy logged on to LexisNexis himself, and did his own research about me. At least my hunch made sense, because that would be the last communication with me from either Billy Langenstein, or from anyone else at the NFL.

Assuming what was likely revealed during everyone's research about me on LexisNexis, it would then explain why City of Santa Clara Attorney Brian Doyle and others at the City of Santa Clara would also want to distance themselves as much as possible and avoid having anything to do with me.

Because yes, I am that guy they researched. And my taking down a hayseed community and police department, bumbling their way trying to handle security at a major NFL team stadium would pale in comparison to what everyone found out about, and also what resulted from of a previous investigation of mine.

But Langenstein and the others had no idea that these days, I was playing a 'deeper game'.

During my Saturday, November 10 phone call with SCPD Captain Tony Parker, my goal was to keep him talking. I wanted to ask as many questions as possible to see just what he would offer, and also what the SCPD knew. One thing was for certain. Parker would not have made that call to me if he knew my history.

My goal with Parker and Langenstein, was to keep them talking to find out anything at all regarding what they knew about the November 1 incident. Another thing was for certain. Neither of them had any idea I would be filing a lawsuit.

What I knew for sure was, if I did file a lawsuit right away, it would have been a long time, if ever, before I could have deposed people like Parker and Langenstein. I would expect the defending attorneys to file Motions to Quash amongst other court procedures to prevent me from talking with several people. Even if I were allowed to depose and question either of these two, or any or all of the other defendants and witnesses, I was certain it would have been quite a battle. The other attorneys would have almost certainly objected to every one of my questions to their clients.

Anticipating these and other procedural challenges upfront, I was prepared, and I had previously planned to do some things 'out of sequence.'

Santa Clara Police Captain Tony Parker didn't know he was my first 'deposition', and the NFL's Billy Langenstein didn't realize he was my second.

CHAPTER 21

"Second Class Citizen"

—ᗰ—

"There's three kinds of folks on this planet. There's people who
make things happen; there's people who *watch* things happen;
and there's people who wonder, what happened?"
David Lee Roth – Lead singer and front man for rock group
Van Halen. (105)

There were actually several 'tipping points' for me throughout
this ordeal that led to filing a lawsuit.

- The 49ers claiming the pair of recent violent and vicious
  beatings resulting in comas to those two 49er fan victims
  attacked at Levi's Stadium that, "Notifying the public
  about the lack of security would discourage use of the
  property and would also serve to invite violent attacks."
- Finding out about all the bad cops involved in Harmon
  and Moneeb/Ikram attacks. And realizing these corrupt
  Santa Clara police officers are the same police officers
  having authority for security as endorsed by the National
  Football league, "as the lead agency for every Levi's
  Stadium game throughout the season."

- The discovery that there is no documentation of a single police officer being terminated or even disciplined for illegally, kicking the doors down on the homes of those two separate residents. And those same bad cops injured both of those residents during that lawlessness. The City of Santa Clara Attorney Bryan Doyle said, "There were no warrants." And the Chief of Police Mike Sellers said, "Our officers' actions were fully within the law and in accordance with accepted police practices." (106) Something just didn't seem right.

- The decisive tipping point was finding out that Deanna Santana was now the new City Manager and CEO of Levi's Stadium Authority. In her 'dual role', Santana is responsible for the operation and security of Levi's Stadium, and managing city government and a group of agencies including the Santa Clara Police Department. Once again, Deanna Santana had personally laundered herself into respectability within a new community leaving behind a wake of litigation, including but not limited to, covering up police misconduct. Her involvement created the guarantee for all of the above illegal actions and security concerns to continue completely unabated... unless someone took corrective measures.

Being treated like a second-class citizen when I was only trying to help was an initial motivation to file a lawsuit. But disappointment and hurt feelings only carry one so far. It was the likelihood that these disturbing findings are absolutely trending toward a first fatality at Levi's Stadium, which really provided the fuel and energy for me to move forward with my case.

There were concerns, however, and I knew full well what I was up against.

The nineteen defendants in my case would certainly not be lying down on this one. Some of the same defendants were involved in all four of the recent personal injury lawsuits mentioned above. High powered, experienced, aggressive, and well-paid attorneys would be hired for this case. And I was a one man show.

There would be demurrers, stays, motions of limine, and a flurry of other legal tactics the defendant attorneys would be using against me. Each one of the causes of action in my lawsuit complaint would be under attack. There would be a tremendous amount of time involved, and then there is the paper. Attorneys can be brutal with the amount of paper they use to bury you.

There were also a couple of other tactics I was immediately concerned with and needed to hopefully engineer a way around. The first of those concerns was a special motion to strike, used by attorneys, pursuant to California's anti-SLAPP statute. If that motion was successful as to *any* of my causes of action, an award of attorney's fees against me would be mandatory.

The acronym SLAPP in the California 'anti-Slapp statute', stands for "Strategic Lawsuits Against Public Participation," and is tied to "a 'disturbing increase' in actions cloaked as tort claims meant to silence legitimate free speech activity. In 1992, California became one of the first states to enact an anti-SLAPP statute." "California's anti-SLAPP statute presents a mechanism to defendants to strike potentially meritless causes of action early in litigation." (107)

By any translation or interpretation of this 'anti-SLAPP statute', this got my attention at 'silencing legitimate free speech'. I wasn't about to let that happen. And further "the special motion may be filed within 60 days of the service of the complaint or, in the court's discretion, at any later time upon terms it deems proper." (108)

The second and equally important of my concerns could potentially take some time, or explode my case at any second, and that concern was judicial bias. My lawsuit was filed in Santa Clara County Superior Court. Not only is this court and its jurisdiction home to the San Francisco 49ers, it is also the heart of Silicon Valley where there is a lot of money, both public and private. And money can help sway a decision. Money can buy lawyers, investigations, and court admissible evidence. Local judges tend to sympathize with local concerns, especially local concerns which are under attack like Levi's Stadium which houses a storied NFL football team such as the 49ers.

But judges don't always side with the local 'brand name'. Judge Simmons denied 84 motions to strike and demurs submitted by PG&E. In the case of PG&E in Hinkley California, as Erin Brockovich exposed during the lawsuit where PG&E was accused of contaminating the residential drinking water wells, the judge hearing the case took a pause. Judge Simmons added, "On a more personal note, as a resident here in Barstow, which is not far from Hinkley, I am disturbed by evidence that suggests that not only was Hexavalent Chromium used, but your clients actually sent these residents pamphlets telling them it was good for them." (109)

For Attorney Ed Masry and Erin Brockovich battling PG&E's poisoning of the local water wells, Judge Simmons's common sense would be what anyone fighting the good fight would want to hear. But there is a flip side. Sometimes local judges can be either 'gotten to' (money) or just go completely and arbitrarily rogue in their decision.

A recent local example of this was in the Brock Turner case.

On January 18, 2015, in Palo Alto, California, a Stanford University student athlete, Brock Allen Turner, sexually penetrated and attempted to rape an intoxicated and unconscious 22-year-old woman. Turner's attempt failed only because of two Stanford international students from Sweden who chanced upon the scene and caught Turner while he attempted to flee as a result. Thus, it took two international students apprehending and restraining Turner until police arrived to take Turner into custody. (110)

Brock Turner was convicted on charges of sexual assault of an unconscious person, sexual assault of an intoxicated person, and sexual assault with intent to commit rape. The presiding judge in the case, Judge Persky sentenced Turner to six months in county jail, of which Brock Turner only served three months, setting off a national outcry. The case prompted public outrage over the sentence, which was widely regarded as lenient.

Turner and his attorney argued on appeal, that Brock had his pants on and fly zipped and only sought "outercourse." "We are not persuaded," wrote Associate Justice Franklin D. Elia. "While it is true that defendant did not expose himself, he was interrupted." Justice Elia wrote that jurors "reasonably could have inferred from the evidence" that if two graduate students had not stopped Mr. Turner when they saw him on top of the unresponsive woman, "he would have exposed himself and raped her." (111) The justices in his appeal also ruled that there was substantial evidence that Mr. Turner knew that the victim was unconscious at the time he sexually penetrated her with his finger and noted that he had lied to a detective in the case about trying to run away.

During the initial trial, the original judge presiding over the case thought differently and went completely rogue against a customary and ordinary 15-year sentence which the prosecution was seeking for Brock Turner. Judge Persky thought since Turner was from a 'good family', according to the judge: "A prison sentence would have a severe impact on him. I think he will not be a danger to others." (112)

114

Even though each of the 'anti-Slapp statute' and judicial bias stood alone as major hurdles, it was the combination of the two which would completely derail my case. The judicial bias could very easily happen with the 'famed' 49ers being considered a 'good family' and thus not deserving to be in the cross hairs and blamed for allowing dangerously inadequate security at their stadium. Besides, no one has died yet at Levi's Stadium (similar to the "not actually been raped" issue in the Brock Turner case).

Related to this concern was the revolving door of judges who can hand off cases in the blink of an eye due to caseload. So just imagine getting another judge like Persky. Same county. Same courthouse. Same drinking fountain as the other judges. Maybe even sharing the same judge's chambers. What if the judge finally assigned to my case is a season ticket holding 49ers fan with a possible bias against a prosecuting, 'self-represented,' long-time season ticket holding Oakland Raider's fan?

Avoiding 'silencing legitimate free speech' with California's anti-SLAPP statute and the potential of a biased judge with a flexible moral compass were now hurdles I needed to clear immediately and convincingly. It was just a matter of how. I needed a strategy.

First Strategy considered

The following is one of the scenes from the movie, <u>Erin Brockovich</u>: (113)

Ed Masry, (Attorney and owner of law firm, Masry & Vititoe)

Erin Brockovich, (Environmental activist with no formal education in the law)

ED'S OFFICE - DAY

ED
I don't know if we can pull this off.

Erin knows how difficult that was for him to say...and she's touched he felt he could say it to her.

ED (cont'd)
This is a monster case...and it's taking time and man-power and money's going out and nothings coming in. I'm going to have to take a second mortgage on the house.

ERIN
So.

ED
(exasperated)
"So"?
(beat)
Look, I have to tell you, I have been making inquiries with other firms. Bigger firms to share some of the cost. They all said no. They say we don't have it.

ERIN
Bullshit! We've got PG&E by the balls...

ED
We've got PG&E Hinkley by the balls. But...unless we can pin this on the corporate PG&E in San Francisco.

ERIN
What do you mean?

116

ED
PG&E Corporate is claiming they had no way of knowing what was going on in Hinkley.

ERIN
Oh, they knew. They had to know.

ED
Show me the document that proves it.

She doesn't have one.

ED (cont'd)
Then they didn't know. And if they didn't know, we can't hit 'em for punitive damages. And with punitive damages, we're talking about the kind of money that could actually have an effect on these people's lives...

ERIN
So, what do we do?

ED
Let's assume there are documents that connect PG&E Hinkley to PG&E corporate. And they know these documents exist.
(more)
We take our four hundred or so plaintiffs and everything you dug up and we file a lawsuit to 'provoke a reaction'... to see if they offer a reasonable settlement or if they just throw more paper at us.

ERIN
(excited)

Well, that sound great! Let's do that!

Ed isn't finished.

ED
There's a down side. PG&E will submit a demur - a list
of reasons attacking each complaint, claiming each cause
of action has no merit. And if the judge agrees with them,
he'll dismiss our lawsuit and PG&E will have no reason
to settle. Then it's all over.

ERIN
So, basically, it's all up to what this one judge decides?

ED
Basically, yeah.

ERIN
Jesus.

They look at each other: Let's hope we get lucky.

Second Strategy considered

Tom Cruise's character 'Maverick' used a strategy in the
movie <u>Top Gun</u>, when he 'hit the brakes' with a Russian MIG
on his tail. (114)

Maverick's co-pilot Merlin
"You haven't lost him yet he's still with us."

Cockpit warning sensors beeping from 'lock' initiated by the MIG

Merlin

"What are you doing, you're slowing down, you're slowin' down?"

Maverick

"I'm bringing him in closer Merlin.

Merlin

"You're gonna do *what*? This is *it* Maverick!"

Maverick

"I'm gonna hit the brakes...he'll fly right by."

Loud amplified warning heard in their cockpit: 'beep, beep, beep, beep'

Merlin

"Shit he's gonna get a lock on us."

Solid uninterrupted warning signal heard in their cockpit

In a split second, Maverick hits 'throttle up' effectively 'braking' the F-14. The MIG flies right by and Maverick locks in on the MIG and fires his remaining rocket exploding the MIG.

(The connection to the story will come later)

Third Strategy considered

The famous comedian Bob Hope used to tell a joke about a Republican and a Democratic senator who ended up having to share a cab to Washington National Airport (now Ronald Reagan Washington National Airport). While the cab driver was loading the luggage in the trunk, the Republican turned to the Democrat and said, "I help our party's cause by always 'tipping big' and then reminding them to vote Republican. The Democrat listened and slyly smiled, and then told the Republican, "I help the Democratic cause and without any of the cost you mention. I don't tip anyone a dime, and then I also remind them to vote Republican."

While the dangerously inadequate security at Levi's Stadium is no joke, the comedy of Bob Hope gave me an idea which was the last piece I needed for an overall strategy I used against all the entities involved with what is soon to be a very deadly situation at Levi's Stadium.

I investigated filing in federal court versus filing in state court. At first, my investigation exposed that my complaint would have a greater chance of being dismissed if I filed in federal court. I initially thought I needed to file federally because of all the out of state entities including the NFL which is based in New York. But then I learned it would be better to file locally in California State court because all of the entities are doing business in the State of California, and specifically in the county of Santa Clara where Levi's Stadium is located. The other benefit of filing in local Superior Court of Santa Clara County, was because this court having jurisdiction for my case was backed up about six months, with their existing caseload. This court backlog of cases would push the date out before any real goings-on took place.

So once again, in an attempt to help, I personally drafted and filed a lawsuit on May 1, 2019, *Frederick Leo Weaver v. San Francisco 49ers Limited, et al.* Santa Clara County Superior Case no. 19CV346749, (2019) (115) (Appendix # 5) My filed Complaint included six Causes of Action:

1. Negligence
2. Premises Liability- Failure to Provide Safe Premise

3. Negligent Stadium Security - Negligent Hiring, Retention, And Supervision
4. Gross Neglect of Duty - Gross Mismanagement
5. Discrimination
6. Conspiracy

The defendants in my lawsuit were the City of Santa Clara who owns Levi's Stadium, the City of Santa Clara Police Department, the San Francisco 49ers and each of their entities, and the National Football League (NFL) including Commissioner Roger Goodell, Senior VP of Security Cathy Lanier, and Billy Langenstein.

After filing the complaint, I was required by the court to 'serve' all of the defendants I named in the complaint. And I also made sure I process served 'courtesy copies' to the 49ers co-owners and two of the Levi's Stadium major advertisers including Levi-Strauss of course, and Intel Corporation the computer chip maker. The idea was to send a direct message to ensure those individuals received their own copy of my lawsuit before any of them 'lawyered up'. Once attorneys get involved, there is usually language in their first communication such as, "Going forward, direct all communications related to this matter to my office."

The list of everyone either served with a courtesy copy or sent a copy via certified mail is included towards the end of this book within, 'List of Individuals, Arranged by Organizational Affiliation'.

My Complaint was filed on May 1, 2019, and all the defendants were officially served by June 14, 2019. Then it was just a matter of waiting for their court required responses...

CHAPTER 22

"This Won't Take Long"

—ᴍ—

"If your opponent is temperamental, seek to irritate him,"
Sun Tzu, *The Art of War.*

Filing a lawsuit and acting as one's own attorney is really no unsurmountable task. The real issue is that acting as your own attorney basically pisses off everyone else involved. Even my process server who owns National Legal Services said, "You know judges don't like when plaintiffs represent themselves." I knew all of the above and more, as this was not the first time, I represented myself in court.

But, when one acts as his or her own attorney or, 'In Pro Per', or 'Per Se', there is a peculiar hubris from the opposing attorneys and sometimes even from the judge sitting the case. After all, an individual acting as his or her own attorney is somewhat of an act of defiance to someone already in that field who has 'earned' their law degree.

However, it should be noted there are several professions where one may perform just as well as a person having a specific degree for a certain field of work. People do their own accounting and taxes all the time. Lots of other people build and remodel their own homes acting as their own general contractor. In either case, if the projects or issues get more complicated, those individuals may then choose to hire someone who is more versed in the complexities of the task.

So even with this lawsuit I filed with six Causes of Action, the legal skills needed are pretty Spartan. Most of the legal procedural information is available out there and on-line, and it is just a matter of going through the motions, getting the right forms and documents for filing, and being aware of times, dates and most importantly, the deadlines set by the court.

But like I mentioned earlier, it really tends to annoy everyone, and especially the opposing attorneys, when you act as your own attorney. "How dare you," they exude in their comments and communication. Adding to this arrogance is a "who do you think you are" attitude usually exhibited during any early communication including phone calls from the defendant's counsel.

I experienced this type of arrogance and hubris during initial communication with the first attorney representing one of the 19 separate defendants in my lawsuit. On Monday, May 20th, 2019, nineteen days after I filed and served my complaint on most of the nineteen defendants, I received an email from an attorney. The attorney contacting me in the email was Ian P. Wilson with the law firm Ericksen Arbuthnot. Ericksen Arbuthnot was representing Landmark Event Staffing Services, the 'mall cops' who help with security at Levi's Stadium, and Attorney Ian Wilson's email to me stated the following:

Dear Mr. Weaver,

This office represents Landmark Event Services in the action you have filed in Santa Clara Superior Court. We have reviewed your Complaint which alleges causes of action arising from a fight that broke out at a Forty Niner's game on November 1, 2018. Per our review of these allegations, we do not believe that the facts, as they are presented, provide you the standing to file suit against our client. We ask that you dismiss our client from your lawsuit. If you would like to discuss this matter and provide a basis as to why you have standing to file suit, please call the undersigned in our firm's San Jose office. Otherwise, our office will file a motion to dismiss the complaint and seek costs against you.

Regards,

Ian P. Wilson, Esq.
ERICKSEN ARBUTHNOT
San Jose, CA 95112

I waited until the following day to respond to Ian, and in a Tuesday May 21, 2019 email, I offered Attorney Wilson the times I would be available for an initial discussion. I wrote:

Dear Mr. Wilson,

I am available this Thursday, May 23rd at 6:00 PM or Friday, May 24th at 5:30 PM.

Do either of these time slots work for you for a phone conversation? Please let me know.

Thank You,

Fred Weaver – Author
Levi's Stadium – Unsafe in Any Seat
fred@UnsafeInAnySeat.com
650 Castro Street, Suite 120-211
Mountain View, CA 94041

I purposely chose the times 6:00 PM and 5:30 PM in the evening, to make it as convenient for me so I could be sitting in front of my laptop and monitor during the call. Attorney Wilson agreed on the Thursday 6:00 PM option and he called me exactly at that time. When I answered, I said, "Hello is this Ian?" and Ian introduced himself and his firm, acknowledging again his firm's representation of Landmark Event Staffing Services. Wilson quickly asked me if I would dismiss the suit against his client, without any discussion or further detail. I pretended as though the phone line broke up and asked Ian to repeat what he said. Ian said, "Mr. Weaver we would like you to dismiss your case against our client, Landmark Event Staffing Services."

I could sense that he was wanting to make quick work of the situation and he was not ready for any sort of lengthy discussion. Perhaps he had only rehearsed, thinking I was going to be emotional, or heated in my exchange with him, and maybe even just hang up on him. But there was no reason for me to be anything but civil and calm, as I wanted Ian to be comfortable in what I had planned, which unanticipated by Ian, was in fact going to be a rather lengthy conversation. Ian seemed impatient, and asked me again, "Mr. Weaver are you going to dismiss my client or not?"

I answered Wilson with a question, "Just like that, Yes or No? It seems rather binary in that you only want one of two answers without hearing and discussing any of the merits of my case." It was then that Ian confirmed, and tried to school me, that the purpose of the call was a Meet and Confer, which is required by the court as an initial communication to try to get a sense of where each party was headed in the lawsuit. A Meet and Confer if properly handled, and in good faith, can sometimes actually turn into a settlement discussion, and or at least benefit in diffusing some of the items in a plaintiff's Complaint. This would be a positive 'quick outcome' that I sensed Ian was ultimately hoping for. But Ian's impatience worked right into my strategy. My goal was simply to keep him on the phone and keep him talking. And to keep Ian talking for as long as possible, I had to remain calm and appear genuinely concerned with the questions I was asking him.

I asked if he was going to reference any type of statute or case law for his argument against the six individual Causes of Action in my Complaint. He then grew irritated, and said, "What do you expect me to do, write a long missive?" I calmly answered Ian and kept looping back and forth with mostly filler conversation, but always returning to my request of him to please try and provide some statutes, or case law or reference, other than just a binary, "Yes or No," request to dismiss his client. I asked if we needed to reconvene the following day, in order for him to come back better prepared, and he then exposed his limitations. "I only have authority from the client for one Meet and Confer." The key takeaway for me in Ian's statement was that Ian didn't have any authority other than hopefully getting a, "Yes I will dismiss Landmark," out of me. I kept trying to keep the clock running, by asking, "But isn't the point of our call to have a meaningful exchange, to discuss points back and forth?" And then I said to Ian, "Wouldn't your client Landmark Event Staffing Services think another call would be beneficial, especially if you were to come prepared to the next call with some sort of argument including statutes or case law?" It was then Ian tried to take some ownership, and said, "I will go back to my client, and see if they will authorize another call."

I offered, "Great, then talk to Landmark, and let's try to schedule a call for tomorrow, if you are available." Wilson then said, "My client isn't Landmark." I knew that Landmark was in the mix during our discussion, but Ericksen Arbuthnot's 'client' wasn't Landmark at all. Attorney Wilson and his firm Ericksen Arbuthnot were hired by the 'insurance company' providing coverage for their 'insured', Landmark Event Staffing Services.

I didn't mind that Wilson and his firm Ericksen Arbuthnot were being dishonest about full disclosure of who they were actually representing, and I decided to let Ericksen Arbuthnot's 'disclosure' work into my favor. I then reset my goal, to keep him on the phone even longer asking questions, now that he and his firm were representing an insurance company.

As a quick note, insurance companies are not really insurance companies 'first'. Insurance companies are first 'investment companies' and they 'invest' money they receive in the form of premiums from you, their 'insured' clients. If you have ever seen the commercial where a tornado has destroyed a family's home, and the insurance company representative shows up and hands a check to the couple standing in what remains of their driveway, well, it doesn't really happen that way. After a disaster or loss, the first thing you have to do is prove you are actually the insurance company's client. The initial conversation usually starts with the question, "What is your policy number?" But, unfortunately, 'Mr. Twister' has archived, literally 'in the cloud', all of your important papers into one or more adjacent zip codes near your loss. And besides, how dare you ask for an insurance company to 'interrupt' their making money with your money, in the form of a payment back to you for your insurable damages. But I digress. However, because of this 'new player' being an insurance company, I was fueled to extend and extrapolate the conversation even further with the already annoyed attorney.

Wilson assured me he would go back to his client, the insurance company for Landmark, and he would try to request another Meet and Confer. This request, if granted, might lead to a meaningful discussion the next time, so Attorney Wilson and Ericksen Arbuthnot can present some statute and or case law supporting their request for my dismissal of their client. I asked him if he would be kind enough to send me an email documenting our phone conversation, and he committed that he would send an email also. We then agreed to finish the phone call, and I hung up after cordially saying, "Good Night."

I had kept Wilson on the phone for a total of forty-two minutes. Mission accomplished.

The following day, I was in meetings, and was keeping an eye out for the promised confirmation email from Ian Wilson. I didn't receive one. I figured he would just default to working on a draft of "a long missive" which he had tried to excuse away in not wanting to initially provide, but would in fact need to eventually provide, just in another format. Because of his frustration with me during the call, I assumed he had no intention at all of trying to get additional approval from his client for another Meet and Confer. My guess was that he was simply drafting the 'eventual' document, a Demurrer, to assist having the judge in my lawsuit, simply dismiss my case against Ericksen Arbuthnot's client.

Since I didn't hear back from Wilson the next morning in either an email or another phone call, I decided to provide a confirmation to him of our discussion from the notes I was typing during our phone conversation. I sent the detailed confirmation in an email during the middle of lunch time at 12:33 PM. Since email is not only cheap, it is free, I decided to 'paper' more than one recipient. Ian had clearly come unprepared the night before to our 'Meet and Confer' and had not readied any statutes or case law against my six individual Causes of Action for us to have a meaningful discussion on. So, I thought with Ian communicating like the low man on the totem pole that he was, or just being the junior member of his law firm, he would need a little help. I copied all forty-two attorneys at Ericksen Arbuthnot. Attorney Wilson and the entire staff of attorneys at Ericksen Arbuthnot received this email from me:

Hey Ian,

Thank you for calling me last night.

Since you did not send an email this morning as you said you would, I just wanted to reiterate and expand a little, and also document our phone conversation last night.

You asked me if I would be willing to dismiss your client from the lawsuit, and I asked If you and your firm would kindly provide in writing some arguments for why your client should be dismissed, including any case law or statutes that your firm believes would support your client's argument.

Unfortunately, Ian, you seemed to want only a 'yes or no' answer on the dismissal. But wasn't the reason for our call to have a meaningful discussion? Upon my asking for some explanation from you and your firm, you seemed completely unwilling to provide any arguments for why your client should be dismissed, including any case law or statutes that you or your firm believes support your argument, and Ian you said, "Do you expect me to write a long missive?"

Please understand, I only made this request, because I don't have anything or any information from you to even consider making an opinion on, much less a decision on, to consider dismissing your client from the lawsuit.

And I have a couple of additional concerns. Ian, you quickly mentioned my Complaint does not have any causations, standings, or mention of injuries. This is quite concerning to me, because my Complaint clearly and succinctly references these even though you later stated the phrase, "rambling in your Complaint." I take no offense to your "rambling" comment but am concerning with your grasp and comprehension of the facts laid out and included as part of the causations within my Complaint. And I am concerned whether or not you personally even read my Complaint, before our phone call.

Ian, at the beginning of our phone conversation last night, I purposely asked you if you personally read my Complaint. Your answer Ian was, "I read it (my Complaint) backwards and forward." I asked this question because I thought maybe you might accidently be referring to another case, or accidently be reading from another Complaint due to the early disconnect of some of your statements and responses to my questions.

Ian, you eventually acknowledged some reference to injuries in my Complaint when you mentioned "your leg". I asked you three times If you saw anywhere in my Complaint where I wrote anything about my leg. And then you went on to confirm, "I may have been told that you suffered a leg injury." Stopping right there, and breaking your statement down a little bit, your use of "I may have been told..." sounds as though someone else read my Complaint, but not you. Again, wouldn't you come prepared, and wasn't the reason for our call to have a meaningful discussion?

To help you out Ian, there is mention of an injury to a 'leg' In my Complaint...but not my leg. The person whose leg was injured, and in fact broken, was Danielle Harmon's leg when the City of Santa Clara Police illegally kicked down her front door without a warrant and broke her leg during this illegal act.

Ian, you also continued and said, "If you Mr. Weaver just happened to see a fight at Levi's Stadium this is not a cause of action. "Mr. Weaver, these things happen. It's a football game, there is an assumption of risk"

Ian, you also mentioned a 'foreseeability issue' three times during our discussion, but you didn't make it clear if you meant a foreseeability issue for me, or for your client Landmark Event Staffing Services (LESS). By the way, it seems to be a fitting acronym for your client, related to the security they *actually* provide versus what your client claims to provide on their website, but I digress.

Assuming Ian, you meant it was a foreseeability issue for your client, I just wanted to bring to your attention:

- In law, a proximate cause is an event sufficiently related to an injury that the courts deem the event to be the cause of that injury.
- "(there is one of several) tests used to determine if an action is close enough to a harm in a "chain of events" to be legally valid. This test is called proximate cause. Proximate cause is a key principle of insurance and is concerned with how the loss or damage actually occurred."

- "A basic rule of negligence law is that a negligent person will not be held liable for unforeseeable consequences of their negligence." But Landmark Event Staffing Services should have been able to 'foresee' the consequences if they are paid to provide qualified trained security services even though Landmark Event Staffing Services was inept and did not provide those security services on November 1, 2018.

- Once a person is held to have behaved negligently, they can, in theory at least, be held liable for foreseeable consequences of that negligence, even if they were of a very low probability. But to remind you (again if you Ian actually read my Complaint) for the November 1, 2018 game between the San Francisco 49ers and the Oakland Raiders, the 49er's and SCPD were expecting a high probability of trouble, with their confirmation of bringing in "well over 400 law enforcement officers," and thus there was not a low probability, but rather a very high probability of trouble expected at Levi's Stadium.

So yes, if you are referring to Landmark Event Staffing Services having a foreseeability issue, I would agree with you, in that LESS did and does have a foreseeability issue. And Ian, again if you read my Complaint, you might be able to understand there is and was a "chain of events." Please read for the first time or re-read my Complaint and try to comprehend the totality of what occurred the night of November 1, 2018.

In fact, the 'chain of events' was actually more of a 'cascading system of failure.' If you are unfamiliar with this term, a 'cascading failure' is a process in a system of interconnected parts in which the failure of one or few parts can trigger the failure of other parts and so on.

As you should be able to comprehend from reading and understanding my Complaint, there is a chain of events which your client, Landmark Event Staffing Services, was and is part of. And Landmark Event Staffing Services is also part of the cascading system of failure. To quickly summarize for you:

- Landmark Event Staffing Services is part of the overall 'security team' at Levi's Stadium.
- According to Defendant NFL Chief of Security Cathy Lanier, "Local police are the lead agency for every game throughout the season."
- The City of Santa Clara Police Department is the "local police," which Cathy Lanier refers to, as the "lead agency" for every game throughout the season.
- The City of Santa Clara Police Department have recently been involved themselves in criminal activity including unlawful acts of kicking down the doors of local residents without legal search or arrest warrants and violating the constitutional rights of those same citizens.
- The City of Santa Clara previously had full knowledge about this.
- The City of Santa Clara Stadium Authority previously had full knowledge about this.
- The San Francisco 49ers previously had full knowledge about this
- The NFL had full knowledge about this

- Landmark Event Staffing Services previously had full knowledge about this
- And now, you, and Landmark Event Staffing Services' Insurance carrier has full knowledge about this
- And all of the above-mentioned entities approve, tolerate, and ratify the recent Illegal actions and unconstitutional conduct of the City of Santa Clara Police Department.

Just to reiterate and clarify. By being knowledgeable of the above, Landmark Event Staffing Services and their Insurance Carrier approve, tolerate, and ratify the recent illegal actions and unconstitutional conduct of the City of Santa Clara Police Department. It will be interesting to see how soon, or even if the Insurance Carrier 'decouples' themselves from their relationship with Landmark Event Staffing Services.

Ian, does the chain of events and cascading system of failure appear more clearly now to you and your client? To even further simplify for you, Landmark Event Staffing Services was and is working with criminals. Landmark Event Staffing Services is working with the criminal City of Santa Clara Police Department including Chief of Police Michael Sellers who fully supports these criminal activities. But don't just take my word for It. Please also refer to and read the two recently filed lawsuits fully explaining these illegal actions. You can find each of these Complaints on my Author's website, on the Sample page. My Author's website is: www.UnsafeInAnySeat.com

Look for:

Moneeb, Ikram and Ikram v City of Santa Clara, Mike Sellers, et al., United States District Court (ND CA 2015), Case no. 5:15-cv-01987-NC,

and:

Danielle Harmon v. City of Santa Clara, City of Santa Clara Police Chief Mike Sellers, et al., United Stated District Court (ND CA 2016) Case no. 5:16-cv-04228-EJD

Ian, during our phone call you also stated, "You (Fred Weaver) even mention Roger Goodell." And then you said, "I shouldn't have said anything, and I apologize about mentioning Goodell." Ian, you don't have to apologize for anything related to your comment on Roger Goodell. Nor would there be any reason for any apology other than perhaps you are apologizing for not reading my Complaint, and your being unprepared for our phone discussion last night. Ian, as we discussed, and as per my recommendation and request of your firm during the end of our phone call, would you please now provide some arguments for why your client should be dismissed, including any case law or statutes that your firm believes would support your client's argument.

You made it clear during our discussion Ian when you said, "I am only authorized to have this call and discussion with you. I will have to see if the carrier (Insurance Company) will approve an additional meet and confer. And, "I will check with my boss about a second email including arguments for why our client should be dismissed, including any case law or statutes that he believes support your argument."

Ian it is also clear to me, if your firm and your firm's client was serious about this first discussion, someone else in your firm with some mettle would have been the participant for last night's phone call. So, I am taking the liberty of including everyone else with your firm to see if anyone can help assist you with these efforts.

It is only my opinion, but my suggestion to you and your firm is you prepare a better defense or get a better class of client. Your client Landmark Event Staffing Services is willingly and knowingly working with criminals as being part of the security staff and personnel at Levi's Stadium. And the carrier for Landmark Event Staffing Services is insuring them to work with these criminals.

I look forward to some semblance of any arguments for why your client should be dismissed, including any case law or statutes that your firm believes support your argument for dismissal of your client, other than just your binary 'yes or no' request.

Please also email the dates you mentioned your firm obtained from the Court Clerk.

I look forward to your response.

Thank You,

Fred Weaver – Author
Levi's Stadium – Unsafe in Any Seat
fred@UnsafeInAnySeat.com
650 Castro Street, Suite 120-211
Mountain View, CA 94041

And then the following day, instead of Attorney Ian P. Wilson responding, the 'heavy' answered in response to my email.

I received the attached response email from Wilson's boss, Attorney Nathanial R. Lucey, a partner with Ericksen Arbuthnot. Lucey, responded in kind like I had done the day before, and copied all other attorneys in his firm on his response to me:

Dear Mr. Weaver,

I am the partner managing this file. Ian Wilson is my associate. Thank you for your comprehensive response. Thank you also for sending it to every lawyer in my firm as I am sure it will be the topic of discussion for a long time to come. Ian has sent you dates for our motion to dismiss. Please select one by Monday. If we do not hear from you, we will assume any of the listed dates will be acceptable.

Understand that California law places a duty on a litigant to call an opposing party before filing a demurrer. The purpose of this call is to advise the party of the motion and request that he dismiss the action or provide some basis as to how he can cure the identified legal deficiencies. Ian was only responsible for telling you that your action is defective and the reason why. He was not responsible for telling you how to fix it.

Reading your e-mail below, I see that you were more concerned with telling your story than listening to what Ian had to say. Therefore, I will repeat our point in this e-mail.

To file suit, a litigant must have standing. This legal principle is in both our federal and state constitutions and acts as a limit on the power of our courts. One must have standing to sue. Standing requires that a plaintiff have an injury for which he or she may seek recovery. It is not enough to just be a "concerned citizen." From everything that you have said below and everything that is in your

Complaint, you have no injury and therefore you do not have standing. You therefore cannot sue.

I am certain that there will be other reasons to dismiss your action, the standing issue is the most obvious. We therefore reserve our right to raise further challenges in our moving papers.

I should advise you that if we prevail on our motion, this firm will seek recovery of the costs expended in defending this action. Therefore, please re-evaluate whether you want to pursue this matter any further.

Regards,

Nathaniel R. Lucey, Esq.
ERICKSEN ARBUTHNOT

I purposely didn't respond. Exactly a week later, on Friday May 24, 2019, I was served via certified mail and email with a copy of Defendant Landmark Event Staffing Services, Inc.'s Notice of Demurrer, which the law firm Ericksen Arbuthnot had already filed with the court. (116) (Appendix # 6) Wilson and company had to prepare and "write a long missive" after all. They knew it. And I knew it. And now I was in possession of it.

I received exactly what I needed, and exactly what I had planned for.

CHAPTER 23

"Hitting the Brakes"

—*ɯ*—

The eighteen other defendants I named in my Complaint included the San Francisco 49er entities, City of Santa Clara and its Police Force, the National Football League (NFL), and three NFL personnel I named 'personally'. Those three separate NFL employees were NFL Commissioner Roger Goodell, NFL Senior V.P. of Security Cathy Lanier and her minion Billy Langenstein.

The San Francisco 49ers entities were all served between the 8th and 11th of May 2019. The City of Santa Clara, its Stadium Authority, and the City of Santa Clara Police Department, along with Chief of Police Mike Sellers, named personally, were all served between May 4th and May 11th, 2019.

For the NFL defendants, other than Roger Goodell who was served on May 7th, it took additional attempts to serve the National Football League, Cathy Lanier, and Billy Langenstein. The NFL got 'cute' after Roger Goodell was served and tried to make it difficult 'process serving' the others with a copy of my Complaint. But my process server, I'll call 'Marty', with National Services was undeterred and within an additional week by May 14th, Marty and his crew had all nineteen defendants in my lawsuit properly served. I hired Marty for his basic processing services, but he had asked me early on if I wanted any 'special process serving'. I wasn't quite sure what he meant by 'special' processing services and assumed he would be able to track someone down and serve them at their residence versus serving them at their place of employment.

Marty smiled as he explained, "For a little extra, I serve wayward NFL players and naughty celebrities, while each of these high-profile types are attending their own news conferences, family weddings, and other public events where there are plenty of people around, including the media. I even get asked to serve a copy on the news media if any are present, to ensure the media has all the details they need, rather than waiting to somehow obtain their own copy." As interesting as this special service sounded, I didn't want to have to wait for the 'off chance' of one of these public events and assured Marty, I just wanted all of the defendants in my lawsuit processed served as quickly as possible.

Even before NFL Defendants Cathy Lanier and Billy Langenstein were properly served June 14, 2019, on Marty's second attempt, I received an email on Monday, June 3rd, 2019, from Joni Gordon, a Legal Assistant with the firm Lombardi, Loper, and Conant. I wasn't who this firm was until I read the email and its attachment:

Good afternoon, Mr. Weaver. In connection with the above-captioned matter, attached please find Mr. Pohle's letter dated today. A copy also has been sent via facsimile.

Joni Gordon
Legal Assistant
Lombardi, Loper & Conant
Oakland, CA 94612

I was driving when I received Gordon's email and waited until I got to my next stop, and then opened the email and letter she had attached. The attachment was a sixteen-page letter from the law firm Lombardi, Loper & Conant, LLP, and prepared by Attorney Taylor J. Pohle. (117) (Appendix # 7)

Pohle's sixteen-page letter started with obligatory, "My firm was recently retained..." and then I realized after a quick read, Attorney Pohle's firm Lombardi, Loper & Conant was representing the balance of *all* of the other eighteen defendants. This meant I would initially be dealing with only two attorneys versus potentially nineteen separate attorneys which was the total number of defendants in my lawsuit. Pohle's letter said:

Dear Mr. Weaver:

My firm was recently retained to represent the San Francisco Forty Niners, Ltd., San Francisco Forty Niners II, LLC, Forty Niners Football Company LLC, San Francisco Forty Niners Foundation, Forty Niners Stadium, LLC, Forty Niners Stadium Management Company LLC, Forty Niners Holdings LP, Forty Niners Holdings LLC, the Forty Niners SC Stadium Company LLC (collectively, the "Forty Niners Entities"), the City of Santa Clara (the "City"), the Santa Clara Stadium Authority (the "Authority"), the Santa Clara Police Department (the "SCPD"), Chief of Police Michael Sellers, City Manager Deanna Santana, the National Football League (the "NFL"), Commissioner Roger Goodell, Vice President Cathy Lanier, and Billy Langenstein (all collectively, the "Defendants") in the above referenced action that you filed on May 1, 2019. Going forward, direct all communications related to this matter to my office.

This letter identifies many deficiencies and defects that appear of the face of your Complaint for Damages and serves as an attempt to initiate a meet and confer discussion. The Complaint is susceptible to demurrer for failure to state causes of action and for uncertainty. *See* Code Civ. Proc. § 430.10(e), (f). The Complaint is also susceptible to a motion to strike because it contains irrelevant, false, and improper matters. *See* Code Civ. Proc. § 436(a). What follows below is not meant to be an exhaustive list, and Defendants reserve all rights related to all potential defenses.

Then completely unlike the earlier and lazy effort I received from Ian Wilson, Pohle continued in his letter with fourteen pages of 'chapter and verse' reference to statutes, legal standards, and case law.

Pohle's 16-page letter concluded with his firm's opinion of why I should dismiss my case against all of the defendants he was representing, and Attorney Taylor's letter also included a reach out to discuss my case on a phone call:

None of the claims contained in the Complaint state a viable cause of action against my clients and there is no reasonable chance to cure the defects based on the allegations. For that reason, the Complaint is susceptible to demurrer and a motion to strike. On behalf of the Forty Niners Entities, the City, the Authority, the SCPD, Mr. Sellers, Ms. Santana, the NFL, Commissioner Goodell, Ms. Lanier, and Mr. Langenstein, I respectfully request that you dismiss your Complaint with prejudice so that we can avoid unnecessary motion practice. To the extent you disagree, please contact me so that we can set time to meet and confer.

Please be advised that in addition to demurring and moving to strike large segments of your Complaint, we will be filing another special motion to strike pursuant to California's antiSLAPP statute. If that motion is successful as to any of your causes of action, an award of attorney's fees against you is mandatory. In the past, we have typically secured awards of fees on such motions in the range of $20,000. I look forward to your response.

Respectfully,

LOMBARDI, LOPER & CONANT, LLP

Taylor J. Pohle

I waited until the following day to respond to Pohle, and in an email, I offered him similar times, late in the day, and later in that week, when I would be available for an initial discussion. I wrote:

Dear Mr. Pohle,

I am available this Thursday, June 6th at 6:00 PM or Friday, June 7th at 5:30 PM.

Do either of these time slots work for you for a phone conversation? Please let me know.

Thank You,

Fred Weaver – Author
Levi's Stadium – Unsafe In Any Seat
fred@UnsafeInAnySeat.com
650 Castro Street, Suite 120-211
Mountain View, CA 94041

Responding to my offer of my two earliest available times, he sent me this email:

Hi, Mr. Weaver:

I am available Thursday at 6:00 pm – 7:00 pm. Friday after 5:00 PM unfortunately doesn't work.

One hour may not be long enough because of the number of issues I raised in my letter, but we can always resume our call next week. What is the best number to reach you?

Thank you,

Taylor J. Pohle
Lombardi, Loper & Conant, LLP

And I responded in kind. But what Pohle didn't realize when he sent his email, was that there was not going to be a need for a 'resume' call:

Hey Mr. Pohle,

Since Thursday at 6:00 PM works for both of us, why don't we at least start then. I am going to be unavailable until late Thursday but may even be able to move the time up on that day to 5:00 PM, and I cannot commit as of this writing, but will advise if I am available earlier.

Unless schedule changes for you, please call me this Thursday, June 6th, at 6:00 PM on my cell phone.

Thank You for your accommodation and talk to you then.

Fred Weaver – Author
Levi's Stadium – Unsafe in Any Seat
fred@UnsafeInAnySeat.com
650 Castro Street, Suite 120-211
Mountain View, CA 94041

Once again, I purposely offered the times 6:00 PM and 5:30 PM in the early evening, to make it as convenient for me. But this time I didn't need to be sitting in front of my computer and screen to take notes. I wasn't concerned in the slightest with what he had to communicate to me. I didn't care because I knew, and I had planned exactly and succinctly for what Pohle and his firm's response would be. There was no other possible option of what their response would or could possibly be, and they had no idea of the direction I was about to take.

I didn't need to be taking notes during this conversation, because if needed, I would basically be referring only to my own. I didn't even plan on referring to any of my written notes, because I had been living 'my notes' since November 1, 2018, and then again on May 1ˢᵗ, 2019 when I filed the Complaint. My conversation was not going to be of a 'read from the prompter or note' type at all. This was going to be a planned one way 'open mic' type of discussion and directed at Pohle. There would be no give and take.

Pohle called me precisely at the agreed scheduled time of 6:00 PM on Thursday, June 6ᵗʰ, 2019. Once again, I answered the phone and cordially asked, "Is this Taylor?"

He said, "Yes, and Mr. Weaver, thank you for scheduling a call with me." He continued, "Mr. Weaver, I am not sure if you were able to read my June 3, 2019 letter which was sent to you?" I then told him, "Yes, I not only read your letter, but I reviewed it quite thoroughly and marked it up and underlined areas considerably."

After my response to his initial question, he cordially suggested since I had read and reviewed his letter if there was any certain area I wanted to discuss first. I thanked him for his detailed sixteen-page letter, and then said, "Why don't we save time here..." and he mildly interrupted and offered, "Well Mr. Weaver since you claim you marked up my letter, you must have some initial concerns?" He must have thought I had changed my demeanor since my email responses and my perceived agreement to potentially discuss his letter over more than one phone call.

I then told Taylor again, "Why don't we save some time here and before we go any further, ...I would like to completely dismiss all of your clients from my lawsuit." There was a short pause and silence before Taylor responded, "Really, Mr. Weaver are you serious?"

There was another purposely delayed response, this time on my part, and then I responded, "Yes, I am willing to fully dismiss all of your clients, with one condition." And my condition was one I was not sure if he could agree to immediately on our phone call, but I hoped given a short period of time my condition would be met. He asked me, "Mr. Weaver, what sort of 'condition' did you have in mind?" I then said, my condition would be to fully dismiss all of his clients from my lawsuit, but 'without prejudice'. He paused as expected, and then said, "Mr. Weaver, I believe dismissing 'without prejudice' would be an option, but of course as you know, I am representing several parties, and would need to obtain their approval and consensus first before agreeing with your request." I said that I understood, and then he offered, "Mr. Weaver, I will immediately try to make contact with all of my clients but I am not sure if I can get an answer immediately, as I have to discuss with all parties, and it may take a couple of days."

I told him, "I understand, and appreciate your initial consideration of my offer to completely dismiss my case against your clients, 'without prejudice.'" He didn't ask me as I had expected, so I then continued with, "Taylor, here is why I had a change of heart." And I knew with him having a 'victory' for his clients, he was a captive audience. He had absolutely no choice. It would not have been prudent for him to want to rush an end to the call. He now had to accommodate and 'nurture' his victory, and not take any chance of letting it slip away with a rude or rushed end of our call. And I knew there would be no reason he wouldn't accommodate a brief reason for my bringing the lawsuit to an end for his clients. But I had no intention on being brief. Pohle unexpectedly received what he ultimately hoped for, and that was closure and or reasonable settlement for his clients. My immediate goal wasn't closure at all. At least not closure with our conversation. My goal was to keep him on the phone as long as possible, and to glean anything he said at all, even though I would be doing most of the talking.

I started by individually mentioning the six causes of action in my Complaint, and briefly going into detail on each of them. I tried to explain as sincerely as I could communicate to him, that my ultimate concern was that someone was going to get killed at

Levi's Stadium due to the complete lack of security I personally witnessed twice, and also documented in photographs I took. I reiterated all of the same discussion points I documented in my email to Attorney Ian Wilson and the rest of his associate lawyers at Ericksen Arbuthnot. I touched on exactly all the same items discussed with Wilson with one difference. This time, I purposely looped my conversation and repeated myself twice on all points. I tried to convey my sincerity to Pohle, and I told him my hope would be during his discussion with his clients regarding the 'dismissal without prejudice' he would echo my concerns to each of them as well. It was then that I told Taylor the reason I wanted the dismissal 'without prejudice'. Taylor might have known, but I acknowledged to him anyway, "Taylor, as you know, by 'dismissing without prejudice', should there be any concern..." at which point Taylor mildly interrupted me and said, "So you could refile the lawsuit if you wanted."

I clocked our conversation and noted that I had kept him on the phone up to that point for a total of one hour and twelve minutes. My other comment and request of him before the end of our discussion was if his firm would be kind enough to prepare the dismissal, assuming Lombardi, Loper & Conant, LLP was able to secure approval from all of their clients, with my request for dismissal without prejudice. He gladly obliged and said upon approval of the dismissal from his clients he would send over the court dismissal form for me to sign. He also mentioned his firm would file the dismissal with the court, pay the related filing fees and once court filed, send me a court date stamped copy.

My sincere "double heartedness" paid off. Exactly one week later I received the court filed document I needed from eighteen of the nineteen defendants, fully dismissing them in my case, but 'without prejudice'. The dismissal 'without prejudice' allowed me to keep a legal cloud hanging over each of these 18 defendants *forever*.

CHAPTER 24

"How Did You Guess?"

—⚹—

"We both guessed the same"

On Wednesday, June 19, 2019 at 10:22 AM, I sent another email to Attorney Ian Wilson at Ericksen Arbuthnot, again, copying the other 42 attorneys with his firm. I attached the court filed document I had received from Attorney Pohle and his firm Lombardi, Loper, and Conant, LLP, dismissing all of their 18 defendant clients named in my lawsuit.

I had received the June 14, 2019 electronically filed copy of the dismissal five days earlier and waited before forwarding a copy to the 43 attorneys at Ericksen Arbuthnot. Wilson didn't wait to respond, however, and I received a call from him within one hour, of my sending the dismissal to his firm. Wilson and Ericksen Arbuthnot had reason to be concerned.

On the phone call, he confirmed receipt of my email, and also the court filed dismissal removing all of the defendants in my lawsuit, other than Ericksen Arbuthnot's client Landmark Event Staffing Services. He then continued and said, "But our firm didn't see our client included within your dismissal, unless you did that on purpose?"

By already having received the dismissal 'without prejudice' from Attorney Pohle and his firm's eighteen other defendants in my lawsuit, it was almost a 'lock' that Wilson and Co. would do the same. I had time for Ericksen Arbuthnot and their client to make that sobering decision.

I was fortunate in negotiating the dismissal 'without prejudice' with Lombardi, Loper, and Conant, LLP and now it was time to leverage that dismissal with the condition I wanted, from Ericksen Arbuthnot and their client. I could take whatever time was needed to get the dismissal from them because there was plenty of time to maneuver. The Santa Clara Superior Court was backlogged for six months.

Rather than wait, however, I was able to quickly negotiate a similar dismissal, without prejudice, with Ericksen Arbuthnot and their client, Landmark Event Staffing Services.

There was one other door I made sure I closed. In dismissing all 19 defendants, I was able to negotiate language such that each of these attorneys would waive 'any fees', meaning of course no charges for their legal time or expenditures defending their clients would be levied against me. That language looked just like what Ericksen Arbuthnot attached to their subsequent court filed dismissal: "The parties Weaver and Landmark ("Weaver," "Landmark"), "parties" will bear their own, individual costs, expenses and/or fees related to the above-titled matter."

I now had exactly what I needed, and what I had planned for, from each law firm and from all 19 of their defendant clients. But only one of the attorneys, the laziest and 'whiniest' of the two came even close to guessing the theme of my little exercise. His comment was, "Unless you did that on purpose?"

Attorney Wilson had no idea, just how correct his guess was on two fronts. Number one, yes, I purposely filed my lawsuit for the sole reason of getting the 19 defendants' court required

responses to my Complaint, and then after receiving those defendants' responses, my plan was to quickly dismiss the lawsuit.

Number two would be something Wilson, and anyone else
who gave the thought any consideration, would have to wait a
little longer to find out exactly the reason behind it. My excuse for
this second part was that I wasn't finished telling this story, nor
would I *ever* be finished with broadly communicating its lesson.
Rather than have that story and lesson, win or lose in a court trial,
then possibly hidden away in some courthouse legal archive, I
had an idea which was my plan all along. I was going to use each
of the efforts of these attorneys, along with their ridiculous and
absurd arguments against why Levi's Stadium and other public
venues should be safer.

But first, I needed to continue writing. Then I needed my
publisher to print it.

CHAPTER 25

"Absurd and Impractical Consequences"

—◊—

"And the judge wasn't gonna look at the twenty-seven
8 x 10 colored glossy pictures with the circles and arrows
and a paragraph on the back of each one..."
from Arlo Guthrie's <u>Alice's</u> <u>Restaurant</u>. (118)

Remember the strategies I gleaned earlier based on the movies Erin Brockovich and Top Gun, and Bob Hope's joke as referenced in Chapter 22 - Second Class Citizen? I combined them all into my consolidated, final, strategy:

(1) File a lawsuit to "provoke a reaction" (Erin Brockovich),
(2) "Hit the brakes" (Top Gun) by immediately filing a dismissal after receiving 'reaction' responses from each of the Defendants' attorney, and
(3) Help my cause without 'any of the cost' (Bob Hope's joke) of a long drawn out court trial

Sometimes life imitates art. The combined strategy worked.

I purposely never had any intention of going forward with a lengthy trial with all the expense, ultimate uncertainty, plus risking the challenges affecting a Per Se, acting as my own attorney. I preplanned utilizing all three of the above strategy 'milestones', combining into one overall strategy. I just needed to carry it out.

I 'provoked a reaction' by filing the lawsuit and received as they say in card playing, 'a look at their hands.' I was able to force the defending attorneys to provide their individual responses to my lawsuit, citing 'chapter and verse', or more properly stated, 'statute and case law'.

I also 'hit the brakes' right after receiving and reviewing their two individually filed 'demurs' by immediately dismissing the case against each of the two attorneys defending the total 19 defendants.

Lastly "I helped my cause without any of the cost," of a full and lengthy trial. A potentially risky trial mind you, with no certain outcome. But there was never a concern, because as the character in Top Gun, pilot Maverick schemed, I hit the brakes and stopped any further court proceedings as soon as I received the Dismissals Without Prejudice. I had budgeted, however, exactly the amount needed to file the case and related costs, and also the cost to dismiss it. I knew both costs, and I also knew I would only be paying 'my side' of the costs. The cost to file my lawsuit complaint was exactly $435 dollars. I also had to pay to 'serve' all the defendants with a copy of my Complaint, and also the cost to serve 'courtesy copies' and certified mailings to other important parties not included as defendants in my lawsuit.

You could say, the costs as compared to a lengthy uncertain trail were minimal. Or you could just parrot the catch phrase in the old American Express commercial: "Priceless."

As I mentioned earlier, I researched, and to get the maximum benefit of filing my complaint in conjunction with the release of this book, it was an easy choice to file locally vs federally. Because the local Santa Clara County Superior Court was backlogged with six months' worth of cases, this would give me the opportunity to complete my book and also provide me with some time for any pre-trial publicity if I wanted.

As planned, and as Arlo Guthrie sings, "the judge wasn't gonna look..."*at anything*, because I planned that there was not going to be any trial. But that certainly isn't the end of things. I did receive as I mentioned, the court required 'Responses' and proposed defenses from both attorneys defending the nineteen defendants. Those were well read, reviewed and marked up. I copied the attorney's responses, scanned them using optical character recognition, and converted the scanned responses into Word files. I then used the attorney's exact language from each of their responses to create the abstract of their arguments below.

I wanted to spare my readers having to read the lengthy 'legalese' within the body of the narrative of this book. Trust me, including those would have severely bogged down the readability. So, I have included my original filed May 1, 2019 lawsuit Complaint, as an (Appendix # 5), and I have included in their entirety, the complete individual responses from each of the attorneys as separate (Appendix # 6) and (Appendix # 7).

Below you will find two abstracts that I prepared from each of the two attorney's responses. The content is verbatim, yet 'abstracted' or in other words, condensed. Read these and then compare to their full versions in the Appendices. But I warn you, even these two abstracts from these attorneys and their client defendants are disturbing and concerning, for a future attendee at Levi's Stadium. See if you agree.

At the end of these two abstract defenses from the attorneys, I have added something very important. Had this case actually gone to trial I would have used the narrative following their full argument responses as part of what I would have used to argue my side of the case. You may be shocked at the similarities. Please keep reading for a further explanation tying it all together.

Here is the first 'abstract' response:

Lombardi, Loper & Conant, LLC - June 3, 2019 Letter attached to his filed Declaration Pursuant to Code of Civil Procedure Section 435.5, Regarding The Forty Niners' Defendants, The City Defendants, and the NFL Defendants' Inability to Meet and Confer

The highlights below, are abstracted from Attorney Taylor Pohle and his law firm Lombardi, Loper & Conant, LLC's arguments contained in the above referenced document filed with the court on June 3, 2019. The abstract is abbreviated at points, but nothing is taken out of context, and Lombardi, Loper & Conant, LLC's full letter can be referenced in (Appendix # 7).

- "The California Government Code 815 holds public entities and their employees to a different legal standard as compared to private entities and individuals. Public entities, and their employees, enjoy an array of immunities many of which relate directly to law enforcement." (page 2)
- "The California Government Code 845 immunizes public entities and their employees 'for failure to provide sufficient police protection service.' The Legislature intended for Section 845 to offer public entities wide protection" (page 2)
- Whether police protection should be provided at all, and the extent to which it should be provided, are political decisions which are committed to the policy making officials of government.

- "Much like the analysis of California Government Code 815, for premises liability, California Government Code 835 also holds public entities to a different standard than their private counterparts.
- First, as stated above, public entities and their employees have statutory immunity against claims of alleged inadequate security, (Gov. Code 845).
- "The Public Entity Defendants are immune for negligence or negligent security.
- Second, public entities are liable only to the extent allowable by statute. (Gov. Code 815). In other words, public entities are not subject to "ordinary care' or "reasonable care."
- Complaint does not indicate any 'despicable conduct.'
- Federal Law Does Not Place an Affirmative Duty on Law Enforcement Officers to Provide Police Protection.
- "And most importantly…police are under no affirmative duty to assist and protect.

Here is the second 'abstract' response:

Ericksen Arbuthnot - May 31, 2019 Defendant Landmark Event Staffing Services - Notice of Demurrer

The highlights below, are abstracted from Attorney Ian P. Wilson and Ericksen Arbuthnot's arguments contained in the above referenced document filed with the court on May 31, 2019. The abstract is abbreviated at points, but nothing is taken out of context, and Ericksen Arbuthnot's full Notice of Demurrer can be referenced in (Appendix # 6).

- "In reality, Plaintiff (Fred Weaver) contends Defendants owed a duty to him to quickly apprehend a person who committed a crime against another person."
- "Plaintiff had no right to have officer assist him in apprehending criminals."
- "Plaintiff also appears to claim that...the Defendants owed him a duty to make sure that no criminal conduct interfered with his enjoyment of the game."
- In any event, the factors above weigh against finding that the Defendant had a duty to apprehend the assailant so that Plaintiff could enjoy the game."
- "There is no disparate conduct."
- "Plaintiff's fourth cause of action for gross negligence focuses on various misdeeds of the Santa Clara Police Department, including falsifying police reports. Plaintiff (Fred Weaver) does not allege how this resulted in any damages to him or anyone else."

This would be one of the first arguments in my case:

Based on the last point of Ericksen Arbuthnot's defense, I would like to present as a legal argument, "Principles of comparable institutions," or in other words utilize a "Brandeis Brief" style of cross-industry-innovation to truly expose "how this will result in damages to anyone." For my argument, we will look at two separate industries, the financial industry and the automotive industry.

Let's look first look at the financial industry using the example of Madoff Investments with Bernie Madoff at the helm.

Thousands of people including Academy Award winning film director Steven Spielberg were investors because Bernie Madoff was a 'trusted name'. They trusted the financial reports that Bernie Madoff provided to them for their consideration in making an investment with his firm. Those people then lost their money due to false reports which were the basis for concealing fraud in the largest swindle on American soil. In fact, a total of $17.5 billion was lost in investments with Bernie Madoff's firm. As a note, Bernie Madoff is currently serving a 150-year prison term.

And then look at the parallels. People put their trust in Bernie Madoff. People put their trust in a Chief of Police like Mike Sellers and the Santa Clara Police Dept.

Let's compare the 'red flags' with each of Bernie Madoff, and Police Chief Mike Sellers:

- Making false financial filings vs making false police reports
- Highly respected position with NASDAQ and Madoff Investments vs highly respected position as Chief of Police for City of Santa Clara
- They both share lies, scandal, moral deterioration, and thousands of people affected
- Bernie Madoff was head of Madoff Investments and in charge of security for those world-wide investments - Mike Sellers is Chief of Police for the "local police". "These local police are the lead agency (handling security and law enforcement) for every game throughout the season," at Levi's Stadium with a 60,000 plus attendance capacity.

Falsified investment reports like what were distributed by Madoff's Investments, gave a false sense of security to his investors. Falsified police reports by the City of Santa Clara Police give a false sense of security to sixty-plus-thousands of fans attending Levi's Stadium each home game.

As the jury in the court of public opinion, do you feel it is fair to compare Bernie Madoff and his firm to Police Chief Mike Sellers and his City of Santa Clara Police Officers?

This would be one of the second arguments in my case, the automotive Industry:

Comstock v. General Motors Corporation - 358 Mich. 163 (1959) 99 N.W.2d 627

Robert Comstock was employed by Ed Lawless Buick Company as a mechanic. While at work on January 18, 1954, he received serious injuries to his right leg. The leg ultimately had to be amputated.

The automobile which struck him was a 1953 Buick Roadmaster equipped with power brakes, owned by Leon Friend. It had been purchased in the spring of 1953 and had been driven 6,000 miles. It was being driven at the time of the accident by Clifford Wentworth, the assistant service manager of Lawless Buick. The accident happened when Wentworth forgot that the power brakes on the Buick in question were not working.

Friend testified that he had first discovered that the brakes on his automobile were not operating on January 17, 1954. The next morning (a Monday) he called Lawless Buick which had sold him the car and talked to Clifford Wentworth who told him that he should bring the car in.

Leon Friend drove the automobile to the garage, with his wife preceding him in another car. He used the emergency brake and employed the car ahead as a bumper.

On arriving at the garage, he brought the car to a stop inside the garage service door. He talked to Wentworth about the brakes and about some other work he wanted done. Wentworth wrote up a service order. Friend asked whether he should leave the car where it was, and Wentworth said to do so.

A few minutes later while Friend was still in the building, Wentworth got into the Buick in question and sought to drive it out of the way into a service stall. He testified that it was a busy morning and that he completely forgot that Friend's Buick had no brakes until he applied them as the car was moving in the direction of another employee, Robert Comstock, who was putting a name plate on the rear of another automobile. The brake pedal went down to the floor board without affecting the progress of the automobile. Although, Wentworth testified, he attempted to apply the emergency brake, the Buick struck Comstock, crushing his right leg against the bumper of the car on which he was working.

Testimony which Robert Comstock points to as establishing negligence on the part of defendant General Motors includes the following:

Wentworth testified that in the fall of 1952, immediately following introduction of the 1953 Buick automobile, difficulties were experienced with the power brake system on the 1953 Buicks resulting in sudden brake failures. In many of those cases it was discovered that failure of an "O" ring sealer in the hydraulic brake master cylinder allowed the brake fluid to escape from the master cylinder. When this happened, the brake foot pedal could be pressed clear to the floorboards without any brake application resulting.

General Motors and Buick knew about the sudden brake failure issues yet did nothing to notify their purchasing customer. They only waited until their customer brought the vehicle in for repair of the faulty brakes. Defendant's Buick division warned its dealers. It did not warn those into whose hands they had placed this dangerous instrument, and whose lives (along with the lives of others) depended upon defective brakes which might fail without notice.

Appellate Justice Edwards rendered a decision overruling the trial judge and sending the case back for a new trial. His words defined certain standards which seem almost elementary:

"The braking system is obviously one of the most crucial safety features of the modern automobile. The greatly increased speed and weight of a modern automobile are factors which must be considered in relation to the care which would be reasonable for a manufacturer to use in designing, fabricating, assembling, and inspecting a power brake. A modern automobile equipped with brakes which fail without notice is as dangerous as a loaded gun."

"Defendant's Buick division warned its dealers. It did not warn those into whose hands they had placed this dangerous instrument, and whose lives (along with the lives of others) depended upon defective brakes which might fail without notice."

"In our view, the facts in this case imposed a duty on defendant to take all reasonable means to convey effective warning to those who had purchased 1953 Buicks with power brakes when the latent defect was discovered."

"If such duty to warn of a known danger exists at point of sale, we believe a like duty to give prompt warning exists when a latent defect which makes the product hazardous to life becomes known to the manufacturer shortly after the product has been put on the market. This, General Motors did not do."

Justice Edward's opinion, rendered on November 25, 1959, sent the case back for a new trial. But General Motors was in no mood to risk another trial against the background of the stinging rebukes and strict guidelines of the Supreme Court of Michigan. The company settled with Comstock for $75,000 as compensation for the loss of his leg. (119)

Bogart v. Cohen-Anderson Motor Co., Inc., 164 Or 233 (98 P2d 720)

In another similar opinion in lawsuit, Bogart v. Cohen-Anderson Motor Co., Inc., 164 Or 233 (98 P2d 720). "The braking system is obviously one of the most crucial safety features of the modern automobile. The greatly increased speed and weight of a modern automobile are factors which must be considered in relation to the care which would be reasonable for a manufacturer to use in designing, fabricating, assembling, and inspecting a power brake. A modern automobile equipped with brakes which fail without notice is as dangerous as a loaded gun. In legal terms, an automobile with defective brakes is clearly a dangerous instrumentality."

As referenced in additional related court cases, "The duty to warn of known danger inherent in a product, or in its contemplated use, has long been a part of the manufacturer's liability doctrine." Clement v. Crosby & Co., 148 Mich. 293 (10 LRA NS 588, 12 Ann Cas 265); Gerkin v. Brown & Sehler Co., 177 Mich. 45 (48 LRA NS 224, 4 NCCA 254); Lovejoy v. Minneapolis-Moline Power Implement Co., 248 Minn 319 (79 NW2d 688); Hopkins v. E.I. DuPont De Nemours & Co. (CCA 3), 199 F2d 930; Tomao v. *177DeSanno & Son (CCA 3), 209 F2d 544; Haberly v. Reardon Company (Mo), 319 S.W.2d 859.

Gerkin v. Brown & Sehler Co., 177 Mich. 45 (48 LRA NS 224, 4 NCCA 254)

In the *Gerkin Case,* the Court said (p 60): "When the fact is once established and demonstrated by experience that a certain commodity, apparently harmless, contains concealed dangers, and when distributed to the public through the channels of trade and used for the purposes for which it was made and sold, is sure to cause suffering to, and injure the health of, some innocent purchaser, <u>even though the percentage of those injured be not large, a duty arises to and a responsibility rests upon the manufacturer and dealer with knowledge, to the extent, at least, of warning the ignorant consumer or user of the existence of the hidden danger. Failing to do so, the dealer, as well as the manufacturer, who has the knowledge and does not impart it, is liable to a subsequent, ignorant purchaser, reasonably within contemplation of the parties to the original sale, for injuries sustained through such hidden dangers.</u> This is by reason of the duty the dealer owes to the public generally, which includes all whom it may concern, to give notice of any concealed dangers in the commodity in which he traffics, and to exercise a reasonable precaution for the protection of others commensurate with the peril involved. We think this principle applicable to the case at bar and fairly deducible from the many authorities touching manufacture and sale of dangerous commodities. *Thornton* v. *Dow,* 60 Wash 622 (111 P. 899, 32 LRA NS 968), and authorities cited and reviewed in *Tomlinson* v. *Armour & Co.,* 75 NJL 748 (70 A 314, 19 LRA NS 923)."

Nine separate court opinions regarding 'concealed dangers' and about the duty of the automotive industry to warn of these known dangers. Within these nine separate court opinions there is clear court direction and requirements of the automotive industry to 'provide ordinary and reasonable care.' But, that is the Automotive Industry.

The National Football League, not unlike General Motors, was and is in a superior position of knowledge and authority to warn sports fans and attendees at NFL games of known and concealed dangers.

The 49er entities, the City of Santa Clara, and the NFL were aware that other assaults of a similar nature to the subject incident on November 1, 2018, had occurred on its premises and thus it had reasonable cause to anticipate the misconduct of third persons. Despite their knowledge about numerous prior assaults and fights at its football games, they failed to provide any warnings whatsoever to its fans about the prior criminal incidents. The 49ers entities, the City of Santa Clara, and the NFL, like the automotive industry, should have given written notice of the history of violent attacks to its season ticket holders and other paying patrons, so they could make an informed decision about whether to attend games with such an increased risk of harm. However, they did not publicize the prior criminal incidents or in any way warn the general public.

In fact, the 49er entities, the City of Santa Clara, and the NFL have actively concealed and have continued to actively conceal the risk of harm to its fan base and have misled its fans into believing that it promotes a safe environment free from intoxication, gang violence and fights or assaults with its highly touted 'Fan Code of Conduct'. The court documented false police reports on security, coupled with the 'Fan Code of Conduct' combine to make a complete misrepresentation that the environment at Levi's Stadium is safe.

The NFL and the 49ers, in no uncertain terms, are currently concealing dangers due to of each of their association, acceptance, and continued use of the corrupt and lawless City of Santa Clara Police, as 'the lead agency' for security at Levi's Stadium.

As clearly stated in my lawsuit, (*Frederick Leo Weaver v. San Francisco 49ers Limited, et al.* Santa Clara County Superior Case no. 19CV346749, 2019), the defendants in my case, the NFL and the 49ers have a duty to warn patrons of known dangers and a duty to take other reasonable and appropriate measures to protect patrons from imminent or "ongoing" aggressive conduct. Such measures include protecting patrons or invitees from an imminent and known peril lurking in the stadium by providing trained security personnel.

I claimed in my lawsuit that each of the defendants had, and continue to have, a special relationship with the patrons and invitees present at Levi's Stadium on NFL game days, an environment where guests should be allowed to enjoy their gameday experience in a safe and enjoyable atmosphere free from fighting, overly intoxicated patrons and gang activity; and thus, had a legal duty to exercise ordinary care to ensure the safety of all persons who were lawfully on the premises of Levi's Stadium.

Sadly, if you read the defenses as presented by each of the two attorneys for the 19 defendants, they don't agree with any part of this at all. This means the NFL and 49ers agree with their attorneys, because the NFL and 49ers hired these attorneys to defend themselves against my documented concerns for security and safety at Levi's Stadium. As a quick summary, the attorneys for the NFL and 49ers argue the following condensed points to defend their clients:

- "Federal Law Does Not Place an Affirmative Duty on Law Enforcement Officers to Provide Police Protection"
- "Police are under no affirmative duty to assist and protect"
- "Public entities are not subject to "ordinary care' or "reasonable care"

Alarmingly, at the height of hypocrisy, the attorney's 'defense' of their 19 clients, directly conflicts with the NFL Fan Code of Conduct (120) and also the Levi's Stadium Security Policies (121) that each of the NFL and Levi's Stadium so highly tout to attending fans.

In plain English, the defense used against my lawsuit by the NFL and 49ers, means at Levi's Stadium, "you are not protected by law enforcement" and "they don't have to care." Those defenses are precisely the absurd and impractical ingredients for the dangerously inadequate security at Levi's Stadium.

I quickly filed and then quickly dismissed my lawsuit for a reason because, "a case in court is a case in court, and that's fine. But there's also the court of public opinion. And the court of public opinion is sometimes the most powerful court." (122)

And as I mentioned earlier, my case Dismissals Without Prejudice allows me to keep a legal cloud hanging over the defendants including the San Francisco 49ers, the National Football League, and City of Santa Clara Police...forever.

The End...for a moment.

Epilogue

—ᴔ—

"I have the world's largest collection of seashells. I keep it
on all the beaches of the world... perhaps you've seen it,"
comedian Steven Wright

Why You Should Be Concerned About This

Unfortunately, on Thursday night, November 1, 2018, my
daughter and I witnessed a brutal and vicious fight between
two San Francisco 49ers fans.

Fortunately, however, I am hoping there is a positive outcome to all that I have encountered, discovered and exposed since
that night.

As far as physical injuries go, I was injured, or at least my
existing injury was aggravated by having to chase and ensure
a felony assailant and his companion didn't hurt anyone else at
Levi's Stadium after the first assault we witnessed. Pain and suffering, yes, but I wasn't looking for a 'trip and fall' type payout
settlement. In fact, I never wanted any money at all for my physical injury. I was in severe pain however, but I was prescheduled
for my total right hip replacement exactly fifteen days later, and
now I am as good as new.

As far as financial injuries, although both attorneys claim I didn't have any, guess what. Do the math. I purchased and brought an $8 twenty-ounce Pepsi back to my seat at the end of halftime and didn't even take a sip out of it before we noticed the fight. The other part of the equation was my purchase of two aftermarket tickets on Ticketmaster at $155 a piece. If you calculate two people missing the entire second half of game, the 'cowboy math' is a loss of $155. Add to this the cost of the unconsumed Pepsi and you would have $163 in total damages.

So, no biggie, and boiled down, it cost me $163 dollars to ensure that the assailant didn't hurt anyone else, and he didn't escape from his assault without being arrested. That was worth it.

But it is the other true damage which really concerns me. The same damage that each of the two attorneys cautiously tried to defend their nineteen clients against. That damage is lurking and concealed at Levi's Stadium just like the faulty brakes on the Buick in the last chapter, which GM knew about, but waited until the customers brought it to their attention before GM would do anything to fix the brake problem.

What you have just read in this book is an exact parallel to the Buicks with bad brakes.

The dangerous lack of security at Levi's Stadium is just like the bad brakes, waiting to harm people, and the entities in control of fixing it—the NFL, the 49ers, and City of Santa Clara who owns Levi's Stadium—are all knowledgeable about the dangers; but the similarity stops there. When this consumer sports fan, (and author of this book) brought it to their attention, unlike GM, they did nothing. Disturbingly, they all conspired further to file false police reports to cover up the events of November 1, 2018, and by 'going dark' they hoped the situation would just go away.

As referenced in the very beginning of this book, "One of *Silent Springs's* lasting effects is that it brought into the consciousness of the public and government the notion that no chemical should be assumed 'safe'."

Even NFL's own Cathy Lanier, Senior Vice President of Security wrote in her 2005 college thesis, "Stadiums are just a few examples of potential targets creating a sense that no one is safe." (123)

I hope my book has a similar impact of bringing into the consciousness of the public and government the notion that no stadium should be assumed "safe."

The specific goal of this book is for Levi's Stadium and all related entities to provide a safe venue for any type of event including, NFL football games, college games, international soccer games, music concerts, and other types of public assembly functions. Hopefully those authorities responsible for all stadium venues worldwide will listen and finally take action before yet another sports fan, concertgoer or other guest is seriously injured or even killed.

Let that sink in...even killed.

Take some of the following information into consideration.

Levi's Stadium Security

If the dangerously inadequate security at Levi's Stadium is not worrisome enough, consider this parallel: Mothers Against Drunk Driving (MADD) have reported, "First-time DUI offenders are rarely first-time drunk drivers," and, "Conservative estimates show that a first-time convicted DUI offender has driven drunk at least 80 times prior to being arrested, (or killing someone)." (124)

The existing data trending at Levi's Stadium far exceeds the numbers and ratios in the above report by MADD. In just 3 (three) recent court documented personal injury lawsuits involving 49ers home games at Levi's Stadium:

- There have been over 500 recent prior assaults and arrests for fighting at 49ers games.
- One fan attending a Kansas City Chiefs at 49ers home game was nearly beaten to death, and suffered a coma requiring brain surgery and ended up partially paralyzed.
- Another fan attending an Arizona Cardinals vs 49ers home game was beaten so badly he also suffered a coma.
- During last year's 'Battle of the Bay' Raiders vs 49ers home game, a single visiting Oakland Raider's fan did the job that 400 plus assigned Law Enforcement officers were incapable of doing, by acting alone in bringing a felony assailant to police custody.
- And during the most recent Seahawks vs 49ers home game, over 630 pictures were taken of Santa Clara Police, other law enforcement, and security not providing any strategic placement or zone coverage, and not observing any of the Levi's Stadium crowd fan base.

The circumstances are too similar to ignore and no one is noticing the red flags. Does someone actually have to be killed at Levi's Stadium before the severe lack of security problems are addressed and properly managed? An alcohol-induced fight between attending fans at Levi's Stadium resulting in a fatality is not a question of 'If' but rather a question of 'When'.

Listed below are some of the other related important items I uncovered as well as the current status:

The National Football League & Roger Goodell

The NFL's unique historical vantage point at the apex of the sport of football, paired with its unmatched resources as the most well-funded organization devoted to the business of the game, has afforded it unparalleled access to data and made it an institutional repository of accumulated knowledge. However, time and time again, the NFL does not learn from its own mistakes, nor does the NFL share information on 'lessons learned' which would benefit all of its 32 teams.

The pattern of lack of security is something that is happening right now, and not just at Levi's Stadium, but at other NFL stadiums as well.

"We again as a league look like amateurs…," one NFC team executive told *Bleacher Report* in a November 30, 2018 interview. (125) "One of the common denominators is that the NFL gets caught flatfooted, says it will handle things better next time, and then when next time arrives, it makes the same mistakes."

Here are some ongoing examples of lessons 'not learned' or shared by the NFL:

- Court filed documents show the City of Santa Clara Police Department have violated 9 (nine) of 14 (fourteen) "Expectations and Standards of Conduct, referenced on page 2 of NFL's policy (Appendix # 1). Roger Goodell has yet to make any response or take any corrective measures, as the NFL continues to use City of Santa Clara Police Department as 'lead agency' for San Francisco 49ers home games at Levi's Stadium

- There are no shared "lessons learned" or NFL's "best security practices" between stadiums. The NFL in their NFL Communications Public Safety statement claim, "The NFL and its teams continually evaluate and improve our comprehensive security plan." But the NFL does not issue it to the teams. "Casey Nice, an assistant sheriff in California's Alameda County, is in charge of overseeing the game-day security operation at all Raiders games at Oakland Coliseum. Nice said he's in occasional contact with the NFL league office, and he attends the league's security seminar each year. But he has not received a list of the NFL's "best practices," (126)

- Even if there was an NFL 'best security practices' shared, it is left up to the local 'lead agency', in this case the corrupt City of Santa Clara Police Department led by Chief Mike Sellers who has been personally named along with his police department for unconstitutional and criminal actions against citizens in both Santa Clara and San Jose.

- In his deposition regarding the temporary seating chaos at Super Bowl XLV, Roger Goodell confirmed there was no document describing what went wrong to ensure it never happens again. Roger said, "I don't know about any document, what we have to do is make sure it doesn't happen again." The NFL spent more than $20 million in attorney's fees defending themselves against the dangerous and chaotic seating mess created at Super Bowl XLV. But the NFL and Roger Goodell didn't spend one dime preparing a report to protect its football fans from a similar seating incident occurring in the future at other stadiums.

- "There is absolutely no unified approach to stadium-alcohol policy outside of not allowing glass bottles and not running the taps after the third quarter, which date back to former NFL Commissioner Paul Tagliabue's reign from 1989 to 2006." (127)

- For Levi's Stadium add the above concern to this one. The 'Dram Shop Act' is case law in 38 states which makes a business which sells alcoholic drinks or a host who serves liquor to a drinker who is obviously intoxicated or close to it, strictly liable to anyone injured by the drunken patron or guest. To the contrary, California, which affects Levi's Stadium, recently passed legislation specifically banning such strict liability.

Ray Rice Incident

The investigative steps that the NFL took in the wake of the Ray Rice incident, are faithfully mirrored in the League's steps taken in the November 1, 2018 assault I personally witnessed.

Similar to my abstract on Cathy Lanier, in my filed lawsuit Complaint, if one takes out and exchanges two items, 'Rice' and 'elevator', with 'November 1, 2018' and 'fight' respectively you will find a very interesting parallel. The lack of League involvement in the November 1, 2018 savage beating is not only a parallel situation, but also a more complex and dangerous one.

It is worth mentioning again, as the League's Cathy Lanier acknowledges, "Local police are the lead agency for every game throughout the season."

Re-read, revisit and focus in the Ray Rice incident on the 'League's longstanding practice of deferring to law enforcement' and think about the local law enforcement involved which the League is 'deferring' to. For every game throughout the season at Levi's Stadium, the League is deferring to the City of Santa Clara Police Department who has recently been involved in multiple false police reports and illegal and unconstitutional actions against citizens.

Within the Ray Rice Report, also revisit NFL Commissioner Roger Goodell's comment, "Our longstanding policy in matters like this – where there is a criminal investigation being directed by law enforcement and prosecutors – is to cooperate with law enforcement and take no action to interfere with the criminal justice system." (Page 43)

- "The League has long-standing relationships with law-enforcement authorities, which are extremely important to the League in the areas of stadium and event security." (Page 53)

- "Finally, deference to law-enforcement officials is a byproduct of the fact that senior management in League Security has traditionally been made up of former law-enforcement officials." (Page 53)

The two bullet point items above may explain why the police "code of silence," is being used to cover up the NFL's relationship with the City of Santa Clara Police Department.

Lisa Gillmor - City of Santa Clara Mayor

- Mayor Lisa Gillmor even before being elected, was no stranger to litigation herself.
- Lisa Gillmor and her father were personally named in a lawsuit for "making illegal cash campaign contributions to several Santa Clara City Council candidates" in violation of Campaign Laws. (128)
- In that lawsuit, Lisa Gillmor used a defense, similar in attitude to comedian Steve Martin's line, "I forgot armed robbery was illegal."
- Lisa Gillmor continued her 'cheer leading' of the 49ers and the new Levi's Stadium, and then turned her back on the 49ers once Levi's Stadium was built when it became convenient to appear to be an advocate against the 49ers, in order to get elected.
- As Mayor, Lisa Gillmor was recently the subject of another lawsuit for not declaring all income sources. (128)

Deanna Santana - City Manager City of Santa Clara

- The City of Santa Clara should also have investigated and been more proactive in due diligence and background checks, especially on someone with Deanna Santana's employment history and background. Unless, of course, bringing in someone with Deanna's 'skill set' as exposed in court documents she was named in, was exactly what the City of Santa Clara and Councilmembers wanted.

City of Santa Clara – Mayor and Council Members

- When you look a little closer, it becomes clear that "politicians are front men in a complex organization" (129)
- "You have to ask yourself why people seek these positions and what their background is," asked recently by an anonymous reader of local publication, *Santa Clara Plays Fair*.
- It's common knowledge, and all one has to do is review the City Council Meeting minutes and videos to see who control the votes. Mayor Lisa Gillmor has a faithful 'crew' in Councilmembers Debi Davis, Teresa O'Neill, and Kathy Watanabe mostly voting together.
- The Mayor and her cronies on the Council, who also run the Stadium Authority, have burned out long ago about maintaining any positive relationship with the Chief of Police Mike Sellers, whose police officers are the 'go-to' for security at Levi's Stadium.
- And with all the above going on, Mayor Gillmor says her critics are too beholden to the 49ers because team officials contribute to their political campaigns.
- And yet, Mayor Lisa Gillmor personally runs fundraising campaigns for the Santa Clara Police Association, although Gillmor and Chief of Police Mike Sellers are publicly at odds with each other.
- If one tried to enter all this in an Excel spreadsheet you would get a 'error' message because of this circular formula.

"In the corporate world there are checks and balances to ensure a CEO doesn't go too far off the rails. Boards hire executive search firms to screen CEOs and other directors," says Dr. Billie Blair, an organizational psychologist who runs Change Strategists Inc. and advises corporate boards and directors. (From the article, "Corporate lessons on ticking time bombs," by Thomas Lee, San Francisco Chronicle, April 30, 2014). (130) In the same article, Wendy Davis, an attorney and business ethics expert at San Diego State University says, "Boards of directors, as soon as they get wind of problems, should immediately open an investigation," "We don't want a person to infect the entire company."

The City of Santa Clara's Mayor and Councilmembers, although a public entity, conduct themselves similarly to a CEO and a Board of Directors in a private company.

- But in City of Santa Clara's case, none of these checks and balances have ever been applied, other than these individuals just being voted in. Who is checking whom? Especially with Lisa Gillmor as Mayor, Deanna Santana as City Manager and their dual roles affecting the Stadium Authority, which controls Levi's Stadium.

- It's hard to keep score of who has been named in more lawsuits, Mayor Lisa Gillmor, City Manager Deanna Santana, or City of Santa Clara Police Chief Mike Sellers.

- As clearly, and court documented, Mayor Lisa Gillmor, City Manager Deanna Santana, and Chief of Police Mike Sellers have each breached the standard of responsibility and conduct demanded of them in their positions of public trust.

Santa Clara Police and Santa Clara Police Association

- "The local police (Santa Clara Police Department) are the lead agency for every game throughout the season."
- As evident and documented in 3 (three) recent court cases, the City of Santa Clara Police don't understand even the most basic fundamentals of implementing security at Levi's Stadium.
- And with the City of Santa Clara Police Department having so much difficulty understanding these simple security concepts, what about potentially highly complex and strategically planned terrorist attacks?
- What about security at all the other types of events including music concerts at Levi's Stadium?
- It is common knowledge that use of non-sworn, non-law enforcement security personnel is not as effective as utilizing law enforcement officers, as non-law enforcement personnel are not as imposing as uniformed officers.
- The 49ers, NFL and SCPD decision to not strategically place uniformed law enforcement officers creates a relaxed, unintimidating atmosphere at Levi's Stadium.
- Perpetrators of violent crime thrive in public places where there is no such physical deterrence, and this is one of the reasons why gang members and other criminal elements are targeting Levi's Stadium.
- Law enforcement agencies and City of Santa Clara Police *'enjoy'* and exploit legal loopholes entirely evading lack of security responsibilities and liabilities as their attorneys at Lombardi, Loper, & Conant confirmed in their filed defense. (Appendix # 7)
- The City of Santa Clara Police are overwhelmed and have neither the manpower, nor resources to adequately and

safely manage security at Levi's Stadium. In an interview, Police Chief Mike Sellers said he didn't even want the stadium.

- Remember, there is not a single City of Santa Clara police officer who was terminated or disciplined for any of their illegal actions involving civil rights violations and personal injury to each of Mohammad Moneeb, Mohammed Ikram, and Danielle Harmon. And there is not even one documented resignation, condemnation or taking a stand against these illegal police activities from the Santa Clara Police Officers Association or any of its members.

- The lack of consequences for violating policy, or even engaging in criminal misconduct, has fostered a culture of impunity to such behavior. The City of Santa Clara police officers observe tacit approval of misconduct by supervisors, commanders, and City of Santa Clara Police Chief Mike Sellers, so the behavior continues.

- Less than five months after unconstitutionally kicking down the second of two local residents' front doors without a warrant, and use of excessive force breaking Danielle Harmon's leg, the Santa Clara Police Officers Association wrote a September 2, 2016 letter to the San Francisco 49ers and its CEO Jed York. Achieving another height of hypocrisy, the SCPOA summarize their letter at the end by stating, "The men and women of the Santa Clara Police Officers Association are sworn to protect the rights of ALL people in the United States, a duty we take very seriously." (Appendix # 2)

- The City of Santa Clara Police Department still have an ingrained attitude about the 49ers and Colin Kaepernick even though Kaepernick is long since gone from the 49ers team and out of the league.

- But the City of Santa Clara police still relish the $65 per hour rate with eight-hour minimum they receive for security services on game day. However, the SCPD have continued their threat from their September 2, 2016 letter to the 49ers of, "choosing not to work." The Santa Clara Police Department noticeably practice a form of 'blue flu' because there is no accountability for their security efforts, other than punching a clock on game day, and 'just showing up.'

- Even with Chief of Mike Seller's pending retirement, don't expect any changes. The next several officer personnel considerations for Police Chief have been with the SCPD for some time now. And again, none of these 'veterans' spoke up about any of their court documented recent illegal police actions. One suggestion might be to even utilize what NFL Senior VP of Security Cathy Lanier wrote on page 43 of her 2005 thesis, "We must undergo some significant changes. Ideally, the structure should be built from the ground up..."(123)

Would it be asking too much, as associate justice on the Supreme Court, Louis D. Brandeis commented long ago, "that government officials be subjected to the same rules of conduct that are commands to the citizen."

Levi's Stadium Ticket Holders, Advertisers, Investors, Partners, and Clients

- With the NFL, 49ers, and the City of Santa Clara continuing to tolerate and endorse corruption throughout the City of Santa Clara Police Department, Levi's Stadium will most certainly lose interest among 49ers Season Ticket purchasers, major advertisers, corporate sponsors, client partners and affiliates. And upcoming music concert promoters and performers will seek to avoid risk by choosing safer venues for themselves and their fans as well.

- With a 'first fatality' looming due to the dangerously inadequate security, this unfortunate occurrence would call into question the future of Levi's Stadium and City of Santa Clara's reputation which would be irreparably compromised.

- Levi's Stadium sponsors include Levi's of course, Intel, Yahoo, Pepsi, and multiple major beer brands.

- One of the most troubling concerns, is whether any of these companies involved, performed any background checks or ongoing due diligence for the dysfunctional individuals associated with the stadium they are sponsoring.

- Continuing to advertise in spite of the known material issues and baggage detailed in recent court documents is a significant risk, for a reputable company.

- And reputation is one of the most valuable assets for any firm. How many of these companies advertising with Levi's Stadium are willing to continue to risk their integrity knowing the corruption throughout the City of Santa Clara Police Department?

- Although I did not name these companies in my Complaint, I had Levi Strauss Corporation and Intel Corporation 'served with courtesy copies' of the lawsuit because each of these two companies are amongst the largest advertising sponsors at Levi's Stadium. Levi Strauss has a '20-year' corporate naming rights on Levi's Stadium. Intel's high definition blue screen monitor at Levi's Stadium's main entrance boldly states, "Experience what's inside ™."

The NFL's unique historical vantage point at the apex of the sport of football, paired with its unmatched resources as the most well-funded organization devoted to the business of the game, has afforded it unparalleled access to data relating to trouble at all NFL team stadiums including dangerous and unsafe conditions and prior assaults and fights and made it an institutional repository of accumulated knowledge about security issues at individual stadiums.

In spite of this knowledge, the NFL, 49ers, and City of Santa Clara Police Department underutilize the physically installed "high-technology security and camera system" security resources in the stadium, in addition to utilizing unmanaged law enforcement officers as security personnel.

The failure of the NFL, 49er entities, and the City of Santa Clara Police Department, to act according to the standard of care, was the proximate and actual cause of Kiran Patel's injuries, victim Crain's injuries, as well as injuries that have already been suffered and will be suffered in the future by other members of the general public unless corrective action is taken.

Throughout the book, I have tried to tell the story in an unbiased manner, but it has been difficult. The fact remains that several of these public servants I encountered along the way are criminals themselves. However, at this time they are STILL in their positions of authority, and it seems likely that based on their history there is still a significant risk to any attendee at Levi's Stadium. And unfortunately, people just like you may still be attending events there.

As a final piece of evidence, for you my readers who are the ultimate jury, and members of the court of public opinion, consider what has transpired since the second time the City of Santa Clara illegally kicked down the front door without a warrant. During the unconstitutional raid without a warrant and forcibly entering her home, it was later discovered that a SCPD 'body cam' worn by the officers was in use while they were violating Danielle Harmon's rights. The 'body cam' videos were meant to be confidential…but they were leaked…"and found their way into the wilds of the internet."

The following information was exposed in an Order by United States Magistrate Judge Nathanael M. Cousins, dated February 5, 2018, granting Plaintiff's Motion to Remove Confidentiality Designation (on the City of Santa Clara Police body cam video):

Due to the constitutional violations, where the body camera captured graphic and alarming footage of police officers hurting a citizen, the parties stipulated to a protective order of the Court. In response to Danielle Harmon's discovery requests the City of Santa Clara produced the roughly 19-minute video of the incident and designated it as confidential pursuant to the stipulated protective order. And then the Santa Clara Police body cam video was leaked to local news outlets and posted on YouTube. Incredulously, the City of Santa Clara asserted that the video's release caused, "extraordinary stress and emotional damages to the involved officers," and indirectly hurt Santa Clara's citizens by compromising the police department.

The City of Santa Clara and its Police Department attempted to 'double down' because of what was captured in the police body camera about Danielle Harmon. After kicking the door down and breaking Danielle Harmon's leg, "the officer wearing the body camera flatly responds, "Stop resisting," and tells Harmon to roll over on her stomach. For the next several minutes, Harmon can be heard and seen on the ground in handcuffs, screaming and writhing in pain, sobbing, exclaiming that her ankle is broken asking for medical help, and eventually vomiting. The officer wearing the body camera and attending to Harmon tells Harmon that she needs to answer some questions before they call an ambulance, and repeatedly tries to calm her down. The officer does not appear to call an ambulance until just over seven minutes into the video." (131)

As detailed in Judge Nathanael M. Cousins' Order, the City of Santa Clara had the unmitigated gall to claim, "extraordinary stress and emotional damages to the involved officers," when Danielle Harmon was effectively 'coerced and tortured' before receiving medical attention.

While it is shocking that the NFL and San Francisco 49ers are so complacent about all of the indications and red flags of lack of security, audit findings, gang presence, and local police ineptitude and corruption, it is beyond comprehension that the NFL and San Francisco 49ers continue to allow the City of Santa Clara Police Department to be the "lead agency" for security at Levi's Stadium.

However, as alarming as all of this may seem, to defend themselves against my lawsuit, the NFL and the San Francisco 49ers joined the legal defense team of law firm, Lombardi, Loper, & Conant, LLP... the same legal defense team hired by the corrupt Santa Clara Police Department. Observe the following timeline:

- I filed my complaint and lawsuit on May 1, 2019.
- The law firm Lombardi, Loper, & Conant, LLP was retained to represent the Forty Niner Defendants on May 8, 2019, and the City Defendants including their Santa Clara Police Department on May 14, 2019.
- On May 24, 2019, the NFL Defendants joined Lombardi, Loper, & Conant, LLP, exactly ten (10) days after the City of Santa Clara Police Department and Police Chief Mike Sellers hired Lombardi, Loper, & Conant, LLP to defend their police officers named in my lawsuit.

This supports the conclusion that the San Francisco 49er organization and the entire NFL organization including Commissioner

Roger Goodell, and Cathy Lanier, have accepted and ratified the multiple recent court documented illegal actions involving the corrupt practices of the City of Santa Clara Police Department and its Police Chief Michael Sellers. (132) (133)

So, my readers, you be the judge and jury. In fact, as my readers, you are the largest jury in the world as the 'court of public opinion'. Put yourselves in the place of Kiran Patel, Mohammad Moneeb, Moneeb Ikram, and Danielle Harmon... and try to decide for yourselves, in an unbiased manner, with all those above responsible parties still calling the shots for stadium security...

Would you TRUST Your SAFETY at Levi's Stadium, the most dangerous venue in North America?

Welcome to Levi's Stadium – Unsafe in Any Seat!

Afterward

—⚏—

To my readers, you are likely to finish this book with a sense that there are still other questions left unanswered. And you are correct. I can assure you I am the possessor of many secrets which still need to be 'shown the light'. I was actually doing research and working on a couple of completely other global topics, when out of pure circumstance, I was embroiled with the November 1, 2018 incident at Levi's Stadium. I decided to write a book related to the incident because the potential for saving lives, starting with dangerously inadequate security at Levi's Stadium, was certainly more important, and gave pause to the other major side projects and issues I was working on.

There are so many related concerns and working solutions needing to be told, which were not included as part of this book. And for editing reasons, there is a lot of information that went to the 'cutting floor'. But after giving it some thought, I decided it would be a shame if I didn't share what was not included in this book. This book reveals a complex set of challenges and because of some recent developments there are dozens of issues, I could not fully go into and reveal with this 'first' book. Yes, I said 'first' book. In the entertainment industry where I have several close friends, they would call the next two books I have coming out, 'back pocket scripts.'

And to my readers, I will let you in on a secret. When I started writing this book and titled it, I used of course a variation on the title of Ralph Nader's automotive safety book, *Unsafe at Any Speed*. By subtitling my book, I thought why not also use, 'Unsafe in Any Seat', as a 'platform'. For starters, it would allow the launch of a grassroots campaign, similar to Ralph Nader's work with the auto industry, in hopes of getting the National Football League and stadium owners to change their ways, methods, and thinking about sports fans and other venue attendee's safety and security.

I knew there would be nothing from our final conversations beyond their receiving a full dismissal, that either Attorneys Ian Wilson or Taylor Pohle would be sharing or downloading with their nineteen defendant clients.

So, in addition to this book I started planning for the platform of 'Unsafe in Any Seat' to be part of a series because there is huge opportunity to offer a new generation of potential life-saving security solutions, and Unsafe in Any Seat could also provide a launchpad to address and tackle other issues and concerns as well. In order to get the word out, books are one thing, but activism is another.

I have already started speaking publicly to groups, started a blog, and video documentaries are also in the works.

And another secret I will let you in on, I initiated a targeted letter campaign. As an early clue, check out some of the names within the 'List of Individuals, Arranged by Organizational Affiliation'. And then look for Sheryl Sandberg. If you would like to see a copy of the letter I wrote her, visit my Author's website: https://unsafeinanyseat.com

Together with the capabilities of all combined efforts, there will be opportunity for real change in stadium security, again starting with Levi's Stadium. Remember, Rachel Carson, Erin Brockovich, and Ralph Nader made an impact in each of their pursuits. Laws were changed, and safety was mandated, all of which have benefitted potentially everyone worldwide.

As Sharlene Martin, president of Martin Literary Agency, wrote in a statement about a Zimmerman juror writing a book. "It could open a whole new dialogue about laws that may need to be revised and revamped to suit a 21st Century way of life," (134)

So, within the next series of books, I will be exposing what I communicated to Attorneys Ian P. Wilson and Taylor Pohle, and their respective law firms Ericksen Arbuthnot and Lombardi, Loper, & Conant LLP. Because just like what Louis Brandeis, as a Supreme Court Justice proposed 110 years ago, "government officials should be subjected to the same rules of conduct that are commands to the citizen." As Louis Brandeis also stated, "Sunshine is the best disinfectant," so, let's start bringing all these issues to light.

And there is certainly hope for the above, and here is just one example of the type of individual whom I might first start working with. Because some of his initiatives are directly related to what you just finished reading about. The following is from a transcript of Santa Clara County District Attorney Jeff Rosen's speech delivered Jan. 23, 2019, at his swearing-in to a third term. (135)

- "The DA's Office has a unique and critical role in safeguarding the public's trust in our democratic institutions and holding public officials accountable for misconduct.
- Who will guard the guards? We did. We are. We will.
- In an extremely difficult and challenging case, Deputy DA Alaleh Kianerci, through hard work and prosecutorial excellence, persuaded a Palo Alto jury to convict Stanford student Brock Turner of raping an unconscious young woman behind a dumpster. At the sentencing hearing, the victim, Emily Doe, read a letter she composed to the

judge explaining the devastating impact of the assault and Turner's lack of remorse. DDA Kianerci urged the court to impose a long prison sentence. Instead, the judge gave Turner a short jail sentence.

- We released Emily's letter hoping that the local newspaper might attach it to their story and perhaps a few hundred people, maybe even a few sexual assault survivors, would read the letter and find their strength and their voice.
- Within days, millions of people around the world had read the letter and demanded that the arc bend. Months later, Alaleh and I persuaded the California legislature to change the law and guarantee that the next Brock Turner go to prison. Then, our office, led by Terry Harman, signed a groundbreaking MOU with all the colleges and universities in our County to prevent future campus sexual assaults by working with law enforcement, encouraging upstanders and raising the status of women. Moreover, led by county Supervisor Cindy Chavez and our entire Board of Supervisors, we are testing rape kits faster than ever before."

Most importantly, the other type of individual I will be working with, is You as my readers. Because like comedian Steven Wright's "world's largest collection of seashells," as an author, with you as my readers, I look to you as the "world's largest Court of Public Opinion."

I look forward to your help!

Meanwhile, look closer at some of the solutions and 'secrets' I have hinted at and embedded within this book, along with ongoing and updated information and the blog available at my Author's website: https://unsafeinanyseat.com

As I mentioned earlier, this discussion and others will continue in my next series of books...

List of Individuals, Arranged by Organizational Affiliation

—ɯ—

THE NATIONAL FOOTBALL LEAGUE

Roger Goodell: Commissioner of the National Football League (NFL). Goodell has authority over all NFL business and related personnel adhering to the National Football League Personal Conduct Policy (136) (Appendix # 1). Court filed documents show the City of Santa Clara Police Department have violated 9 (nine) of 14 (fourteen) "Expectations and Standards of Conduct, referenced on page 2 of NFL's policy. Roger Goodell has yet to make any response or take any corrective measures, as the City of Santa Clara Police continue to be the 'lead agency' for security on all NFL game days at Levi's Stadium.

Billy Langenstein: Director, Investigations & Security Services for the National Football League (NFL) CSSP. Langenstein called me back January 8, 2019 on behalf of his boss Cathy Lanier, Senior Vice President of Security National Football League. Langenstein tipped his hand stating the NFL uses LexisNexis and the NFL was fully aware of Kiran Patel's personal injury lawsuit from a near-fatal beating from two gang members at a

49ers Levi's Stadium home game. After our twenty-five-minute discussion, Langenstein officially emailed me from the NFL later that night saying, "I will follow up with the 49ers on the active investigation that you referenced." I never heard again from Billy Langenstein or anyone else with the NFL.

Cathy L. Lanier: Senior Vice President of Security National Football League (NFL). Lanier was previously the Chief of Police for Washington D.C. In an October 26, 2017 interview with *ESPN*, (137) Lanier claimed, "I look at every attack that takes place everywhere," which prompted me to call and leave Lanier a voicemail on January 7, 2019. Lanier had her errand boy Billy Langenstein return her call instead.

CITY OF SANTA CLARA POLICE

Captain Steve Buress: Arresting City of Santa Clara Police Officer who worked security November 1, 2018, at Levi's Stadium. Captain Steve Buress took my statement after I restrained and brought to arrest the assailant Steve Guardado who viciously attacked and injured another 49er fan during a home game against the Oakland Raiders that night. I received Captain Buress' cell phone number and email address on November 2, 2018 from a female desk officer during my initial visit to the City of Santa Clara Police Department.

Officer Keith Busmire: City of Santa Clara Police Officer who heard me yelling at law enforcement to help stop and arrest assailant Steve Guardado who I restrained to keep from hurting any additional Levi's Stadium patrons. Officer Busmire only stood and watched as a visiting California Highway Patrol officer took my request to restrain the assailant and observe the assailant's bloody hands. Officer Busmire's Original Police Report can be found on my Author's website: https://unsafeinanyseat.com/wp-content/uploads/2019/03/181101-Santa-Clara-Police-Dept.-Report-Suspect-Steve-Guardado-ORIG.pdf

Ray Carreira: Global Security Event Manager at Facebook. Ray Carreira was previously a Lieutenant with the City of Santa Clara Police Department, from June 2000 to September 2018. It was during this unfortunate time on October 4, 2014, while attending a game at Levi's Stadium, when Kiran Patel was nearly beaten to death by two drunken gang members. Nine months earlier, Officer Carreira deliberately made false statements, and filed false police reports to obtain an illegal search warrant for the home of Mohammad Moneeb. Lieutenant Carreira and his police unit kicked the door down to Moneeb's home as Moneeb sat hand-cuffed in Carreira's police car with his house keys in his pocket.

Marci Cremer: Police Chief Mike Seller's Assistant. I received Marci Cremer's contact information November 28, 2018 from female police desk officer during my second visit to the City of Santa Clara Police Station. I left a voicemail that same day for Cremer requesting to meet and speak with Chief Mike Sellers about the lack of security and November 1, 2018 incident at Levi's Stadium. I never received a response from her or Police Chief Mike Sellers.

Grant McCauley: Member of the Santa Clara Police Chief's Advisory Committee. McCauley and I never talked, and he never received any direct communication or emails from me. However, McCauley viewed my LinkedIn profile on December 12, 2018, exactly one month after my phone conversation with Captain Tony Parker on November 10, 2018, the date when Parker and the City of Santa Clara Police Department ceased all communication with me.

Officer Nick Cusimano: City of Santa Clara Police Officer I met with during my second trip to the Santa Clara Police Station, to discuss the November 1, 2018 incident at Levi's Stadium. Cusimano was nervous while talking with me through the glass partition and he said, "This is an ongoing investigation and you (Fred Weaver) are not an 'integral' part of the case." If Cusimano only knew…or did he?

Captain Wahid Kazem: Kazem is spokesperson for the City of Santa Clara Police Department. On Friday, November 2, 2018, in an interview with *ABC News 7*, Kazem told reporter Chris Nguyen, "To identify the person and apprehend them is just fantastic work, and it's the type of luck we've continuously had at the stadium, given the stadium's technology, and the security personnel." (138) Additionally, on November 2, 2018, Kazem told reporter Eric Ting with *SF Gate*, "The description of the man was pretty vague, so to get proper information out and to identify one person among 62,000 was pretty impressive." (139)

Officer Steve Medina: Medina was standing near Levi's Stadium egress area of exit gate F, when he heard commotion from me screaming for law enforcement help. Medina only stood and watched as another officer, a 'visiting' California Highway Patrol officer took the assailant I was restraining into custody. Officer Medina's Supplement No. 0001 Police Report can be found on my Author's website: https://unsafeinanyseat.com/wp-content/uploads/2019/03/181101-Santa-Clara-Police-Dept.-Report-Suspect-Steve-Guardado-SUPP-0001.pdf

Captain Tony Parker: Parker called me on Saturday morning, November 10, 2018. During the phone conversation with Captain Parker, he acknowledged that, "there were well in excess of 400 (four hundred) law enforcement officers working the game," the night of November 1, 2018. Parker also confirmed during that call, positive identification of me in that evening's Levi's Stadium security tapes. After that phone call, Captain Parker and the City of Santa Clara Police Department 'went dark' on any further communication with me.

Chief Mike Sellers: Chief of Police with the City of Santa Clara Police Department. Chief Mike Sellers has been personally named in two recent lawsuits involving identical charges of kicking down residents' doors and arresting those citizens without a warrant. Sellers said, "Our officers' actions were fully within the law and in accordance with accepted police practices." 2016 'Candidate' for Chief of Police, Michael J. Sellers number one slogan on his campaign website page under, 'My Top 3 Priorities' was, "Maintain an open dialogue with community members and businesses." Police Chief Mike Sellers never returned one of my phone calls, responded to any emails, nor responded to any of my meeting requests. As of this writing, Sellers is planning his retirement in September 2019.

Staff Sargeant Alex Torke: Torke was the investigating Detective for the November 1, 2018 incident at Levi's Stadium and is currently Interim President and Board Member of Santa Clara Police Officer's Association. Torke was identified as Investigating Detective by Officer Nick Cusimano when I visited the City of Santa Clara Police for the second time. On the evening of November 1. 2018, as Sargent Torke wrote in his police report, he was watching delayed social media. Twenty minutes prior to his even becoming aware, I had already restrained and had the assailant Steve Guardado in custody and under arrest. Sergeant Torke's Supplement No. 0002 Police Report can be found on my Author's website: https://unsafeinanyseat.com/

wp-content/uploads/2019/03/181101-Santa-Clara-Police-Dept.-Report-Suspect-Steve-Guardado-SUPP-0002.pdf

SAN FRANCISCO 49ERS

Al Guido: President of the San Francisco 49ers. On May 6, 2019, Al Guido received via certified mail a Sealed Envelope containing a courtesy copy of my Complaint filed May 1, 2019, along my author business cards stapled to color copies of the front and rear covers of my upcoming book.

Hannah Gordon: Chief Administration Officer & General Counsel for the San Francisco 49ers. On May 6, 2019, Hannah Gordon received via certified mail a Sealed Envelope containing a courtesy copy of my Complaint filed May 1, 2019, along my author business cards stapled to color copies of the front and rear covers of my upcoming book.

Jim Mercurio: Vice President and Stadium Operations and General Manager for Levi's Stadium. Mercurio is currently under investigation for conflict of interest for purchasing stock in two companies doing business with Levi's Stadium. Mercurio is also currently being accused of breach of contract for improper bidding and minimum wage practices involving contracts at Levi's Stadium. (140) (141)

Mark Wan: Co-Owner of the San Francisco 49ers. Mark Wan is a venture capitalist with Causeway Media Partners and is also a Boston Celtics limited partner. Wan like his other co-owner Gideon Yu, was oblivious to the accounting requirements required for Levi's Stadium security budgets, which an outside audit determined the 49ers had failed to produce for two years. On May 21, 2019, Mark Wan was 'process served' a Sealed Envelope containing a courtesy copy of my Complaint filed May 1, 2019, along my author business cards stapled to color copies of the front and rear covers of my upcoming book.

Jed York: York is CEO of the San Francisco 49ers NFL franchise. York graduated from the University of Notre Dame with a BA in Finance and History. 'Historians' can note that York's financial education didn't help his understanding for the need to provide two year's security budgets, required for where his 49ers play at Levi's Stadium. On May 8, 2019, Jed York received via certified mail a Sealed Envelope containing a courtesy copy of my Complaint filed May 1, 2019, along my author business cards stapled to color copies of the front and rear covers of my upcoming book.

Gideon Yu: Co-Owner & Former President of the San Francisco 49ers. Gideon Yu was Chief Financial Officer of both Facebook and YouTube and was honored by Fortune and Forbes magazines. Although an accountant, Yu was oblivious to the accounting requirements required for Levi's Stadium security budgets, which an outside audit determined the 49ers had failed to produce for two years. On May 6, 2019, Gideon Yu received via certified mail a Sealed Envelope containing a courtesy copy of my Complaint filed May 1, 2019, along my author business cards stapled to color copies of the front and rear covers of my upcoming book.

CITY OF SANTA CLARA (142)

Debi Davis: Council Member of the City of Santa Clara. As an elected member of the City Council, Davis also serves on the governing board for the (Levi's) Stadium Authority. Davis received a personal copy of my UPS overnighted November 26, 2018 letter, documenting concerns about the lack of security at

195

Levi's Stadium. Davis is a loyal part of Mayor Lisa Gillmor's majority voting 'crew'.

Brian Doyle: City Attorney for the City of Santa Clara. Doyle never responded to any of my requests for meetings, but viewed my LinkedIn profile on November 15, 2018, after my second visit to City Hall and handwritten note left for him, attached to my business card. After a $6.7 million-dollar settlement for one of the City of Santa Clara Police Department's excessive force lawsuits, City Attorney Brian Doyle confirmed, "...there was no dispute that the plaintiff sustained a broken ankle in the course of the (City of Santa Clara Police) entry to the plaintiff's home without a warrant."

Lisa M. Gillmor: Mayor of the City of Santa Clara, and City Council Member. As an elected member of the City Council, Gillmor also serves on the governing board as Chairperson, for the (Levi's) Stadium Authority. Gillmor was a previous City of Santa Clara Councilmember prior to becoming Mayor. Gillmor was an original 'cheerleader' for bringing the San Francisco 49ers to Santa Clara and building Levi's Stadium until Gillmor turned an about face on both. Mayor Lisa Gillmor and her staff including City Attorney Brian Doyle refused to see me during two separate trips to City Hall. Mayor Lisa Gillmor received a personal certified copy of my UPS overnighted November 26, 2018 letter, documenting concerns about the lack of security at Levi's Stadium. As a public servant, Mayor Lisa Gillmor never responded to any of my communication attempts.

Patrick Kolstad: Council Member for the City of Santa Clara. Kolstad received a personal copy of my UPS overnighted November 26, 2018 letter, documenting concerns about the lack of security at Levi's Stadium. In November 2018, Kolstad was not re-elected.

Patricia Mahan: Private attorney and Council Member for the City of Santa Clara. As an elected member of the City Council, Mahan also serves on the governing board for the (Levi's) Stadium Authority. Mahan was elected mayor for the City of Santa Clara in 2002, 2006, and 2010. Mahan received a personal copy of my UPS overnighted November 26, 2018 letter, documenting concerns about the lack of security at Levi's Stadium. Mahan is part of the Council minority and vocal adversary to Mayor Lisa Gillmor. As a three-time ex-Mayor, Mahan's support from and relationship with the 49ers management, outweighs her duty as a public servant to respond to my security concerns at Levi's Stadium.

Teresa O'Neill: Council Member for the City of Santa Clara. As an elected member of the City Council, O'Neill also serves on the governing board for the (Levi's) Stadium Authority. O'Neill received a personal copy of my UPS overnighted November 26, 2018 letter, documenting concerns about the lack of security at Levi's Stadium. O'Neill is a loyal part of Mayor Lisa Gillmor's majority voting 'crew'.

Deanna Santana: City Manager for the City of Santa Clara. Santana also serves on the governing board as Executive Director, for the (Levi's) Stadium Authority. Santana has been a serial suppressor of police misconduct reports while in her similar official capacity at other Bay Area Cities. Santana is no stranger to being named in litigation herself. Santana was *the* 'tipping point' and reason for my filing a lawsuit in an attempt to stop her 'cancer' from spreading.

Kathy Watanabe: Council Member for the City of Santa Clara. As an elected member of the City Council, Watanabe also serves on the governing board for the (Levi's) Stadium Authority. Watanabe received a personal copy of my UPS overnighted November 26, 2018 letter, documenting concerns about the lack of security at Levi's Stadium. Watanabe is a loyal part of Mayor Lisa Gillmor's majority voting 'crew'.

OTHER RELEVANT INDIVIDUALS

Megan Cacace: Attorney and Partner at Relman, Dan & Colfax, in Washington D.C. Cacace's practice combines civil rights litigation and civil rights counseling. Cacace led the Facebook Civil Rights Audit - Progress Report issued June 30, 2019. On July 11, 2019, Cacace received a certified mail copy of my July 9, 2019 letter of concern to Sheryl Sandberg, regarding Facebook's Global Security Special Event Manager, Ray Carreira.

Danielle Harmon: San Jose resident whose front door was kicked in without a warrant by the City of Santa Clara Police Department officers. As captured on their police 'body cam', the SCPD officers forcefully threw Danielle through a doorway breaking her leg and ankle, and then handcuffed her while telling her, "to calm down." The City of Santa Clara asserted that the video's release caused, "extraordinary stress and emotional damages to the involved officers," and indirectly hurt Santa Clara's citizens by compromising the police department.

Mohammad Moneeb: Santa Clara resident and law enforcement officer of the United States Department of Homeland Security. On two separate occasions without a warrant, February 10, 2014 and then again on March 27, 2014, the City of Santa Clara Police Department officers filed false police reports to obtain warrants to illegally search Moneeb's home. Facebook's Global Security Special Event Manager, Ray Carreira, was SCPD officer who wrongfully procured a search warrant by judicial deception to illegally search Moneeb's home.

Judge Peter Kirwan: Santa Clara County Superior Court Judge Kirwan was assigned my complaint, *Frederick Leo Weaver vs. San Francisco Forty Niners, Limited, et al*, Santa Clara County Superior Court Case No. 19CV346749 (2019). Fred Weaver, the author of this book, reassigned the case to the Court of Public Opinion.

Laura Murphy: President of Laura Murphy & Associates. A national civil liberties and civil rights leader and policy strategist. Laura Murphy serves as a senior advisor to Airbnb. Murphy is part of the Audit Team for the *Facebook Civil Rights Audit - Progress Report* issued June 30, 2019. On July 11, 2019, Murphy received a certified mail copy of my July 9, 2019 letter of concern to Sheryl Sandberg, regarding Facebook's Global Security Special Event Manager, Ray Carreira.

Kiran Patel: San Francisco 49ers season ticket holder who was savagely beaten by two drunken gang member brothers less than five minutes after entering Levi's Stadium on October 4, 2014. Kiran Patel suffered a coma, brain surgery, and partial paralysis. During Kiran Patel's personal injury lawsuit, court documents revealed the San Francisco 49ers and the City of Santa Clara and Stadium Authority, had specific knowledge of reports of more than 500 recent prior assaults and fights at San Francisco 49ers home games.

Sheryl Sandberg: Chief Operating Officer at Facebook. Former Vice President, Online Sales and Operations at Google. Co-author of *Lean In: Women, Work, and the Will to Lead*. On June 30, 2019, Sandberg posted on Facebook, *A Second Update on Our Civil Rights Audit*. Included within the audit, 'The purpose of the Task Force', page 27, item 3, "Ensure civil rights concerns raised by outside groups are escalated promptly to decision-makers so that they can be considered and acted on quickly, without having to go through layers of management." As an 'outside group' I wrote a July 9, 2019 letter of concern to Sandberg, regarding Facebook's Global Security Special Event Manager, Ray Carreira. My letter was sent via certified mail and received by Sandberg on July 10, 2019. I am still awaiting an answer from her.

Seth Jaffe: Executive Vice President & General Counsel at Levi Strauss & Co. On May 20, 2019, Jaffe was 'process served' a Sealed Envelope containing a courtesy copy of my Complaint filed May 1, 2019, along my author business cards stapled to color copies of the front and rear covers of my upcoming book.

Chip Bergh: President & Chief Executive Officer at Levi Strauss & Co. On May 20, 2019, Bergh was 'process served' a Sealed Envelope containing a courtesy copy of my Complaint filed May 1, 2019, along my author business cards stapled to color copies of the front and rear covers of my upcoming book.

Andy D. Bryant: Chairman of the Board at Intel Corporation. Bryant's Intel Corporation is one of the most prominent advertisers at Levi's Stadium with a trademark slogan, "Look What's Inside." On May 15, 2019, Bryant received via certified mail, a Sealed Envelope containing a courtesy copy of my Complaint filed May 1, 2019, along my author business cards stapled to color copies of the front and rear covers of my upcoming book.

Steven R. Rodgers: General Counsel at Intel Corporation. On May 15, 2019, Rogers received via certified mail, a Sealed Envelope containing a courtesy copy of my Complaint filed May 1, 2019, along my author business cards stapled to color copies of the front and rear covers of my upcoming book.

Allon Stabinsky: Chief Deputy General Counsel at Intel Corporation. On May 15, 2019, Stabinsky received via certified mail, a Sealed Envelope containing a courtesy copy of my Complaint filed May 1, 2019, along my author business cards stapled to color copies of the front and rear covers of my upcoming book.

Stephen C. Neal: Attorney and Chairman of the law firm Cooley in their Palo Alto, California office. Neal is Chairman of the Board of Directors of Levi Strauss & Co. On May 15, 2019, Neal received via certified mail, a Sealed Envelope containing a courtesy copy of my Complaint filed May 1, 2019, along my author business cards stapled to color copies of the front and rear covers of my upcoming book.

Robert Swan: Chief Executive Officer of Intel Corporation. Swan's Intel Corporation is one of the most prominent advertisers at Levi's Stadium with a trademark slogan, "Look What's Inside." On May 15, 2019, Swan received via certified mail, a Sealed Envelope containing a courtesy copy of my Complaint filed May 1, 2019, along my author business cards stapled to color copies of the front and rear covers of my upcoming book.

Fred Weaver: Author of this book and devout season ticket holding, Oakland Raider's Fan. On November 1, 2018, with over 400 law enforcement officers on duty, Weaver provided the only line of defense to keep and restrain assailant Steve Guardado after his vicious attack on another 49ers fan, from hurting any additional Levi's Stadium patrons, before having him arrested. Acting as his own attorney, he personally drafted and filed a Complaint on May 1, 2019 against the NFL, the San Francisco 49ers entities, City of Santa Clara, City of Santa Clara Police Department, and Landmark Event Security, for their part in the dangerously inadequate security at Levi's Stadium. His book *Levi's Stadium - Unsafe in Any Seat* is only the first in a series...

Sources

—𝕿—

The bulk of this book was drawn from the research and experience of Fred Weaver. The sources and notes below include citations for court records, academic papers and police and security manuals. Most of them are available as public record, or available for download online, as well as from my Author's Website, www.UnsafeInAnySeat.com Other material in this book comes from previously unpublished research and interviews by the author. Material not listed in these notes was generally drawn from readily accessible databases, news reports, and reference works. The Internet references cited in this publication were valid as of August 2019. Given that URL's and web sites are in constant flux, the author cannot vouch for their current validity.

For research, I reviewed:

- Thousands of pages of legal filings and trial documents including more than 50 related recent court cases involving personal injury due to lack of security, negligent stadium security, premise liability, and gross neglect of duty.
- Over 600 local and national articles on concerns of security and safety at professional football stadiums and concert venues.
- More than 30 police 'best practices', police accountability, and law enforcement intelligence reports.

During research for this book, in addition to Levi's Stadium, I have recently surveyed these national and international stadiums and venues for NFL, MLB, NBA, NHL, FIFA (soccer) and NCAA football:

- Oracle Park (previously AT&T Park) - MLB Baseball-San Francisco, CA
- Oakland Coliseum - Oakland, CA
- Oracle Arena - Oakland, CA
- SAP Center - San Jose, CA
- Denver Rockies - MLB Baseball - Denver, CO
- Soldier's Field - Chicago, IL
- Sanford Stadium - Athens, GA
- Busch Stadium - St. Louis, MO
- Qualcomm Stadium - San Diego, CA
- Hong Kong (Island) soccer field - Hong Kong
- Shanghai Stadium - Shanghai, China

Introduction - 'Reactive Only' Responses

(1)　September 11 attacks. (n.d.) *Wikipedia*, retrieved July 5, 2019 from: https://en.wikipedia.org/wiki/September_11_attacks

(2)　Baker, Kenneth. "Out of Our Hands." *San Francisco Chronicle*, March 23, 2014.

(3)　"Blaze ignites propane tanks, sets off explosions." *SFGate,* November 1, 2005, https://www.sfgate.com/bayarea/article/Blaze-ignites-propane-tanks-sets-off-explosions-2575224.php

(4)　*Kiran Patel and Amish Patel v. San Francisco Forty Niners, et al.*, Santa Clara County Superior Court Case no. 115CV286138, (2015), The pdf of this lawsuit can also be found on my Author's website at: https://unsafeinanyseat.

204

com/wp-content/uploads/2019/03/150925-Complaint-For-Damages-Kiran-Patel-vs-San-Francisco-Forty-Niners-Limited.pdf

(5)   *People v. Brock Allen Turner,* Santa Clara County Superior Court Case no. B1577162, (2015) People's Sentencing Memorandum, May 27, 2016. https://www.paloaltoon-line.com/media/reports/1465602925.pdf The pdf of this lawsuit can also be found on my Author's website.

(6)   *IN RE Ghost Ship Fire Litigation,* Alameda County Superior Case no. RG16843631 (2017), https://www. maryalexanderlaw.com/uploads/2017/05/Ghost-Ship-Master-Complaint-file-endorsed.pdf The pdf of this law-suit can also be found on my Author's website at: https://unsafeinanyseat.com/wp-content/uploads/2019/08/IN-RE-Ghost-Ship-Fire-Litigation-Master-Complaint-Superior-Court-for-County-of-Alameda-Case-no.-RG16843631-2017.pdf

(7)   *KNBR* Staff. "Fights Break Out in Stands During 49ers-Raiders Game." *KNBR 680 - 1050 AM*, San Francisco, November 1, 2018. (www.knbr.com - has denied access to this video) The video of this fight can be found on my Author's website at: https://unsafeinanyseat.com/wp-con-tent/uploads/2019/08/181101-49ers-vs-Raiders-Steve-Gonzales-Guardado-fight-EXTENDED.mp4

Chapter 1 - The Lonely Chase

(8)   Gafni, Matthias. "Fans Beaten, Shot at 49ers-Raiders Game Last Year Sue." *Daily Democrat* [Woodland, CA] August 30, 2018, https://www.dailydemocrat.com/2012/08/23/fans-beaten-shot-at-49ers-raiders-game-last-year-sue/

(9)   Salonga, Robert. "Raiders vs. 49ers: Security Stepped Up at Levi's Stadium to Thwart Any Rivalry Violence."

The Mercury News [San Jose] October 31, 2018, https://www.mercurynews.com/2018/10/31/raiders-vs-49ers-security-stepped-up-at-levis-stadium-to-thwart-any-rivalry-violence/

- "David Aguilera Gonzales, 34, of Madera, was charged with assault by means of force causing great bodily injury — in this case a brain injury leading to the victim becoming comatose — after allegedly punching a man multiple times during a confrontation after the game against the Arizona Cardinals."
- "For a typical NFL game at Levi's, Santa Clara police employ over 100 out-of-town officers to work at the stadium."

(10)   Area KPIX CBS SF Bay Area Staff. "Extra Security At 49ers-Raiders Game to Police Rival Fans." *KPIX CBS, YouTube Bay Area* Nov 1, 2018, https://www.youtube.com/watch?v=tMRBtHUjZ4o

- more visible and in uniform

(11)   Thompson, Tisha and Sciallo, Michael. "From Teen Mother to NFL Security Chief, Cathy Lanier's Rise Through the Law Enforcement Ranks" *ESPNW.com* October 26, 2017, http://www.espn.com/espnw/culture/feature/article/20994956/from-teen-mother-nfl-security-chief-cathy-lanier-rise-law-enforcement-ranks

(12)   Busmire, Keith. Santa Clara Police Department. Police Report 18-10404 **Supplement No. ORIG**. Santa Clara, CA: Santa Clara Police Dept., 11-01-2018. Print. The pdf of this can be found on my Author's website at: https://unsafeinanyseat.com/wp-content/uploads/2019/03/181101-Santa-Clara-Police-Dept.-Report-Suspect-Steve-Guardado-ORIG.pdf

(13)   Medina, Steve. Santa Clara Police Department. Police Report 18-10404 **Supplement No. 0001**. Santa Clara,

CA: Santa Clara Police Dept., 11-01-2018. Print. The pdf of this can be found on my Author's website at: https://unsafeinanyseat.com/wp-content/uploads/2019/03/181101-Santa-Clara-Police-Dept.-Report-Suspect-Steve-Guardado-SUPP-0001.pdf

(14)   Torke, Alex. Santa Clara Police Department. Police Report 18-10404 **Supplement No. 0002**. Santa Clara, CA: Santa Clara Police Dept., 11-01-2018. Print. The pdf of this can be found on my Author's website at: https://unsafeinanyseat.com/wp-content/uploads/2019/03/181101-Santa-Clara-Police-Dept.-Report-Suspect-Steve-Guardado-SUPP-0002.pdf

(15)   NEWOFF, New Officer. Santa Clara Police Department. Police Report 18-10404 **Supplement No. 0003**. Santa Clara, CA: Santa Clara Police Dept., 11-01-2018. Print. The pdf of this can be found on my Author's website at: https://unsafeinanyseat.com/wp-content/uploads/2019/03/181101-Santa-Clara-Police-Dept.-Report-Suspect-Steve-Guardado-SUPP-0003.pdf

(16)   *KNBR* Staff. "Fights Break Out in Stands During 49ers-Raiders Game." *KNBR 680 - 1050 AM* November 1, 2018, http://www.knbr.com/2018/11/01/fights-break-out-in-stands-during-49ers-raiders-game/
   • Note: 2 fight videos including Guardado and Crain have been removed

Extras sources:

Gutierrez, Paul. "Goodbye to the Sneaky Bitter Rivalry Known as The Battle of the Bay," *ESPN* November 1, 2018, http://www.espn.com/blog/oakland-raiders/post/_/id/22298/goodbye-to-the-sneaky-bitter-rivalry-known-as-the-battle-of-the-bay

- "True fans were at Candlestick. I've been to Levi's four or five times and it's just not the same. It's kind of like the fans don't go for the entertainment of the game; they go for the entertainment of the stadium. It's the Silicon Valley crowd."

KPIX Staff. "Extra Security At 49ers-Raiders Game To Police Rival Fans" *KPIX CBS YouTube Bay Area* November 1, 2018, https://www.youtube.com/watch?v=tMRBtHUjZ4o
- "more visible and in uniform"
- Includes video of Kirin Patel assault by two gang members

Nguyen, Chris. "Dozens of Arrests During Oakland Raiders-SF 49ers 'Battle of the Bay' Game at Levi's Stadium," *ABC 7 News* Friday November 2, 2018, https://abc7news.com/sports/dozens-of-arrests-during-battle-of-the-bay-at-levis-stadium/4602099/
- Includes video and picture of assailant Steve Guardado
- "Santa Clara police say they were able to identify and locate him before he was able to exit the stadium. Law enforcement had been monitoring social media throughout the game, saw the video, and was able to send out a picture and description for personnel to be on the lookout."
- "Police say there were able to identify and locate the subject before he could exit the stadium because the fight was quickly posted to social media which law enforcement had been monitoring throughout the game."
- Actual Quote by Kazem: "To actually identify the person, find the person and apprehend them is just

fantastic work. And it's the type of luck that we've continuously had at the stadium 'uh' given the stadium's technology as well as the security personnel."

- Typed News Quote: "To identify the person and apprehend them is just fantastic work, and it's the type of luck we have continuously have at the stadium, given the stadium's technology, and the security personnel," said Capt. Wahid Kazem, spokesperson for the Santa Clara Police Department.

Chapter 2 - How Media Shapes Policy

(17)   Carson, Rachel. *Silent Spring: the Classic That Launched the Environmental Movement*. Boston: Houghton Mifflin, 2002, c1962. Print.

(18)   Banks, Sedina. "The "Erin Brockovich Effect:" How Media Shapes Toxics Policy" U.C. Davis, Environs Environmental Law & Policy Journal, 2003, https://environs.law.ucdavis.edu/volumes/26/2/banks.pdf

(19)   Excerpt from DDT, A Review of Scientific and Economic Aspects of the Decision To Ban Its Use as a Pesticide, prepared for the Committee on Appropriations of the U.S. House of Representatives by EPA, (July 1975), (EPA-540/1-75-022), https://archive.epa.gov/epa/aboutepa/ddt-regulatory-history-brief-survey-1975.html

(20)   NRDC. "The Story of Silent Spring." *NRDC* August 13, 2015, https://www.nrdc.org/stories/story-silent-spring

(21)   *An Unreasonable Man*. Dir. Henriette Mantel and Steve Skrovan. Perf. Ralph Nader, Pat Buchanan, Phil Donahue, William Greider, Eric Alterman, James Ridgeway. IFC Films, 2006. Film.

(22)   Nader, Ralph. *Unsafe at Any Speed; the Designed-in Dangers of the American Automobile*. New York: Pocket Books, a division of Simon & Schuster, Inc., 1965.

(23)   Ralph Nader. (n.d.) *Wikipedia*, retrieved July 5, 2019 from: https://en.wikipedia.org/wiki/Ralph_Nader

(24)   Abraham Ribicoff. (n.d.) *Wikipedia*, retrieved July 5, 2019 from: https://en.wikipedia.org/wiki/Abraham_Ribicoff

(25)   Directed by Steven Soderbergh and starring Julia Roberts, *Erin Brockovich* was based on the true story of how one company contaminated a small Californian desert town's water supply with chromium 6. *Erin Brockovich* (Universal Studios Mar. 2000): see eg. Andrew Gumbel, This Woman is at a Film Premiere, but She is Not a Film Star, Indep. (London), Apr. 1, 2000, Features at 1, http://www.lexis.com

(26)   Sharp, Kathleen. "Erin Brockovich: The Real Story." *Salon Arts & Ent.*, April 14, 2000, https://www.salon.com/2000/04/14/sharp/

(27)   Welkos, Robert W. "Digging For the Truth." *Los Angeles Times* March 12, 2000, https://www.latimes.com/archives/la-xpm-2000-mar-12-ca-7856-story.html

(28)   Koutsky, Joe. "Executive Officer's Report: PG&E Hinkley and the Film Erin Brockovich." Lahontan Regional Water Quality Control Board, General # 23, March 2000, https://www.waterboards.ca.gov/lahontan/publications_forms/available_documents/e_o_reports/2000/march.shtml (General # 23)

(29)   An Overview of a Natural Gas Compressor Station, BSI Group, at: https://standardsdevelopment.bsigroup.com/committees/50002609

(30)   Factsheet: Eliminating Hexavalent Chrome From Cooling Towers, L.A. Board of Public Works: Hazardous and

Toxic Materials Office, April 6, 2006, available at http://
www.gfxtechnology.com/CR6.pdf

(31) *California Utility Agrees to Settle Suit by Residents for
$50 Million to $400 Million*, BNA Toxics L. DAILY, May
11, 1995, available at: http://www.lexis.com

(32) Koutsky, Joe. "Executive Officer's Report: Public
Health Assessment for Pacific Gas and Electric site in
Hinkley, San Bernardino County." Lahontan Regional
Water Quality Control Board, Feb. 2001, available at:
https://www.waterboards.ca.gov/lahontan/water_issues/
projects/pge/

- "PG&E's natural gas Compressor Station is located
  approximately two miles southeast of the town of
  Hinkley and a dozen miles west of Barstow in the
  Mojave Desert of San Bernardino County. Between
  1952 and 1966, PG&E used hexavalent chromium,
  also known as chromium 6, to fight corrosion in
  cooling tower water. The wastewater from the cooling
  towers was discharged to unlined ponds at the site.
  Some of the wastewater percolated to the groundwater, resulting in hexavalent chromium pollution.
  The chromium affects an area of groundwater at
  least eight miles long and two miles wide. Chromium
  plume maps through time are listed on the bottom of
  this webpage."
- "PG&E is under orders from the Lahontan Water
  Board to stop plume expansion and clean up the chromium plume. Monthly monitoring reports by PG&E
  demonstrate that the chromium plume is currently
  being contained south of Thompson Road."
- "Below are certain documents related to some of these
  corrective actions. All documents associated with the
  project are available at the Lahontan Water Board

office in Victorville and on the State Water Board's database called Geotracker at http://geotracker.waterboards.ca.gov/."

(33) Ascenzi, Joseph. "Toxics suit cites PG&E in 4 deaths: Action by 56 plaintiffs says toxic water used to fill swimming pools." Bus. Press/Cal. August. 14, 2000, available at: http://www.lexis.com

Extras sources:

Graham, Frank Jr. "Fifty Years After Silent Spring, Attacks on Science Continue." *YaleEnvironment360*, New Haven, June 21, 2012, available at: https://e360.yale.edu/features/fifty_years_after_rachel_carsons_silent_spring_assacult_on_science_continues

• "The parallels with today's assault on climate science are striking. The personal, vitriolic attacks that were leveled at Carson are echoed today in the organized assault on the scientists who bring us uncontroverted evidence that greenhouse gases are rapidly warming the planet."

"The Movie Erin Brockovich." *Sample Experimental Ethics Papers, University of Minnesota*, Duluth, available at:
http://www.d.umn.edu/~scastleb/Sample%20Experiential%20%20Ethics%20Papers/Movie%20(Erin%20Brockovich).pdf

Chapter 3 - A Quietly Escalating Issue of the NFL

(34) Babb, Kent and Rich, Steven. "A Quietly Escalating Issue for NFL: Fan Violence and How to Contain It." *Chicago*

Tribune October 28, 2016, available at: https://www.chicagotribune.com/sports/football/ct-nfl-fan-violence-stadium-20161028-story.html

- "A significant problem, particularly in some locations, is that there is disagreement among the league, teams and local enforcement on who is ultimately responsible for fan safety."
- "The data show per-game arrests over the past five seasons were highest at San Diego's Qualcomm Stadium, where police instituted stricter policies in 2013 following a violent parking lot brawl that involved thrown glass bottles. Following San Diego, where police made 24.58 arrests per game between 2011 and 2015, were the stadiums in New York (21.96 arrests per game), Oakland (17.78) and Pittsburgh (16.75). The NFL sees high arrest numbers at its stadiums in San Diego, New York and Pittsburgh as byproducts of those franchises' zero-tolerance policies; Oakland, though, is continually on the league's radar, along with San Francisco, Cincinnati, Cleveland and Philadelphia."
- "But the potential for trouble is hardly confined to those sites. Last October, a man was shot outside a Dallas Cowboys game at A&T Stadium and later died. A year earlier, a man at Levi's Stadium in Santa Clara, California, home of the 49ers, was beaten so badly, his attorney said, the man now suffers from permanent seizure activity. In 2013, a 30-year-old man was beaten to death in the parking lot at Kansas City Arrowhead Stadium."
- "Casey Nice, an assistant sheriff in California's Alameda County, is in charge of overseeing the game-day security operation at all Raiders games at

Oakland Coliseum. Nice said he's in occasional contact with the NFL league office, and he attends the
league's security seminar each year. But he has not
received a list of the NFL's "best practices."

(35)   Lo, Karen. "Bud Light Signs Multi-Year Renewal as
NFL's Official Beer Sponsor, with Access to Game
Footage." *The Daily Meal*, November 6, 2015, available
at: https://www.thedailymeal.com/drink/bud-light-signs-
multi-year-renewal-nfl-s-official-beer-sponsor-access-
game-footage

(36)   The Ray Carreira statement is recorded in the "Confidential
Videotaped Deposition of Ray Carreira," October 21,
2016, *Kirin Patel and Amish Patel v. San Francisco Forty
Niners, et al.*, Santa Clara County Superior Court Case
no. 115CV286138, (2015)

Extra Sources:

Notte, Jason. "The NFL Isn't Admitting it Has a Drinking
Problem." *MarketWatch* September 23, 2015, available
at: https://www.marketwatch.com/story/the-nfl-isnt-
admitting-it-has-a-drinking-problem-2015-09-23

• "A fight in a Levi's Stadium bathroom last year
resulted in the victim having a portion of his skull
removed surgically and an assailant sentenced to five
years in prison."

• "There is absolutely no unified approach to stadium-alcohol policy outside of not allowing glass bottles and not running the taps after the third quarter,
which date back to former NFL Commissioner Paul
Tagliabue's reign from 1989 to 2006."

- "The NFL doesn't have to ban beer or turn into a teetotaler to build a better, more functional alcohol policy. It just has to try before someone forces it to."

Chapter 4 - "Jerry...remember Jerry? It's a lawsuit about Jerry"

(37) *Steve Simms, et al., vs. Jerral "Jerry" Wayne Jones, National Football League, et al.,* 3:11-cv-00248-M, 2011, Dallas. The pdf of this lawsuit can also be found on my Author's website at: https://unsafeinanyseat.com/wp-content/uploads/2019/05/NFL-Am-Compl.pdf

(38) Charles F. Sabel & William H. Simont. "The Duty of Responsible Administration and the Problem of Police Accountability." *Yale Law School Legal Scholarship Repository.* (2016), available at:
https://digitalcommons.law.yale.edu/yjreg/vol33/iss1/4
- "... Need to reassess routines in the light of changing circumstances." Page 165
- "... court-supervised reforms in New York, Cincinnati, (and Oakland) ...," Page 165.
- "Public officials have a duty of responsible administration that consists of three elements. It requires that officials articulate reflectively the policies and principles that govern their work. It demands that they monitor the activities of peers and subordinates to induce compliance with these policies and principles. And finally, the duty mandates frequent reassessment of these policies and principles in light of the officials' own experience and that of comparable institutions." Page 166.
- "(Need a) comprehensive reform of city's policing practices." Page 169.

(39)   The complete original 1907 Brandeis Brief can be referenced at: *"The Brandeis Brief."* Louis D. Brandeis School of Law Library. Louisville (1907), https://louisville.edu/law/library/special-collections/the-louis-d.-brandeis-collection/the-brandeis-brief-in-its-entirety

(40)   Roger Goodell's complete answers and statements can be found in, "Videotaped Deposition of Roger Goodell", Friday, August 9, 2013, *Steve Simms, et al., vs. Jerral "Jerry" Wayne Jones, National Football League, et al., 3:11-cv-00248-M, 2011, Dallas.* The pdf of this file can be found on my Author's website at: https://unsafeinanyseat.com/wp-content/uploads/2019/03/130809-Videotaped-Deposition-of-Roger-Goodell.pdf

Extra sources:

Heitner, Darren. "After Four Years, Super Bowl XLV Ticket Seating Scandal Finally Settles." *Forbes Magazine* May 24, 2017, https://www.forbes.com/sites/darrenheitner/2017/05/24/after-4-years-super-bowl-xlv-ticket-seating-scandal-finally-settles/#1d2e7a730a83

"Photos: See the seat issues at Cowboys Stadium." *SportsDay* February 2011, https://sportsday.dallasnews.com/dallascowboys/cowboysheadlines/2011/02/06/photos-see-the-seat-issues-at-cowboys-stadium

Chapter 5 - "Honey, you really knock me out!"

(41)   "Robert S. Mueller III's Report on Ray Rice Domestic Violence Case." *New York Times* January 8, 2015, https://www.nytimes.com/interactive/2015/01/08/sports/

football/document-robert-s-mueller-iiis-report-on-ray-rice-domestic-violence-case.html

(42) *"National Football League Personal Conduct Policy,"* National Football League, December 10, 2014, (Appendix #1) https://static.nfl.com/static/content/public/photo/2014/12/10/0ap3000000441637.pdf

(43) Bensen, Jackie and Cook, Gina. "NFL Security Chief Cathy Lanier Addresses Assault Cases, Says League Has Improved," *NBC4 Washington*, December 10, 2018, https://www.nbcwashington.com/news/sports/NFL-Security-Chief-Cathy-Lanier-Addresses-Assault-Cases-502318241.html

- "There was (were) extensive reforms that we put in place post Robert Mueller's report from Ray Rice and that is detailed investigative protocol that we follow," Lanier said.

(44) Garcia, Ahiza. "NFL Picks Washington D.C. Police Chief to Head Security." *CNN Money Cable News Network* August 16, 2016, https://money.cnn.com/2016/08/16/news/nfl-cathy-lanier-dc-police-chief/index.html

- "She will oversee the league's security department and will work with its 32 teams and federal, state and local law enforcement."
- "Lanier will coordinate security of fans, players, staff, venues and infrastructure at all games, including the Super Bowl and international games."

(45) Freeman, Mike. "Kareem Hunt Video Shows NFL Still Has No Idea How to Address Its Biggest Problem," *Bleacher Report* November 30, 2018, https://bleacher-report.com/articles/2808663-kareem-hunt-video-shows-nfl-still-has-no-idea-how-to-address-its-biggest-problem

- "In 2014, Ray Rice knocked his then-fiancee, Janay Palmer, in an elevator—and the NFL said it had not heard of a video that was eventually found by TMZ. The league only reacted sternly once those horrific images from that elevator surfaced."

- "But what happened with Rice was supposed to change everything. At least, that's what we were told. But now we have Hunt's actions of February 2018, and, again, a league with enormous financial and investigative resources was outhustled by TMZ."

- "What we do know is the NFL utilizes a private army full of ex-cops, FBI agents and former investigators."

- "And yet TMZ could get this tape but a billion-dollar league couldn't?

- "We again as a league look like amateurs on this issue," one NFC team executive told Bleacher Report on Friday."

- "But it is totally fair to wonder if the NFL didn't want to find a video. The league's history has lost it the benefit of the doubt on that."

Extra sources:

"NFL Owners Endorse New Personal Conduct Policy." *NFL. com National Football League News* December 19, 2014, http://www.nfl.com/news/story/0ap3000000441758/ article/nfl-owners-endorse-new-personal-conduct-policy
- "This policy applies to the Commissioner; all owners; all employees of the NFL, NFL clubs, and all NFL-related entities, including players under contract, coaches, game officials; all rookie players selected in the NFL college draft and all undrafted rookie players, unsigned veterans who were under contract in the

prior League Year; and other prospective employees once they commence negotiations with a club concerning employment. Clubs and league staff are strongly encouraged to communicate this policy to independent contractors and consultants and to make clear that violations of this policy will be grounds for terminating a business relationship."

Brennan, Christine. "Brennan: NFL Cleared on Rice Video, But Owners See Lessons." *USA Today Gannet Satellite Information Network* January 8, 2015, https://www.usatoday.com/story/sports/nfl/2015/01/08/national-football-league-ray-rice-video-roger-goodell-robert-mueller-report/21457367/

Pelissero, Tom. "Mueller report: NFL Had Not Seen Elevator Video Before Punishing Ray Rice." *USA Today Gannet Satellite Information Network* January 8, 2015, https://www.usatoday.com/story/sports/nfl/2015/01/08/robert-mueller-report-ray-rice-vide-roger-goodell/21450561/

Chapter 6 - Levi's Stadium Security - "How do you work this thing?"

(46)   Brown, Elizabeth and Sellers, Mike. "Policing the 2016 Super Bowl Stadium," *ICMA.org* December 12, 2015, https://icma.org/articles/pm-magazine/policing-2016-super-bowl-stadium
 •   "Santa Clara would have one of the smallest law enforcement agencies in the country to protect an NFL stadium."

- In turn, this model has also strengthened relationships between the Santa Clara Police Department (SCPD) and federal, state, and local law enforcement jurisdictions.
- The unit studied 21 stadium operations across the country and created an operations plan and manual for all events at Levi's Stadium based on National Football League best practices.

(47)   Thompson, Tisha and Sciallo, Michael. "From Teen Mother to NFL Security Chief, Cathy Lanier's Rise Through the Law Enforcement Ranks," *ESPNW Internet Ventures* October 26, 2017, http://www.espn.com/espnw/culture/feature/article/20994956/from-teen-mother-nfl-security-chief-cathy-lanier-rise-law-enforcement-ranks

(48)   Waitt, Tammy. "Levi's Stadium Invests in Unified VMS & Access Control Systems (Video)," *American Security Today* October 26, 2016, https://americansecuritytoday.com/levis-stadium-invests-unified-vms-access-control-systems-video/

(49)   "3U IP Video Surveillance Strong System." IP Video Surveillance Storage - COLDSTORE 3U-Long Retention IP Video Storage. http://www.veracityglobal.com/products/storage-systems-for-video-surveillance/cold-store-3u.aspx

(50)   Torke, Alex. "Police Report Supplement No. 0002," Santa Clara Police Dept., November 1, 2018. The pdf of this can be found on my Author's website at: https://unsafeinanyseat.com/wp-content/uploads/2019/03/181101-Santa-Clara-Police-Dept.-Report-Suspect-Steve-Guardado-SUPP-0002.pdf

(51)   Nguyen, Chris. "Dozens of Arrests During Oakland Raiders-SF 49ers 'Battle of the Bay' Game at Levi's Stadium," *ABC 7 San Francisco* November 2, 2018,

https://abc7news.com/sports/dozens-of-arrests-during-battle-of-the-bay-at-levis-stadium/4602099/

Extra Sources:

Roberts, Michelle. "State-of-the-Art Security Technology at Levi's Stadium in Time for Super Bowl 50," *NBC Bay Area* September 29, 2015, https://www.nbcbayarea.com/news/local/State-of-the-Art-Security-Technology-at-Levis-Stadium-in-Time-for-Super-Bowl-50-330016471.html

Sprig Electric Wires Comprehensive Security System at Levi's Stadium.
http://www.sprigelectric.com/documents/The_VOICE_Levis.pdf

- "State-of-the-art security is in place at the new Levi's® Stadium, thanks to the installation of a $1,000,000 security system wired by Sprig Electric, Inc."
- "Security for the stadium begins in the main parking lot, where 60 pole-mounted cameras can pan the surrounding area on a 360-degree scan, providing surveillance of all visitors. Security cameras are also mounted above the solar energy bridges which are used as a walkway into the stadium."
- "Cameras are installed at the stadium's entry gates, throughout the facility (offices areas, walkways, etc.), as well as within the stadium seating area. Over 240 cameras are mounted within nine levels of walkways, and some 50 cameras are mounted on pedestals in the seating area."

"The Silicon Valley Wire - The Latest News From the Electrical Industry in Silicon Valley" *NECA-IBEW*, 1st Quarter 2015, https://www.scvneca.com/wp-content/uploads/SVWire_1Q15.pdf

- "Cameras are installed at the stadium's entry gates, throughout the facility (offices areas, walkways, etc...), as well as within the stadium seating area."
- "Over 240 cameras are mounted within nine levels of walkways and some 50 cameras are mounted on pedestals in the seating area." Page 7.

Chapter 7 - "Two times Zero equals Zero"

(52) "All animals are equal, but some animals are more equal than others." *Dictionary.com* https://www.dictionary.com/browse/all-animals-are-equal--but-some-animals-are-more-equal-than-others

(53) *Moneeb, Ikram and Ikram v City of Santa Clara, Mike Sellers, et al.*, United States District Court (ND CA 2015), Case no. 5:15-cv-01987-NC. The pdf of this lawsuit can also be found on my Author's website at: https://unsafeinanyseat.com/wp-content/uploads/2019/05/Complaint.First-Amended.FILED-Doc.-25.pdf

(54) Haddad & Sherwin LLP, "$499,000 for Federal Law Enforcement Officer whose Home Was Illegally Raided by Santa Clara Police." *Haddad & Sherwin LLP website* April 27, 2016, https://www.haddadandsherwin.com/2016/04/27/499000-for-federal-law-enforcement-officer-whose-home-was-illegally-raided-by-santa-clara-police/

(55) *Danielle Harmon v. City of Santa Clara, City of Santa Clara Police Chief Mike Sellers, et al.*, United Stated

District Court (ND CA 2016) Case no. 5:16-cv-04228-EJD. The pdf of this lawsuit can also be found on my Author's website at: https://unsafeinanyseat.com/wp-content/uploads/2019/03/160727-Danielle-Harmon-v-City-of-Santa-Clara-et-al-Complaint-for-Damages.pdf

(56)   ABC 7 KGO Staff. "Santa Clara Settles Police Excessive Force Lawsuit for $6.7 million," *ABC 7 News San Francisco* September 28, 2017, https://abc7news.com/santa-clara-settles-police-excessive-force-lawsuit-for-$67-million/2464559/

- Link includes 'police body cam' of door being kicked down and Danielle Harmon's injuries.
- Santa Clara's City Attorney, Brian Doyle said, "Although there was significant disagreement about the extent of the injury, there was no dispute that the plaintiff sustained a broken ankle in the course of the entry to the plaintiff's home without a warrant. The city's insurer determined that the most prudent course of action was for it to pay an amount that would result in settlement."
- "Police Chief Mike Sellers says he's extremely disappointed with the settlement and would have liked to have presented all the evidence and video to a judge. He says his officers acted within the law and was surprised how quickly the city settled with the plaintiff."

(57)   Herhold, Scott. "Police Chief Sellers Should Retire." *The Mercury News* October 5, 2017, https://www.pressreader.com/usa/the-mercury-news/20171005/282604558055565

- "Our officers' actions were fully within the law and in accordance with accepted police practices," said Chief Mike Sellers in a prepared statement.

(58)   Santa Clara Police Officers Association Board of Directors. Untitled - letter to Mr. Jed York San Francisco 49ers. September 2, 2016. (Appendix #2) The pdf of this letter can also be found on my Author's website at: https://unsafeinanyseat.com/wp-content/uploads/2019/03/160902-SCPOA-BOD-letter-to-Jed-York.pdf

Extra sources:

Green, Jason. "Santa Clara Settles Federal Civil Rights Suit Alleging Police Illegally Searched Muslim Family's Home — twice." *Marin Independent Journal* April 28, 2016, https://www.marinij.com/2016/04/28/santa-clara-settles-federal-civil-rights-suit-alleging-police-illegally-searched-muslim-familys-home-twice/

- "Mohammad Moneeb and his parents, Mohammad and Hazakat Ikram, claim that officers investigating the alleged theft of a $300 dashboard camera illegally entered and searched their home on the 1100 block of Lincoln Street around 1:15 a.m. on Feb. 10, 2014."

Chapter 8 - September 2, 2016 - SCPOA letter to Jed York

(59)   Santa Clara Police Officers Association Board of Directors. Untitled - letter to Mr. Jed York San Francisco 49ers. September 2, 2016. (Appendix #2) The pdf of this letter can also be found on my Author's website at: https://unsafeinanyseat.com/wp-content/uploads/2019/03/160902-SCPOA-BOD-letter-to-Jed-York.pdf

Chapter 9 - Colin Kaepernick

(60) "Sympathy for the Devil." Beggars Banquet. By Mick
      Jagger and Keith Richards. Rolling Stones. Rec. 4-5, 8-10
      June 1968. Jimmy Miller, 1968. Vinyl.
      • Stones opening track on their 1968 album,
        Beggars Banquet.
      • https://www.youtube.com/watch?v=qmppOF0_DHE

(61) Santa Clara Police Officer's Association Board of
      Directors. "To Mr. Jed York." September 26, 2016. Santa
      Clara, California. 1-2. (Appendix #2)

(62) White, Kenon. "Oakland Police Scandal Underscores
      Importance of Kaepernick's Protest" *News One*
      September 8, 2016, https://newsone.com/3532567/
      oakland-police-scandal-colin-kaepernick/
      • "At least a dozen Oakland, California, cops were ter-
        minated as a result of a sexual misconduct scandal
        that began in September 2015."
      • "A 19-year-old Hispanic teen prostitute told authori-
        ties she had sex with approximately thirty law enforce-
        ment officials. Four of the cops allegedly had sex with
        the young woman before she turned eighteen."
      • "You can't have this kind of widespread misconduct
        and not have some supervisors know something about
        it." John Burris, Civil Rights Attorney.
      • He continued, "When you have officers conducting
        misconduct while on the job and engaging in crim-
        inal activity, it's very difficult for the citizens in the
        community to have trust and faith in the department
        notwithstanding all the other issues."
      • "News One news host Roland Martin said the scandal
        in Oakland is an example of what San Francisco
        49ers QB Colin Kaepernick is protesting. Amazingly

enough, after the news of the scandal broke, no other law enforcement officials have come out to condemn the actions of the cops involved in this massive scandal."

- Martin asked, "Where are all these police associations, the Fraternal Order of Police, issuing the statements of condemnation of these officers?"
- "No other Police Officers are on record condemning these actions."
- "Clear abuse of their authority."

(63)   Bakkila, Blake. "Police Union Says Officers Might Not Work at 49ers Games Amid Colin Kaepernick's Continued Protests." *People* September 9, 2016, https://people.com/celebrity/police-officers-might-not-work-at-49ers-games-amid-kaepernick-controversy/

- "Many of us in the law enforcement community have been saddened and angered by Kaepernick's words and actions," Sellers wrote. "As distasteful as his actions are, these actions are protected by the Constitution. Police officers are here to protect the rights of every person, even if we disagree with their position."
- "I will urge the POA leadership to put the safety of our citizens first," he wrote. "I will work with both sides to find a solution. I will ensure we continue to provide a safe environment at Levi's Stadium."

(64)   Herhold, Scott. "Police Chief Sellers Should Retire." *The Mercury News* October 5, 2017, https://www.pressreader.com/usa/the-mercury-news/20171005/282604558055565

- "Our officers' actions were fully within the law and in accordance with accepted police practices," said Chief Mike Sellers in a prepared statement.

(65)   Voter's Edge. Candidates. City of Santa Clara
         Candidate for Chief of Police. https://votersedge.org/
         en/ca/ballot/election/area/42/contests/contest/14425/
         candidate/134461?election_authority_id=43
         From "My Top 3 Priorities." Priority # 1:
         •   "Maintain an open dialog with community members
             and businesses. Focus on SCPD's long-standing tra-
             dition of honest, transparent, ethical law enforcement
             while maintaining fiscal responsibility. Become the
             safest city in America."

Extra sources:

BondGraham, Darwin and Winston, Ali. "Badge of
Dishonor: Top Oakland Police Department Officials
Looked Away as East Bay Cops Sexually Exploited
and Trafficked a Teenager." *East Bay Express*
[Oakland] June 15, 2016 https://www.eastbayexpress.
com/oakland/badge-of-dishonor-top-oakland-police-
department-officials-looked-away-as-east-bay-cops-
sexually-exploited-and-trafficked-a-teenagerdepartmen/
Content?oid=4832543&storyPage=3
•   "No matter how one parses the legal and ethical
    aspects of the case, Lutnick said the scandal involves
    multiple departments across jurisdictions, and that
    this "highlights the need for a hard look at the cul-
    tures within police departments."

Herhold, Scott. "How Kaepernick's socks play in Santa
Clara police chief race." *The Mercury News* September 12,
2016, https://www.mercurynews.com/2016/09/11/how-
kaepernicks-socks-play-in-santa-clara-police-chief-race/

- "Competing statements from Police Chief Mike Sellers and Mayor Lisa Gillmor"
- "Meanwhile, an audit of the stadium's financial operation is being undertaken by Harvey Rose Associates, a step that was suggested by a civil grand jury last June."

Hamilton, Matt. "Santa Clara Police Union Urges Officers to Work at 49ers Game, Despite 'Concerns' Over Kaepernick's Comments." *Los Angeles Times* September 8, 2016, http://www.latimes.com/local/lanow/la-me-ln-santa-clara-police-kaepernick-20160908-snap-story.html
- "About 70 officers from the Santa Clara Police Department patrol Levi's Stadium when the 49ers play there; the officers are paid as stadium security."

Perez, A.J. "Santa Clara Police Might Not Work 49ers Games Amid Colin Kaepernick Protest." *USA Today Gannett Satellite Info Network* September 3, 2016, https://www.usatoday.com/story/sports/nfl/niners/2016/09/02/colin-kaepernick-anthem-protest-santa-clara-police-union/89799328/

Belson, Ken. "Colin Kaepernick's Collusion Case Against the N.F.L. Will Advance." *New York Times* Aug. 30 2018, https://www.nytimes.com/2018/08/30/sports/colin-kaepernick-collusion-case-nfl.html
- "discovery, question witnesses, and present this full case in front of the arbitrator."
- "During discovery, Kaepernick's lawyers have requested hundreds of pages of documents from the league office and teams."

Reid, Jason. "Colin Kaepernick Won. Period." *The Undefeated* February 15, 2019, https://theundefeated.com/features/colin-kaepernick-won-period/

- "The NFL is the most powerful sports league on the planet. It has virtually inexhaustible financial resources. It has top-notch lawyers. And it is fiercely protective of its image — the whole thing about not tarnishing the shield and all."
- "Kaepernick's grievance was expected to go to a full hearing sometime this year, and the NFL was facing the possibility of massive financial liability if it lost. Without a winning hand, the NFL decided to fold, said Stanford Law School professor William B. Gould IV."

Chapter 10 - Kiran Patel

(66)   Brown, Elizabeth and (Chief) Sellers, Mike. "Policing the 2016 Super Bowl Stadium." *ICMA.org* December 11, 2015, https://icma.org/articles/pm-magazine/policing-2016-super-bowl-stadium

- "Santa Clara would have one of the smallest law enforcement agencies in the country to protect an NFL stadium."
- "Santa Clara has been able to develop a comprehensive law enforcement plan involving federal, state, and local partners."
- "The plan identified the need for a law enforcement coalition for the stadium that included SCPD; 49ers security team; homeland security partners; contracted security officers; Santa Clara County Sheriff's Department; California Highway Patrol; and neighboring Sunnyvale's Public Safety Department."

- "The position would be categorized as "as needed, at will," but the special events officer would have full police powers in deployment in and around the stadium to provide crowd and traffic control, arrest of offenders, report writing, and general enforcement duties.""
- "Levi's Stadium hosted more than 200 events in 2014, ranging from corporate meetings to charity events to large-attendance athletic competitions. Most of them were easily handled by stadium security backed up by regular law enforcement services provided by SCPD.""

(67) *Kiran Patel and Amish Patel v. San Francisco Forty Niners, et al.*, Santa Clara County Superior Court Case no. 115CV286138, (2015). The pdf of this lawsuit can also be found on my Author's website at: https://unsafeinanyseat.com/wpcontent/uploads/2019/03/150925-Complaint-For-Damages-Kiran-Patel-vs-San-Francisco-Forty-Niners-Limited.pdf

(68) CBS 5 KPIX 5 Staff. "Santa Clara Police Urging More Witnesses to Come Forward in Levi's Stadium Assault Caught On Camera." *CBS 5 KPIX SF Bay Area* October 16, 2014, https://sanfrancisco.cbslocal.com/2014/10/16/santa-clara-police-urging-more-witnesses-to-come-forward-in-levis-stadium-beating-caught-on-camera/

Extra Sources:

Eisler, Geoffrey. "Levi's Stadium Bathroom Assault Victim 'Close to Death,' Prosecutors Say." *NBC Bay Area* The Faithful - Coverage of the San Francisco 49ers, October 8, 2014, https://www.nbcbayarea.com/news/local/Levis-Stadium-Bathroom-Assault-Was-Not-A-Fight-Prosecutors-Say-278588731.html

Chapter 11 - "And the Award goes to..."

(69)   "Levi's Stadium Named 2017 Facility of Merit by NFL and National Sports and Security Conference," *Levi's Stadium website* June 7, 2017, http://www.levisstadium. com/2017/06/levis-stadium-named-2017-facility-of-merit-by-nfl-and-national-sports-safety-and-security-conference/

(70)   The Jim Mercurio statement is recorded in the "Confidential Videotaped Deposition of Jim Mercurio," March 13, 2017, *Kiran Patel and Amish Patel v. San Francisco Forty Niners, et al.,* Santa Clara County Superior Court Case no. 115CV286138, (2015)

(71)   "Jim Mercurio, Levi's Stadium," *Sports Business Journal Daily* June 19, 2017, https://www.sportsbusinessdaily. com/Journal/Issues/2017/06/19/Power-Players/Jim-Mercurio.aspx

Chapter - 12 - Levi's Stadium Incident - November 1, 2018 - Part 2

(72)   Anderson, et al. v. Pacific Gas and Electric: Superior Court for County of San Bernardino, Barstow Division, Case no. BCV 00300 (1993).

(73)   "Welcome to the City Manager's Office," City of Santa Clara, http://santaclaraca.gov/government/departments/city-manager

(74)   Winston, Ali. "Deanna Santana Tried to Alter Damning Report." *East Bay Express* [Oakland] September 19, 2012, https://www.eastbayexpress.com/oakland/deanna-santana-tried-to-alter-damning-report/Content?oid=3341245

(75) Frazier Group, LLC. *"Independent Investigation Occupy Oakland Response,"* October 25, 2011 (Frazier Report), Frazier Group LLC - June 14, 2012.

(76) *Daryelle Lawanna Preston v. City of Oakland; Deanna Santana, et al.,* Alameda Superior Court Case no. RG14-717585, (2014). The pdf of this can be found on my Author's website at: https://unsafeinanyseat.com/wp-content/uploads/2019/08/Daryelle-Lawanna-Preston-v.-City-of-Oakland-Deanna-Santana-et-al.-Alameda-Superior-Court-Case-no.-RG14-717585-2014.pdf

(77) BondGraham, Darwin. "Jury Awards Whistleblower $613,302 in Lawsuit Against City of Oakland," *East Bay Express* September 24, 2015, https://www.eastbayexpress.com/SevenDays/archives/2015/09/24/jury-awards-whistleblower-613302-in-lawsuit-against-oakland

• Reference: *Daryelle Lawanna Preston v. City of Oakland; Deanna Santana, et al.,* Alameda Superior Court Case no. RG14-717585, (2014)

• The pdf of this lawsuit can be found on my Author's website at: https://unsafeinanyseat.com/wp-content/uploads/2019/08/Daryelle-Lawanna-Preston-v.-City-of-Oakland-Deanna-Santana-et-al.-Alameda-Superior-Court-Case-no.-RG14-717585-2014.pdf

(78) *IN RE Ghost Ship Fire Litigation Master Complaint*: Superior Court for County of Alameda, Case no. RG16843631 (2017). The pdf of this lawsuit can be found on my Author's website at: https://unsafeinanyseat.com/wp-content/uploads/2019/08/IN-RE-Ghost-Ship-Fire-Litigation-Master-Complaint-Superior-Court-for-County-of-Alameda-Case-no.-RG16843631-2017.pdf

(79) BondGraham, Darwin. "Oakland Firefighters Say Their Department Is So Badly Managed, Ghost Ship Warehouse Wasn't Even In Its Inspection Database,"

East Bay Express December 7, 2016, https://www.
eastbayexpress.com/oakland/oakland-firefighters-say-
their-department-is-so-badly-managed-ghost-ship-
warehouse-wasnt-even-in-its-inspection-database/
Content?oid=5055245

(80) "2016 Oakland warehouse fire." *Wikipedia*,
retrieved from https://en.wikipedia.org/
wiki/2016_Oakland_warehouse_fire

(81) *'HLN Ghost Ship' Warehouse Fire: Interview with Attorney
Mary Alexander."* December 26, 2016. https://www.you-
tube.com/watch?time_continue=474&v=l-TpnbnN5BY
- "Notice to the City" (at 7:40)
- "Only 600 feet from the Fire Department"

(82) Schuk, Carolyn. "Santa Clara Subject of State Pension
Investigation." *The Silicon Valley Voice* October 12, 2018,
https://www.svvoice.com/santa-clara-subject-of-state-
pension-investigation/

Extra sources:

Ramona Giwargis, "Internal Affairs: Santa Clara
Appoints Deanna Santana as New City Manager." *The
Mercury News* August 24, 2017, https://www.mercury-
news.com/2017/08/23/internal-affairs-santa-clara-ap-
points-deanna-santana-as-new-city-manager/

Gammon, Robert. "Oakland's Latest Mess," *East Bay
Express* Friday, August 24, 2012, https://www.east-
bayexpress.com/SevenDays/archives/2012/08/24/
oaklands-latest-mess
- "Attorneys John Burris and Jim Chanin, who are also
involved in monitoring OPD, are now demanding an

investigation into who leaked Santana's allegations to the press."

- "They note that the timing of the allegations is suspicious because court monitor Warshaw has been highly critical of OPD and its failure to implement the reforms it agreed to make. Warshaw and his team are also close to releasing new progress reports on the department."

BondGraham, Darwin. "Damning Report of OPD," *East Bay Express* June 20, 2012, https://www.eastbayexpress. com/oakland/damning-report-of-opd/Content?oid= 3244833

Chapter - 13 - Levi's Stadium Incident - November 1, 2018 - Part 3

(83) *Kiran Patel and Amish Patel v. San Francisco Forty Niners, et al.*, Santa Clara County Superior Court Case no. 115CV286138, (2015). The pdf of this lawsuit can also be found on my Author's website at: https://unsafeinanyseat. com/wpcontent/uploads/2019/03/150925-Complaint-For-Damages-Kiran-Patel-vs-San-Francisco-Forty-Niners-Limited.pdf

(84) *The State of California v Gonzales*, David Aguilera, Santa Clara County Superior Court Case No. C1802883, (2018)

Chapter - 14 - Levi's Stadium Incident - November 1, 2018 - Part 4

(85) Babb, Kent and Rich, Steven. "A Quietly Escalating Issue for NFL: Fan Violence and How to Contain It," *Washington Post* October 28, 2016, https://www.

chicagotribune.com/sports/football/ct-nfl-fan-violence-stadium-20161028-story.html

(86)   Harvey M. Rose Associates, LLC. *"Comprehensive Audit of Stadium Authority Finances prepared for the Stadium Authority Board, Santa Clara Stadium Authority, City of Santa Clara,"* pages 18 & 73 (included in City of Santa Clara. Agenda Report, August 24, 2017, Agenda Item # 8.C.). Available at: https://unsafeinanyseat.com/wp-content/uploads/2019/03/170824-Comprehensive-Audit-of-Stadium-Harvey-M-Rose-Associates-LLC-St.pdf

Extra sources:

Meacham, Jody. "49ers-Santa Clara Audit Dispute Moves From Mean to Nasty." *Silicon Valley Business Journal* [San Jose] November 1, 2016, https://www.bizjournals.com/sanjose/news/2016/11/01/49ers-santa-clara-audit-dispute-moves-from-mean-to.html

- "Incumbent Chief Mike Sellers has been criticized by Gillmor for an alleged failure to cooperate fully with auditors. The mayor supports challenger Pat Nikolai for chief."
- "The city staff time that Broussard was referring to in his comments has to do with police assigned to the stadium for NFL games. Whether the team or the city has paid for that security is uncertain and resolution of that issue has been complicated by the fact that the city's police department has one of the few elected chiefs in the state. His job is also up for grabs in next week's election."

CBS 5 KPIX CBS SF Bay Area Staff. "Levi's Stadium Financial Politics Pits Police Chief

Against Mayor." *CBS 5 KPIX* August 25, 2017, https://sanfrancisco.cbslocal.com/2017/08/25/levis-stadium-financial-politics-police-chief-mayor/

- "Santa Clara Police Chief Mike Sellers is giving full voice to months of frustration, accusing Mayor Lisa Gillmor of putting her ego, her agenda and her personal grievances against the 49ers, ahead of the city's best interests."

Koehn, Josh. "Civil Grand Jury Investigates Stadium Authority for Levi's Stadium, Site of Super Bowl 50." *San Jose Inside* February 3, 2016, http://www.sanjoseinside.com/2016/02/03/civil-grand-jury-investigates-stadium-authority-for-levis-stadium-site-of-super-bowl-50/

- "Fuentes, and by extension other top city staff, are suspected of withholding and/or obfuscating information related to the operations of Levi's Stadium, the two-year home of the San Francisco 49ers."
- "The San Francisco 49ers have a keen interest in the direction of the Santa Clara's City Council." (caption under picture in ribbon cutting ceremony)
- "A particularly worrisome lack of information concerns stadium security and related costs attributed to Santa Clara police and the city's general fund."
- "I think we're going to have to get much more sophisticated as a local government." - Councilwoman O'Neill direct quote
- "We're seeing a lot of dirty laundry in the council chambers, which is good, because it's being transparent, but it's not good because we're seeing our city break down in its effectiveness to work together." - Kirk Vartan owner of pizzeria, A Slice of New

York, and former digital content director for NBC in New York.

1. Kirk Vartan's pizza passes the fold test. It collapses easily in the hand, and, when held over a paper plate, drips bright orange grease. It's a classic slice of New York pizza, which is probably why Vartan named his joint A Slice of New York.

2. A former digital content director for NBC in New York, Vartan moved to San Jose in 1998 to work for Cisco before opening the pizzeria eight-and-a-half years ago. Hard pressed to pack more than five people inside at a time, we sit on the patio looking out over Stevens Creek Boulevard as evening commuters make their way home, the occasional street bike popping a wheelie.

3. In regards to oversight of operations at Levi's Stadium, few Santa Clarans have witnessed as closely as Vartan the unusual manner in which council members Gillmor, O'Neill and Davis have been brushed off.

4. "They're asking for very specific accounting records, and still to this day I've never seen them provided," he said. "It hasn't happened.

Chapter 15 - "Tale of the Tape"

(87) Thompson, Tisha and Sciallo, Michael. "From Teen Mother to NFL Security Chief, Cathy Lanier's Rise Through the Law Enforcement Ranks," *ESPNW.com* October 26, 2017, http://www.espn.com/espnw/culture/feature/article/20994956/from-teen-mother-nfl-security-chief-cathy-lanier-rise-law-enforcement-ranks

- "NFL security chief Cathy Lanier details the precautions the league has taken to make fans safer at NFL events."
- "I look at every attack that takes place everywhere," Lanier says
- "The league isn't quite like a police department, tasked with collecting and presenting evidence -- nor is it quite like a judge," Lanier says. She never wants to interfere with or jeopardize an ongoing criminal investigation. The toughest cases, in her opinion, are when criminal charges get dropped -- something that often happens in cases with domestic or sexual violence, when victims refuse to cooperate. If prosecutors don't move forward with a criminal case, her team will reach out to the accuser to see if that person will cooperate with them. They don't always agree. "I think people don't realize that we can't just, you know, make assumptions. We have to have something to support that there was a violation of the policy."

(88) CBS KPIX 5 Staff. "Santa Clara Police Urging More Witnesses to Come Forward In Levi's Stadium Assault Caught On Camera." *KPIX CBS SF Bay Area* October 16, 2014, https://sanfrancisco.cbslocal.com/2014/10/16/santa-clara-police-urging-more-witnesses-to-come-forward-in-levis-stadium-beating-caught-on-camera/

- "The Robollero's each wore tattoos associated with the Norteño criminal street gang."

Chapter 16 - "November 26, 2018 Letter to City Hall"

(89)   Weaver, Fred. "Thursday, November 1, 2018, Raiders at 49'ers Night Game - 49 fans savage assault" November 26, 2018.

Chapter 17 - "November 28, 2018 City of Santa Clara response"

(90)   Armas, Jose. "Your letter regarding the Raiders at 49ers Night Game on November 1, 2018 was received on November 27, 2018." November 28, 2018. (Appendix # 3)

Chapter 19 - There's a New Sheriff in Town

(91)   Wilson, James Q. *Varieties of Police Behavior: The Management of Law and Order in Eight American Communities,*" Harvard University Press, Cambridge, Mass., 1968
        For further reference, see also:
        James Q. Wilson. (n.d.) *Wikipedia,* retrieved July 5, 2019 from https://en.wikipedia.org/wiki/James_Q._Wilson

(92)   Lanier, Cathy L. *"Preventing Terror Attacks in The Homeland: A New Mission for State and Local Police."* Diss. Naval Post Graduate School, September 2005. https://calhoun.nps.edu/bitstream/handle/10945/1957/05Sep_Lanier.pdf?sequence=1&isAllowed=y

(93)   Broken windows theory. (n.d.) *Wikipedia,* retrieved July 5, 2019 from https://en.wikipedia.org/wiki/Broken_windows_theory

(94)   Thompson, Tisha and Sciallo, Michael. "From Teen Mother to NFL Security Chief, Cathy Lanier's Rise Through the Law Enforcement Ranks." *ESPNW.com*

October 26, 2017, http://www.espn.com/espnw/culture/feature/article/20994956/from-teen-mother-nfl-security-chief-cathy-lanier-rise-law-enforcement-ranks

(95) Davis, Paul and Jenkins, Brian. "Deterrence and Influence in Counterterrorism: A Component in the War on Al Qaeda" *RAND*, Santa Monica, CA 2002, https://www.rand.org/content/dam/rand/pubs/monograph_reports/2005/MR1619.pdf

(96) Scheider, Matthew and Chapman, Robert. "Community Policing and Terrorism," RAND, Santa Monica, CA April 2003, https://www.ncjrs.gov/App/Publications/abstract.aspx?ID=200121

(97) Carter, David. *"Law Enforcement Intelligence: A Guide for State, Local and Tribal Law Enforcement Agencies"* (U.S. Department of Justice, Office of Community Oriented Policing Services, 2003). https://ric-zai-inc.com/Publications/cops-p064-pub.pdf

(98) Lanier, Cathy. *"Evolving Threats to the Homeland,"* Committee on Homeland Security and Government Affairs, United States Senate, September 13, 2018. https://www.hsgac.senate.gov/imo/media/doc/Testimony-Lanier-2018-09-13.pdf

  • "To help the clubs in this difficult environment, the NFL has developed and published best practices and standards for responding to... incidents. These best practices...are incorporated into our overall best practices for stadium security..." Cathy Lanier, page 3.

(99) Babb, Kent and Rich, Steven. "A Quietly Escalating Issue for NFL: Fan Violence and How to Contain It." *Washington Post* October 28, 2016, https://www.chicagotribune.com/sports/football/ct-nfl-fan-violence-stadium-20161028-story.html

- "Casey Nice, an assistant sheriff in California's Alameda County, is in charge of overseeing the game-day security operation at all Raiders games at Oakland Coliseum."
- "As local law enforcement, Nice attends the NFL league's security seminar each year, but has never received a list of the NFL's "best practices.""

(100) Clarke, Liz. "Former Police Chief's Focus in New NFL Gig is Protecting the League's Image," *Washington Post* February 1, 2017, https://www.abqjournal.com/940611/former-police-chiefs-focus-in-new-nfl-gig-is-protecting-the-leagues-image.html

- "But there is a fundamental difference between protecting the public and protecting a corporate brand – the NFL or, to insiders, "the Shield." In this context, Lanier's charge isn't simply to keep fans safe. It's also to protect the league's image."
- "For all its popularity, the NFL has an image problem that some believe is cutting into unrivaled hold on U.S. sports fans. The roots of that image problem are complex and lie, in large part, in the league's delayed response to the dangers."

Chapter 20 - "Out of Sequence"

(101) Water Cribs in Chicago. (n.d.) *Wikipedia*, retrieved August 3, 2019 from https://en.wikipedia.org/wiki/Water_cribs_in_Chicago

(102) Carter, Elliot. "Chicago Water Cribs." *Atlas Obscura* January 9, 2017, https://www.atlasobscura.com/places/chicago-water-cribs

(103) LexisNexis - Legal & Professional Solutions, Risk Solutions, https://www.lexisnexis.com/en-us/gateway. page

(104) Langenstein, Billy. "Re: Follow Up." Message to Fred Weaver. 8 January 2019. E-mail. Included as an (Appendix #4) The pdf of this email can also be found on my Author's website at: https://unsafeinanyseat.com/wpcontent/ uploads/2019/01/190108-Follow-Up-email-from-Billy-Langenstein-NFL-Director-Investigations-Security-Services-COPY.pdf

Chapter 21 - "Second Class Citizen"

(105) Brown, Mike. "Van Halen's David Lee Roth: 'I've always been a show-off' – a classic interview from the vaults," *The Guardian* January 4, 2012, https://www.theguardian.com/music/musicblog/2012/ jan/04/valen-halen-david-lee-roth

(106) Herhold, Scott. "Police Chief Sellers should retire." *The Mercury News* October 5, 2017, https://www. pressreader.com/usa/the-mercury-news/20171005/ 282604558055565

   • "Our officers' actions were fully within the law and in accordance with accepted police practices," said Chief Mike Sellers in a prepared statement."

(107) Stahl, Ryan. "California's Anti-Slapp Statute - A Powerful Tool for Litigators," *SFBar.org* 2016, https://www.sfbar. org/forms/sfam/q22016/anti-slapp.pdf

(108) "Code of Civil Procedure - Section 425.16 California's Anti-SLAPP Law." *California Anti-SLAPP Project*, 2019, http://www.casp.net/california-anti-slapp-first-amendment-law-resources/ statutes/c-c-p-section-425-16/

(109)   *Anderson, et al. v. Pacific Gas and Electric* (Superior Ct. for County of San Bernardino, Barstow Division, file BCV 00300)

(110)   *People v. Brock Allen Turner,* Santa Clara County Superior Court Case no. B1577162, (2015) People's Sentencing Memorandum, May 27, 2016. https://www.paloaltoon-line.com/media/reports/1465602925.pdf The pdf of this lawsuit can also be found on my Author's website.

(111)   Hauser, Christine. "Brock Turner Loses Appeal to Overturn Sexual Assault Conviction." *New York Times* August 9, 2018, https://www.nytimes.com/2018/08/09/us/brock-turner-appeal.html

(112)   Stack, Liam. "Light Sentence for Brock Turner in Stanford Rape Case Draws Outrage." *New York Times* June 6, 2016, https://www.nytimes.com/2016/06/07/us/outrage-in-stanford-rape-case-over-dueling-statements-of-victim-and-attackers-father.html?action=click&mod-ule=RelatedCoverage&pgtype=Article&region=Footer

(113)   Erin Brockovich. Dir. Steven Soderbergh. With Julia Roberts, Albert Finney. Universal Pictures and Columbia Pictures 2012.
   • Grant, Susan. *Erin Brockovich: The Shooting Script.* New York: Newmarket Press, 2000.

(114)   Top Gun. Dir. Tony Scott. with Tom Cruise, Val Kilmer, and Kelly McGillis. Paramount Pictures 1986. "Hit the brakes," YouTube, https://www.youtube.com/watch?v=hp4cy2NXblc

(115)   *Frederick Leo Weaver v. San Francisco 49ers Limited, et al.* Santa Clara County Superior Case no. 19CV346749, (2019), (Appendix #5) The pdf of this lawsuit can also be found on my Author's website at: https://unsafeinan-yseat.com/wp-content/uploads/2019/05/190501-Weaver-v-49ers-Complaint-filed.pdf

Chapter 22 - "This Won't Take Long"

(116)   (Appendix #6) - May 31, 2019 - Ericksen Arbuthnot - Responses to Weaver Complaint

Chapter 23 - "Hitting the Brakes"

(117)   (Appendix #7) - June 3, 2019 - Lombardi, Loper, & Conant, LLP- Responses to Weaver Complaint

Chapter 25 - "Absurd and Impractical Consequences"

(118)   "Alice's Restaurant." Alice's Restaurant. By Arlo Guthrie. Rec. 1967. Fred Hellerman, 1967. Vinyl.

(119)   *Comstock v. General Motors Corporation* - 358 Mich. 163 (1959) 99 N.W.2d 627

(120)   "NFL Fan Code of Conduct." *National Football League* Updated July 26, 2012. http://www.nfl.com/news/story/09000d5d809c28f9/article/nfl-teams-implement-fan-code-of-conduct

   • Author's note: As a pleasant irony, the link at the top of this website says, "Not Secure - nfl.com"

(121)   "Levi's Stadium Security Policies - Code of Conduct." *Levi's Stadium website*, 2019. http://www.levisstadium.com/security-policies/

(122)   Hartman, Rome. Interview. "Mike Moore vs. The Opioid Industry." *60 Minutes* June 30, 2018. https://www.cbsnews.com/news/mike-moore-vs-the-opioid-industry-60-minutes-2019-06-30/

Epilogue

(123) Lanier, Cathy L. *"Preventing Terror Attacks in The Homeland: A New Mission for State and Local Police."* Diss. Naval Post Graduate School, September 2005. https://calhoun.nps.edu/bitstream/handle/10945/1957/05Sep_Lanier.pdf?sequence=1&isAllowed=y

(124) Umhoefer, Dave. "MADD says most drunken-driving deaths caused by first-time offenders." *PolitiFact Wisconsin* (in partnership with Journal Sentinel) February 24, 2014, https://www.politifact.com/wisconsin/statements/2014/feb/24/mothers-against-drunk-driving/madd-says-most-drunken-driving-deaths-caused-first/

(125) Freeman, Mike. "Kareem Hunt Video Shows NFL Still Has No Idea How to Address Its Biggest Problem." *Bleacher Report* November 30, 2018, https://bleacher-report.com/articles/2808663-kareem-hunt-video-shows-nfl-still-has-no-idea-how-to-address-its-biggest-problem

(126) Babb, Kent and Rich, Steven. "A Quietly Escalating Issue for NFL: Fan Violence and How to Contain It." *Washington Post* [Washington D.C.] October 28, 2016, https://www.chicagotribune.com/sports/football/ct-nfl-fan-violence-stadium-20161028-story.html

(127) Notte, Jason. "The NFL isn't admitting it has a drinking problem." *MarketWatch* September 23, 2015, https://www.marketwatch.com/story/the-nfl-isnt-admitting-it-has-a-drinking-problem-2015-09-23
  - "A fight in a Levi's Stadium bathroom last year resulted in the victim having a portion of his skull removed surgically and an assailant sentenced to five years in prison."
  - "There is absolutely no unified approach to stadium-alcohol policy outside of not allowing glass

bottles and not running the taps after the third quarter, which date back to former NFL Commissioner Paul Tagliabue's reign from 1989 to 2006."

- "The NFL doesn't have to ban beer or turn into a teetotaler to build a better, more functional alcohol policy. It just has to try before someone forces it to."

(128)   Deruy, Emily. "Santa Clara Mayor Sued For Allegedly Failing to Disclose Income." *The Mercury News* October 24, 2018, https://www.mercurynews.com/2018/10/24/santa-clara-mayor-sued-for-allegedly-failing-to-disclose-income/

(129)   Wolff, Michael. *Fire and Fury: Inside the Trump White House*. New York: Henry Holt & Company, page 3, 2018. Print.

(130)   Lee, Thomas. "Corporate lessons on ticking time bombs." *San Francisco Chronicle* April 30, 2014, https://www.pressreader.com/usa/san-francisco-chronicle-late-edition/20140430/281500749258175/textview

(131)   *Danielle Harmon v. City of Santa Clara, City of Santa Clara Police Chief Mike Sellers, et al.*, United Stated District Court (ND CA February 5, 2018) Case no. 5:16-cv-04228-EJD, Order Granting Plaintiff's Motion to Remove Confidentiality Designation and Granting In Part Defendant's Motions For Sanctions.

(132)   *Moneeb, Ikram and Ikram v City of Santa Clara, Mike Sellers, et al.*, United States District Court (ND CA 2015), Case no. 5:15-cv-01987-NC. The pdf of this lawsuit can also be found on my Author's website at: https://unsafeinanyseat.com/wp-content/uploads/2019/05/Complaint.First-Amended.FILED-Doc.-25.pdf

(133)   *Danielle Harmon v. City of Santa Clara, City of Santa Clara Police Chief Mike Sellers, et al.*, United Stated District Court (ND CA 2016) Case no. 5:16-cv-04228-EJD.

The pdf of this lawsuit can also be found on my Author's website at: https://unsafeinanyseat.com/wp-content/uploads/2019/03/160727-Danielle-Harmon-v-City-of-Santa-Clara-et-al-Complaint-for-Damages.pdf

Afterward

(134) Rakes, Amanda. "Zimmerman juror to write a book," Fox 59 News,
https://fox59.com/2013/07/15/zimmerman-juror-to-write-a-book/
- From Bill Kirkos (CNN) — "One of the six women who served on the jury that acquitted George Zimmerman will be writing a book about her experiences, literary agent Sharlene Martin said Monday."

(135) Silicon Valley Newsroom. "Santa Clara County DA: 'No Matter How Long It Takes, We Will Bend the Arc Toward Justice," *San Jose Inside* January 24, 2019, https://www.sanjoseinside.com/2019/01/24/santa-clara-county-da-no-matter-how-long-it-takes-we-will-bend-the-arc-toward-justice/

List of Individuals, Arranged by Organizational Affiliation

(136) National Football League Personal Conduct Policy 2018 (Appendix #1)
https://nflcommunications.com/Documents/2018%20Policies/2018%20Personal%20Conduct%20Policy.pdf

(137) Thompson, Tisha and Sciallo, Michael. "From Teen Mother to NFL Security Chief, Cathy Lanier's Rise Through the Law Enforcement Ranks." *ESPNW.com* October 26, 2017, http://www.espn.com/espnw/culture/

feature/article/20994956/from-teen-mother-nfl-security-chief-cathy-lanier-rise-law-enforcement-ranks

(138) Nguyen, Chris. "Dozens of Arrests During Oakland Raiders-SF 49ers 'Battle of the Bay' Game at Levi's Stadium." *ABC7News.com* November 2, 2018, https://abc7news.com/sports/dozens-of-arrests-during-battle-of-the-bay-at-levis-stadium/4602099/

- "To identify the person and apprehend them is just fantastic work, and it's the type of luck we have continuously have at the stadium, given the stadium's technology, and the security personnel," – Friday, November 2, 2018 *ABC News 7* interview with Chris Nguyen.

(139) Ting, Eric. "32 Rowdy Fans Arrested at 49ers-Raiders Game After Brawls Break Out." *SF Gate* November 2, 2018, https://www.sfgate.com/49ers/article/fans-Raiders-fight-brawl-Levis-Stadium-arrests-13358779.php

- "The description of the man was pretty vague, so to get proper information out and to identify one person among 62,000 was pretty impressive," Kazem said. Police arrested Steve Gonzalez Guardado in connection to the assault seen in the video.

- "The vast majority of the arrests on Thursday were for public intoxication, although there were three people arrested for assault. One of the assaults was caught on video and shared on social media, and police were able to quickly identify the suspect and make an arrest."

(140) Vo, Thy. "State Investigates Levi's Stadium Manager for Conflicts of Interest." *The Mercury News* May 17, 2019, https://www.mercurynews.com/2019/05/28/state-eth-ics-agency-investigating-levis-stadium-manager-for-con-flicts-of-interest/?utm_campaign=socialflow&utm_

content=fb-mercurynews&utm_source=facebook.
com&utm_medium=social&fbclid=IwAR2KhwwB-
v3zSex9XK2ad4M8x4h9prP_dkay5EoAsy6-trBM-
W3NAhk7ZrXPs

- The stadium's manager, Jim Mercurio, bought stock in two companies that do work for the stadium

(141) NBC Bay Area Staff. "Santa Clara Accuses Levi's Stadium Manager, 49ers of Contract Breach" *Bay City News* March 27, 2019,

https://www.nbcbayarea.com/news/local/
Santa-Clara-Accuses-Levis-Stadium-Manager-
49ers-of-Contract-Breach-507763641.html?_osource=So-
cialFlowFB_BAYBrand&fbclid=IwAR0bMVhGOyCee
PYYaaj8UJqJ0bdRJ9yjwdFAghAWu
Gon0lcePMatiHtaUZ0

- In an email to 49ers president Al Guido on Friday, City Manager Deanna Santana said stadium manager Jim Mercurio did not provide documentation showing proper bidding and minimum wage practices in securing the flooring contract.
- The scuffle comes after years of bad blood between the Santa Clara Stadium Authority and the 49ers over increased rent, a 10 p.m. curfew, and financial transparency.
- Used also in Epilogue

(142) *City of Santa Clara website. Government. Santa Clara Stadium Authority Board.* 2019.

http://santaclaraca.gov/government/stadium-authority/
stadium-authority-board

- "In addition to serving on the City Council, the Mayor and Council Members also serve as Board Members of the Santa Clara Stadium Authority which owns Levi's Stadium."

Appendix # 1
National Football League Personal Conduct Policy
- Author's note: I reference the 2014 version of this because this was the National Football League Personal Conduct Policy in place during the illegal activities of the City of Santa Clara Police Department. The NFL policy has since been updated 2018 and is available at: https://nflcommunications.com/Documents/2018%20Policies/2018%20Personal%20Conduct%20Policy.pdf

Appendix # 2
September 2, 2016 - SCPOA letter to Jed York

Appendix # 3
"November 28, 2018 City of Santa Clara response"

Appendix #4
Follow Up email from Billy Langenstein - NFL Director, Investigations & Security Services

Appendix #5
The Complaint: *Frederick Leo Weaver v. San Francisco 49ers Limited, et al.* Santa Clara County Superior Case no. 19CV346749, (2019)

Appendix #6
May 31, 2019 - Ericksen Arbuthnot - Responses to Weaver Complaint

Appendix #7
June 3, 2019 - Lombardi, Loper, & Conant, LLP- Responses to Weaver Complaint

APPENDIX # 1

National Football League Personal Conduct Policy

—m—

NATIONAL FOOTBALL LEAGUE

PERSONAL CONDUCT POLICY

It is a privilege to be part of the National Football League. **Everyone** who is part of the league must refrain from "conduct detrimental to the integrity of and public confidence in" the NFL. This includes owners, coaches, players, other team employees, game officials, and employees of the league office, NFL Films, NFL Network, or any other NFL business.

Conduct by anyone in the league that is illegal, violent, dangerous, or irresponsible puts innocent victims at risk, damages the reputation of others in the game, and undercuts public respect and support for the NFL. We must endeavor at all times to be people of high character; we must show respect for others inside and outside our workplace; and we must strive to conduct ourselves in ways that favorably reflect on ourselves, our teams, the communities we represent, and the NFL.

To this end, the league has increased education regarding respect and appropriate behavior, has provided resources for all employees to assist them in conforming their behavior to the standards expected of them, and has made clear that the league's goal is to prevent violations of the Personal Conduct Policy. In order to uphold our high standards, when violations of this Personal Conduct Policy do occur, appropriate disciplinary action must follow.

This Personal Conduct Policy is issued pursuant to the Commissioner's authority under the Constitution and Bylaws to address and sanction conduct detrimental to the league and professional football.

This policy applies to the Commissioner; all owners; all employees of the NFL, NFL clubs, and all NFL-related entities, including players under contract, coaches, game officials; all rookie players selected in the NFL college draft and all undrafted rookie players, unsigned veterans who were under contract in the prior League Year; and other prospective employees once they commence negotiations with a club concerning employment. Clubs and league staff are strongly encouraged to communicate this policy to independent contractors and consultants and to make clear that violations of this policy will be grounds for terminating a business relationship.

December 2014

Expectations and Standards of Conduct

It is not enough simply to avoid being found guilty of a crime. We are all held to a higher standard and must conduct ourselves in a way that is responsible, promotes the values of the NFL, and is lawful.

If you are convicted of a crime or subject to a disposition of a criminal proceeding (as defined in this Policy), you are subject to discipline. But even if your conduct does not result in a criminal conviction, if the league finds that you have engaged in any of the following conduct, you will be subject to discipline. Prohibited conduct includes but is not limited to the following:

- Actual or threatened physical violence against another person, including dating violence, domestic violence, child abuse, and other forms of family violence;
- Assault and/or battery, including sexual assault or other sex offenses;
- Violent or threatening behavior toward another employee or a third party in any workplace setting;
- Stalking, harassment, or similar forms of intimidation;
- Illegal possession of a gun or other weapon (such as explosives, toxic substances, and the like), or possession of a gun or other weapon in any workplace setting;
- Illegal possession, use, or distribution of alcohol or drugs;
- Possession, use, or distribution of steroids or other performance enhancing substances;
- Crimes involving cruelty to animals as defined by state or federal law;
- Crimes of dishonesty such as blackmail, extortion, fraud, money laundering, or racketeering;
- Theft-related crimes such as burglary, robbery, or larceny;
- Disorderly conduct;
- Crimes against law enforcement, such as obstruction, resisting arrest, or harming a police officer or other law enforcement officer;
- Conduct that poses a genuine danger to the safety and well-being of another person; and
- Conduct that undermines or puts at risk the integrity of the NFL, NFL clubs, or NFL personnel.

2

What Happens When a Violation of This Policy is Suspected?

Evaluation, Counseling, and Services – Anyone arrested or charged with violent or threatening conduct that would violate this policy will be offered a formal clinical evaluation, the cost of which will be paid by the league, and appropriate follow-up education, counseling, or treatment programs. In cases reviewed for possible disciplinary action, the employee's decision to make beneficial use of these clinical services will be considered a positive factor in determining eventual discipline if a violation is found. These evaluations will be available at designated facilities around the country on a confidential basis. The employee may select the particular provider at the designated facility.

In appropriate cases (for example, cases involving domestic violence or child abuse), the league will make available assistance to victims and families, as well as the employee. This assistance may include providing or direction to appropriate counseling, social and other services, clergy, medical professionals, and specialists in dealing with children and youth. These resources will be provided through specialized Critical Response Teams affiliated with the league office and with member clubs. These teams will develop standard protocols based on experts' recommendations of appropriate and constructive responses to reported incidents of violence, particularly incidents of domestic violence, child abuse, or sexual assault. These response teams will assist victims and families in matters of personal security and other needs following a reported incident. In addition, information about local non-league resources to help victims and family members will be provided to affected parties.

Investigations – Whenever the league office becomes aware of a possible violation of the Personal Conduct Policy, it will undertake an investigation, the timing and scope of which will be based upon the particular circumstances of the matter. Any such investigation may be conducted by NFL Security, independent parties, or by a combination of the two. In cases that are also being investigated by law enforcement, the league will work to cooperate with and to avoid any conflict or interference with the law enforcement proceedings.

In conducting investigations, the league office will make reasonable efforts to safeguard requests for confidentiality from witnesses and others with information. In addition, the league will not tolerate any retaliation against anyone who in good faith reports a possible violation or provides truthful information during an investigation. Any person who directly or indirectly through others interferes in any manner with an investigation, including by retaliating or threatening to retaliate against a victim or witness, will face separate disciplinary action under this policy. Prohibited retaliation includes, but is not

3

254

limited to: threats, intimidation, harassment, any other adverse action threatened, expressly or impliedly, or taken against anyone who reports a violation or suspected violation of this Policy or who participates in an investigation of a complaint.

In investigating a potential violation, the league may rely on information obtained by law enforcement agencies, court records, or independent investigations conducted at the direction of the NFL. League and team employees are required to cooperate in any such investigation and are obligated to be fully responsive and truthful in responding to requests from investigators for information (testimony, documents, physical evidence, or other information) that may bear on whether the Policy has been violated. A failure to cooperate with an investigation or to be truthful in responding to inquiries will be separate grounds for disciplinary action. Players who are interviewed in the course of an investigation may be accompanied by an NFLPA representative as provided by Article 51, Section 11 of the CBA.

Because the Fifth Amendment's protection against self-incrimination does not apply in a workplace investigation, the league will reserve the right to compel an employee to cooperate in its investigations even when the employee is the target of a pending law enforcement investigation or proceeding. An employee's refusal to speak to a league investigator under such circumstances will not preclude an investigation from proceeding or discipline from being imposed.

Leave with Pay – You may be placed on paid administrative leave or on the Commissioner Exempt List under either of the following circumstances:

First, if you are formally charged with a crime of violence, meaning that you are accused of having used physical force or a weapon to injure or threaten another person, of having engaged in a sexual assault by force or a sexual assault of a person who was incapable of giving consent, of having engaged in other conduct that poses a genuine danger to the safety or well-being of another person, or of having engaged in animal abuse. The formal charges may be in the form of an indictment by a grand jury, the filing of charges by a prosecutor, or an arraignment in a criminal court.

Second, if an investigation leads the Commissioner to believe that you may have violated this Policy by committing any of the conduct identified above, he may act where the circumstances and evidence warrant doing so. This decision will not reflect a finding of guilt or innocence and will not be guided by the same legal standards and considerations that would apply in a criminal trial.

In cases in which a violation relating to a crime of violence is suspected but further investigation is required, the Commissioner may determine to place a player or other employee on leave with pay on a limited and temporary basis to permit the league to conduct an investigation. Based on the results of this investigation, the player or employee may be returned to duty, be placed on leave with pay for a longer period, or be subject to discipline.

A player who is placed on the Commissioner Exempt List may not practice or attend games, but with the club's permission he may be present at the club's facility on a reasonable basis for meetings, individual workouts, therapy and rehabilitation, and other permitted non-football activities. Non-player employees placed on paid administrative leave may be present only on such basis as is approved by the Commissioner or the league disciplinary officer and only under circumstances in which they are not performing their regular duties.

Leave with pay will generally last until the league makes a disciplinary decision and any appeal from that discipline is fully resolved.

Discipline – You have violated this policy if you have a disposition of a criminal proceeding (as defined), or if the evidence gathered by the league's investigation demonstrates that you engaged in conduct prohibited by the Personal Conduct Policy. In cases where you are not charged with a crime, or are charged but not convicted, you may still be found to have violated the Policy if the credible evidence establishes that you engaged in conduct prohibited by this Personal Conduct Policy.

Initial decisions regarding discipline will be made or recommended by a disciplinary officer, a member of the league office staff who will be a highly-qualified individual with a criminal justice background. The disciplinary officer will follow the process outlined below and will make the initial decision on discipline pursuant to a delegation of the Commissioner's authority, subject to any appeal. In cases involving league staff, decisions may also be made by senior Human Resources executives consistent with the terms of this Policy.

To assist in evaluating a potential violation, expert and independent advisors may be consulted by the disciplinary officer, the Commissioner, and others as needed. Such advisors may include former players and others with appropriate backgrounds and experience in law enforcement, academia, judicial and public service, mental health, and persons with other specialized subject matter expertise.

Employees who are subject to discipline will be given notice of the potential violation for which discipline may be imposed. The employee will be furnished with the records and other reports that the

5

disciplinary officer has relied on in addressing the matter, including records from law enforcement and a copy of any investigatory report and any documents relied upon by a league investigator in generating the report. The employee will be permitted to submit information in writing to rebut or otherwise respond to the report. In addition, the employee will have the opportunity to meet with the investigator and disciplinary officer in advance of discipline being imposed. In cases where there has been a criminal disposition, the underlying disposition may not be challenged in a disciplinary hearing and the court's judgment and factual findings shall be conclusive and binding, and only the level of discipline will be at issue. Once the record is complete, the disciplinary officer will issue a written decision setting forth the reasons for as well as the amount and nature of the discipline to be imposed.

Depending on the nature of the violation and the record of the employee, discipline may be a fine, a suspension for a fixed or an indefinite period of time, a requirement of community service, a combination of the three, or banishment from the league. Discipline may also include requirements to seek ongoing counseling, treatment, or therapy where appropriate as well as the imposition of enhanced supervision. It may also include a probationary period and conditions that must be met for reinstatement and to remain eligible to participate in the league. Repeat offenders will be subject to enhanced and/or expedited discipline, including banishment from the league. In determining discipline, both aggravating and mitigating factors will be considered.

Ownership and club or league management have traditionally been held to a higher standard and will be subject to more significant discipline when violations of the Personal Conduct Policy occur.

With regard to violations of the Personal Conduct Policy that involve assault, battery, domestic violence, dating violence, child abuse and other forms of family violence, or sexual assault involving physical force or committed against someone incapable of giving consent, a first offense will subject the offender to a baseline suspension without pay of six games, with consideration given to any aggravating or mitigating factors. The presence of possible aggravating factors may warrant a longer suspension. Possible aggravating factors include, but are not limited to, a prior violation of the Personal Conduct Policy, similar misconduct before joining the NFL, violence involving a weapon, choking, repeated striking, or when an act is committed against a particularly vulnerable person, such as a child, a pregnant woman, or an elderly person, or where the act is committed in the presence of a child. A second offense will result in permanent banishment from the NFL. An individual who has been banished may petition for reinstatement after one year, but there is no presumption or assurance that the petition will be granted.

6

257

Appeals of any disciplinary decision will be processed pursuant to Article 46 of the Collective Bargaining Agreement for players or pursuant to the applicable league procedures for non-players. The Commissioner may name a panel that consists of independent experts to recommend a decision on the appeal.

Reporting – Clubs are obligated to promptly report any matter that comes to their attention (through, for example, victim or witness reports, law enforcement, media reports) that may constitute a violation of this Policy. Clubs are expected to educate their employees on this obligation to report. League employees who are aware of an incident that may violate this Personal Conduct Policy have a similar obligation to report the matter. Reports should be made to any of Robert Gulliver or Tara Wood of Human Resources, Jeffrey Miller of NFL Security or Adolpho Birch of the Management Council legal staff. Questions about whether an incident triggers a reporting obligation should be directed to a member of the Management Council legal staff.

Failure to report an incident will be grounds for disciplinary action. This obligation to report is broader than simply reporting an arrest; it requires reporting to the league any incident that comes to the club's attention which, if the allegations were true, would constitute a violation of the Personal Conduct Policy.

It is important to remember that the obligation to report is a continuing one, and is not satisfied simply by making an initial report of an incident. The obligation includes reporting on a timely basis all information of which a club becomes aware. If a club learns additional information, including but not limited to information regarding the nature of an incident, the identity of witnesses, statements regarding the incident (including by the accused), or the existence of evidentiary material (such as documents, electronic communications such as emails or text messages, medical reports, photographs, audio or video recordings, or social media activity), it must promptly report that information to the league office.

Anyone who believes that he or she is a victim of conduct that violates the Personal Conduct Policy or who learns of or witnesses such conduct is strongly encouraged to report the matter to the club or the league office. Reports will be addressed promptly and confidentially, and the Critical Response Team will be available to address issues regarding victim and family security and other support services. Any employee with questions regarding either this reporting obligation or any other aspect of this Personal Conduct Policy may contact either the Security or Human Resources department, or the NFL Management Council.

7

December 2014

258

Conduct Committee – To ensure that this policy remains current and consistent with best practices and evolving legal and social standards, the Commissioner has named a Conduct Committee. This committee will be made up of NFL owners, who will review this policy at least annually and recommend any appropriate changes in the policy, including investigatory practices, disciplinary levels or procedures, or service components. The committee will receive regular reports from the disciplinary officer, and may seek advice from current and former players, as well as a broad and diverse group of outside experts regarding best practices in academic, business, and public sector settings, and will review developments in similar workplace policies in other settings.

Definitions –

"Disposition of a Criminal Proceeding" – Includes an adjudication of guilt or admission to a criminal violation; a plea to a lesser included offense; a plea of nolo contendere or no contest; or the disposition of the proceeding through a diversionary program, deferred adjudication, disposition of supervision, conditional dismissal, or similar arrangements.

"Probationary Period" – Persons found to have violated this policy may be placed on a period of probation as determined by the Commissioner. During such period, restrictions on certain activities, limitations on participation in Club activities, or other conditions may be imposed. Failure to comply with such conditions may result in additional discipline including an extension of the period of suspension.

"Repeat Offenders" – Persons who have had previous violations of law or of this policy may be considered repeat offenders. When appropriate, conduct occurring prior to the person's association with the NFL will be considered.

"Workplace Setting" – the workplace setting means any location or conveyance used in connection with NFL activities, including the club facility, training camp, stadium, locker room, location at which a club-sponsored event takes place, and while traveling on team or NFL-related business.

APPENDIX # 2

September 2, 2016 - SCPOA
letter to Jed York

—⁓—

Santa Clara Police Officer's Association
P.O. Box 223
Santa Clara, CA 95052
Phone: (408) 243-COPS
"Courage – Honor – Commitment"

Mr. Jed York   September 2, 2016
San Francisco 49ers
4949 Marie P. DeBartolo Way
Santa Clara, CA 95054

Mr. York,

The members of the Santa Clara Police Officers' Association (SCPOA) have a long history of working with the San Francisco 49ers organization. This relationship was greatly expanded with the construction of Levi's stadium. Our officers and 49er employees have worked incredibly well together to create a safe and enjoyable environment for guests and employees. This partnership has made Levi's stadium the premier sports venue in the world as evident in the extremely successful Super Bowl 50 operation.

Unfortunately, some recent actions by a 49ers employee have threatened our harmonious working relationship. On August 26, 2016, prior to the start of the 49er pre-season football game at Levi's stadium, on duty 49er employee Colin Kaepernick made the decision to exercise his right of free expression and not stand to honor the National Anthem. This expression caught the attention of the media. Following the game, your employee explained to the media that his actions were an attempt to get public attention to the oppression of African Americans and minorities in the United States by police officers. Your employee then insinuated that police officers are being placed on paid leave for murdering minorities. This statement is obviously insulting, inaccurate and completely unsupported by any facts.

On August 28, 2016, at 49er training facility in Santa Clara, Mr. Kaepernick again made the allegation that police officers are getting paid to murder people. Your employee further insulted all law enforcement officers in America by stating, "There is police brutality. People of color have been targeted by police." Mr. Kaepernick then made inaccurate and untrue statements about the level of training that is required to be a police officer.

On August 31, 2016, it was learned by the members of the SCPOA that the 49er organization has been allowing Mr. Kaepernick to wear exposed socks with the image of a pig wearing a police hat during practices at the training camp in Santa Clara. Photos of Mr. Kaepernick wearing these socks with the derogatory image have been broadcast nationally.

Our membership acknowledges that police officers are human and are not perfect. However, blanket statements that police officers in general, murder minorities is completely false and insulting to the dedicated men and women in law enforcement agencies across America.

These intentional acts and inflammatory statements by Mr. Kaepernick are insulting to the members of the SCPOA. It is apparent, that the 49ers organization is aware of Mr. Kaepernick's actions. These actions have occurred while Mr. Kaepernick was acting as an employee of the 49ers and at 49er facilities in Santa Clara. The 49ers organization has taken no action to stop or prevent Mr. Kaepernick from continuing to make inaccurate, incorrect and inflammatory statements against police officers, which include members of the Santa Clara Police Officers

Association. Furthermore, your organization has made no statement disagreeing with Mr. Kaepernick's accusations. It is the unanimous opinion of the SCPOA that the 49ers organization has failed to address your employee's inappropriate workplace behavior. The board of directors of the Santa Clara Police Officers Association has a duty to protect its members and work to make all of their working environments free of harassing behavior. SCPOA members have worked thousands of hours at Levi's stadium, 49er training camp and headquarters protecting guests, players and fellow employees. Our officers voluntarily agree to work these assignments. If the 49ers organization fails to take action to stop this type of inappropriate workplace behavior, it could result in police officers choosing not to work at your facilities. Please contact us as soon as possible with the corrective actions your organization intends on implementing.

The men and women of the Santa Clara Police Officers Association are sworn to protect the rights of ALL people in the United States, a duty we take very seriously. Our members, however, have the right to do their job in an environment free of unjustified and insulting attacks from employees of your organization.

SCPOA Board of Directors

Cc: Rajeev Batra
    Chief Mike Sellers

APPENDIX # 3

"November 28, 2018 City of Santa Clara Response

—ɯ—

**City of
Santa Clara**
The Center of What's Possible

Mayor

Lisa M. Gillmor

Council Members

Debi Davis
Patrick Kolstad
Patricia M. Mahan
Teresa O'Neill
Kathy Watanabe

November 28, 2018

Fred Weaver
650 Castro Street, Suite 120-211
Mountain View, CA 94041

Dear Mr. Weaver:

Your letter regarding the Raiders at 49ers Night Game on November 1, 2018 was received on November 27, 2018. Your letter will be distributed to the Mayor and Councilmembers, as well as the City Manager's Office, for their review.

Sincerely,

Jose Armas
Office Records Specialist
Mayor and Council Offices

City of Santa Clara
The Center of What's Possible

Mayor and Council Offices
1500 Warburton Avenue
Santa Clara, CA 95050

US POSTAGE PITNEY BOWES

28P 95050 $ 000.47⁰
02 4W
0000326799 NOV 28 2018

Fred Weaver
650 Castro Street, Suite 120-211
Mountain View, CA 94041

94041$2093 C079

APPENDIX # 4

Follow Up email from Billy Langenstein - NFL Director, Investigations & Security

—ᘑ—

Subject:	Follow Up
Date:	Tuesday, January 8, 2019 at 4:39:37 PM Pacific Standard Time
From:	Langenstein, Billy
To:	Fred Weaver
Attachments:	image001.jpg

Good Afternoon Fred-

Thank you for your time on the phone today and I appreciated the conversation. If you would like, I would be interested in you sending me the photos, I believe you said over 600 that you have taken.

We work with our stadiums and clubs to carry out our standards to deliver a world class, safe and secure environment for our fans. Again, I appreciate you taking the time to speak with me and I will follow up with the 49ers on the active investigation that you referenced.

Thank you and have a great night,

Billy

Billy Langenstein, CSSP
Director, Investigations & Security Services
National Football League
345 Park Avenue, 6th Floor
New York, NY 10154

APPENDIX # 5

The Complaint - *Weaver v. San Francisco 49ers, et al.*

FREDERICK LEO WEAVER
650 Castro Street, Suite 120-211
Mountain View, CA 94041
Telephone:
Facsimile:
Fred@UnsafeInAnySeat.com

(ENDORSED)

FILED

MAY 1 2019

Clerk of the Court
Superior Court of CA County of Santa Clara
BY_____Y. Lai_____DEPUTY

SUPERIOR COURT OF THE STATE OF CALIFORNIA

COUNTY OF SANTA CLARA

FREDERICK LEO WEAVER,	Case No.: **1 9 C V 3 4 6 7 4 9**
Plaintiff,	
vs.	**PLAINTIFF'S COMPLAINT FOR DAMAGES**
SAN FRANCISCO FORTY NINERS, LIMITED; SAN FRANCISCO FORTY NINERS II, LLC; FORTY NINERS FOOTBALL COMPANY, LLC; SAN FRANCISCO FORTY NINERS FOUNDATION; FORTY NINERS STADIUM, LLC; FORTY NINERS STADIUM MANAGEMENT COMPANY, LLC; FORTY NINERS HOLDINGS LP; FORTY NINERS HOLDINGS LLC; FORTY NINERS SC STADIUM COMPANY, LLC; CITY OF SANTA CLARA; SANTA CLARA STADIUM AUTHORITY; CITY OF SANTA CLARA CITY MANAGER DEANNA SANTANA; CITY OF SANTA CLARA POLICE DEPARTMENT; CITY OF SANTA CLARA POLICE CHIEF MICHAEL SELLERS; NATIONAL FOOTBALL LEAGUE; NATIONAL FOOTBALL LEAGUE COMMISSIONER ROGER GOODELL; NATIONAL FOOTBALL LEAGUE SENIOR VICE PRESIDENT OF SECURITY CATHY LANIER; NATIONAL FOOTBALL LEAGUE DIRECTOR INVESTIGATIONS & SECURITY SERVICES BILLY	**COUNTS:** **1. NEGLIGENCE;** **2. PREMISES LIABILITY – FAILURE TO PROVIDE SAFE PREMISE – DANGEROUS CONDITION OF PUBLIC PROPERTY;** **3. NEGLIGENT STADIUM SECURITY – NEGLIGENT HIRING, RETENTION, AND SUPERVISION;** **4. GROSS NEGLECT OF DUTY – GROSS MISCONDUCT;** **5. DISCRIMINATION;** **6. CONSPIRACY** **DEMAND FOR JURY TRIAL** **UNLIMITED CIVIL CASE**

Fred Weaver – Plaintiff in Pro Per – www.UnsafeInAnySeat.com

1

PLAINTIFF'S COMPLAINT FOR DAMAGES

272

1	LANGENSTEIN; LANDMARK EVENT
2	STAFFING SERVICES, INC; and DOES 1 through 100,
3	INCLUSIVE,
4	Defendants.

5

6   Plaintiff FREDERICK LEO WEAVER, (hereinafter referred to as "PLAINTIFF", "FRED

7 WEAVER" or "WEAVER") complains and alleges as follows:

8   **THE PARTIES**

9 **The PLAINTIFF**

10   Plaintiff FREDERICK LEO WEAVER is and was at all times relevant herein an individual

11 and a citizen of California who resides in Santa Clara County, California.

12

13 **The DEFENDANTS**

14   1.   Plaintiff is informed and believes and thereon alleges that FORTY NINERS,

    LIMITED, is a Delaware limited liability company with offices located in Santa Clara County,

15 California;

16   2.   Plaintiff is informed and believes and thereon alleges that SAN FRANCISCO

17 FORTY NINERS II, LLC, is a Delaware limited liability company with offices located in Santa

18 Clara County, California;

19   3.   Plaintiff is informed and believes and thereon alleges that FORTY NINERS

20 FOOTBALL COMPANY, LLC, is a Delaware limited liability company with offices located in

21 Santa Clara County, California;

22   4.   Plaintiff is informed and believes and thereon alleges that FORTY NINERS

    HOLDINGS LP, is a Delaware limited liability company with offices located in Santa Clara

23 County, California;

24   5.   Plaintiff is informed and believes and thereon alleges that FORTY NINERS

25 HOLDINGS LLC, is a Delaware limited liability company with offices located in Santa Clara

26 County, California;

27

28

2

PLAINTIFF'S COMPLAINT FOR DAMAGES

Fred Weaver – Plaintiff in Pro Per – www.UnsafeInAnySeat.com

1   6.   Plaintiff is informed and believes and thereon alleges that SAN FRANCISCO

2 FORTY NINERS FOUNDATION, is a Delaware limited liability company with offices located

3 in Santa Clara County, California;

4   7.   Plaintiff is informed and believes and thereon alleges that FORTY NINERS

5 STADIUM MANAGEMENT COMPANY, LLC, is a Delaware limited liability company with

6 offices located in Santa Clara County, California;

7   8.   Plaintiff is informed and believes and thereon alleges that FORTY NINERS SC

8 STADIUM COMPANY, LLC, is a Delaware limited liability company with offices located in

Santa Clara County, California;

9   9.   The entities referenced in paragraphs 1-8 are herein collectively referred to as the

10 "**FORTY NINER DEFENDANTS**". Plaintiff is informed and believes and thereon alleges that

11 the FORTY NINERS DEFENDANTS and DOES 1 through 20, inclusive, were doing business

12 in the County of Santa Clara, which included owning, operating, controlling and managing a

13 professional football team within the National Football League known as the "San Francisco

14 49ers" that now, and at all times herein mentioned did play its home games at Levi's Stadium,

15 located at 4900 Marie P. DeBartolo Way, Santa Clara, California.

16   10.   Plaintiff is informed and believes and thereon alleges that, at all times herein

mentioned, and prior thereto, Defendants **CITY OF SANTA CLARA, SANTA CLARA**

17 **STADIUM AUTHORITY** and DOES 21 through 40, inclusive were public entities, that

18 Defendant CITY OF SANTA CLARA is a public entity established under the laws and

19 Constitution of the State of California, and that it owns, operates, manages, directs, and controls

20 the **SANTA CLARA POLICE DEPARTMENT** which employs other DOE Defendants in this

21 action. Plaintiff is informed and believes and thereon alleges that the elected members of the

22 Santa Clara City Council serve as the governing board for the **SANTA CLARA STADIUM**

23 **AUTHORITY**.

24   11.   Plaintiff is informed and believes and thereon alleges that Defendant **DEANNA**

SANTANA (hereinafter referred to as either "DEANNA SANTANA", or "SANTANA") is, and

25 at all times herein mentioned was, a resident of Santa Clara County, California and the City

26 Manager of the CITY OF SANTA CLARA, and that, in her capacity as City Manager, she serves

27 as Executive Director of the SANTA CLARA STADIUM AUTHORITY.

28

3

PLAINTIFF'S COMPLAINT FOR DAMAGES

12. Plaintiff is informed and believes and thereon alleges that Defendant **BRIAN DOYLE** is, and at all times herein mentioned was, a resident of Santa Clara County, California and the City Attorney of the CITY OF SANTA CLARA, and that, in his capacity as City Attorney, he serves as General Counsel of the SANTA CLARA STADIUM AUTHORITY.

13. Plaintiff is informed and believes and thereon alleges that Defendant **CITY OF SANTA CLARA POLICE DEPARTMENT** (hereinafter referred to as either "SANTA CLARA POLICE DEPARTMENT", or "SCPD") is, and at all times herein mentioned was a separate public entity or a department of the City of Santa Clara.

14. Plaintiff is informed and believes and thereon alleges that Defendant **MICHAEL SELLERS** (hereinafter "SELLERS") is, and at all times herein mentioned was, a resident of Santa Clara County, California and the Chief of Police of the Santa Clara Police Department and was acting within the course and scope of that employment. Plaintiff is informed and believes and thereon alleges that, in that capacity, Defendant SELLERS is and was a policy making officer for the CITY OF SANTA CLARA POLICE DEPARTMENT. Plaintiff is informed and believes and thereon alleges that DOES 41 through 60, inclusive, were and are employees of the SANTA CLARA POLICE DEPARTMENT, CITY OF SANTA CLARA, and at the time of these events were acting as agents of Defendant CITY OF SANTA CLARA, SANTA CLARA STADIUM AUTHORITY, FORTY NINER DEFENDANTS, and the NATIONAL FOOTBALL LEAGUE, acting within the course and scope of that relationship.

15. Plaintiff is informed and believes and thereon alleges that Defendants **NATIONAL FOOTBALL LEAGUE**, (hereinafter referred to as either "NATIONAL FOOTBALL LEAGUE", or "NFL", is, and at all times herein mentioned was, an unincorporated association consisting of separately owned and independently-operated professional football teams which operate out of many different cities and states within this country, including the State of California (and, more specifically, Levi's Stadium in Santa Clara), with its headquarters located in New York. The NFL is engaged in interstate commerce in the business of, among other things, promoting, operating, organizing, and regulating the major professional football league in the United States. The United States Supreme Court held in American Needle, Inc. v NFL, 130 S. Ct. 14 2201, 2212-13, (2010) that each team that is a member of the NFL is a legally distinct and separate entity from both the other teams and the NFL itself.

4

Fred Weaver – Plaintiff in Pro Per – www.UnsafeInAnySeat.com

16.   Plaintiff is informed and believes and thereon alleges that Defendant **ROGER GOODELL,** an individual whose residence in unknown, is and, at all material times was NFL Football Commissioner and was acting within the course and scope of that employment.

17.   Plaintiff is informed and believes and thereon alleges that Defendant **CATHY LANIER,** an individual whose residence is unknown, is and, at all material times was NFL Senior Vice President of Security and was acting within the course and scope of that employment.

18.   Plaintiff is informed and believes and thereon alleges that Defendant **BILLY LANGENSTEIN,** an individual whose residence is unknown, is and, at all material times was Director, Investigations & Security Services – National Football League and was acting within the course and scope of that employment.

19.   Plaintiff is informed and believes and thereon alleges that DOES 61-70 are individuals or business entities that are part of NATIONAL FOOTBALL LEAGUE.

20.   Plaintiff is informed and believes and thereon alleges that Defendants **LANDMARK EVENT STAFFING SERVICES, INC.,** (hereinafter referred to as either "LANDMARK EVENT STAFFING SERVICES, INC", "LANDMARK DEFENDANTS" or "LANDMARK"), is a Delaware corporation doing business in Santa Clara County, California, and that it and DOES 71 through 80, inclusive, are and were, at all times herein mentioned, doing business in the State of California, which included providing security services to Levi's Stadium, located in the City and County of Santa Clara, before, during and after NFL games.

21.   In accordance with California Government Code sections 900 eq. seq., on December 17, 2018, Plaintiff filed government claims against Defendants CITY OF SANTA CLARA, SANTA CLARA STADIUM AUTHORITY, and CITY OF SANTA CLARA POLICE DEPARTMENT. On March 1, 2019, Plaintiffs' claims were rejected.

22.   Plaintiff is informed and believes, and thereon alleges, that at all times herein mentioned, and prior thereto, the FORTY NINER DEFENDANTS, CITY OF SANTA CLARA, SANTA CLARA STADIUM AUTHORITY, CITY OF SANTA CLARA POLICE DEPARTMENT, NATIONAL FOOTBALL LEAGUE, LANDMARK EVENT STAFFING SERVICES, INC., and DOES 1 through 100, inclusive, owned, leased, operated, managed, controlled, maintained, inspected and/or surveilled the San Francisco 49ers' home stadium,

5

PLAINTIFF'S COMPLAINT FOR DAMAGES

known as "Levi's Stadium," located in Santa Clara, California, and/or provided security services to said stadium on National Football League ("NFL") game days. In that capacity, at all times herein mentioned, and prior thereto, the FORTY NINER DEFENDANTS, CITY OF SANTA CLARA, SANTA CLARA STADIUM AUTHORITY, CITY OF SANTA CLARA POLICE DEPARTMENT, NATIONAL FOOTBALL LEAGUE, LANDMARK EVENT STAFFING SERVICES, INC., and/or DOES 1 through 100, inclusive, were responsible for selecting, hiring, supervising, evaluating, and retaining security personnel for Levi's Stadium on NFL game days.

23. Defendants DOES 1 through 100, inclusive, are sued herein by fictitious names because Plaintiff is ignorant of the true names or capacities of these defendants but will insert the same herein when ascertained. Plaintiff is informed and believes and thereon alleges that each of the defendants designated herein as a DOE legally and proximately caused injury and damage to Plaintiff and the general public as herein alleged and is therefore responsible to Plaintiff for the damages and attorney's fees herein requested.

24. Plaintiff is informed, believes, and thereon alleges, that, at all times herein mentioned, each Defendant was acting as an agent, servant, employee, special employee, alter ego, successor in interest, partner, joint venturer, lessee, and licensee of each of the other defendants, and was acting within the course and scope of said relationship. In addition, Plaintiff is informed, believes and thereon alleges, that each Defendant has ratified and approved the acts of each of the other Defendants.

25. Plaintiff is informed and believes and thereon alleges that each of the Defendants sued herein was negligently, wrongfully, and otherwise responsible in some manner for the events and happenings as hereinafter described, and proximately caused injuries and damages to Plaintiff and the general public.

JURISDICTION AND VENUE

26. This Court has jurisdiction over this matter because all DEFENDANTS conduct business in, and have substantial contacts, within the State of California.

27. Venue is proper in the County of Santa Clara because Defendants SAN FRANCISCO FORTY NINERS, LIMITED; SAN FRANCISCO FORTY NINERS II, LLC; FORTY NINERS FOOTBALL COMPANY, LLC; SAN FRANCISCO FORTY NINERS FOUNDATION; FORTY NINERS STADIUM, LLC; FORTY NINERS STADIUM

6

Fred Weaver – Plaintiff in Pro Per – www.UnsafeInAnySeat.com

MANAGEMENT COMPANY, LLC; FORTY NINERS HOLDINGS, LP; FORTY NINERS HOLDINGS LLC; FORTY NINERS SC STADIUM COMPANY, LLC, CITY OF SANTA CLARA, SANTA CLARA STADIUM AUTHORITY, and CITY OF SANTA CLARA POLICE DEPARTMENT are headquartered in Santa Clara County, State of California, and the acts and omissions alleged herein occurred in Santa Clara County, California.

SUMMARY OF ALLEGATIONS

28. The rivalry between the San Francisco 49ers and the Oakland Raiders has existed for years with both teams based in the San Francisco Bay Area. The rivalry known as the "Battle of the Bay" intensified since both teams met during a preseason game in August 20, 2011.

29. In previous litigation, after the infamous August 20, 2011 49ers-Raiders game, according to two lawsuits filed in San Francisco Superior Court, the San Francisco 49ers failed to "proactively create an environment that was free from fighting...and gang activity." Statements were taken from San Francisco 49er Hall of Fame quarterback Joe Montana mentioning the team advising 49ers players to keep their families at home during Raiders games because of safety concerns. "Tell your families to sit this one out and watch it on TV," Montana recalled Coach Bill Walsh saying in an interview, "It just wasn't that safe to be around."

30. Beginning with the 2014 season, the DEFENDANTS sold alcohol for all San Francisco 49ers games at Levi's Stadium. Plaintiff is informed and believes and thereon alleges that the FORTY NINER DEFENDANTS, Defendant CITY OF SANTA CLARA, Defendant SANTA CLARA STADIUM AUTHORITY, and the NATIONAL FOOTBALL LEAGUE created an alcohol-induced atmosphere of violence at Levi's Stadium, based on the on and off field violence of the San Francisco 49ers and other NFL football players and the enabling of excessive alcohol consumption by the fans. The FORTY NINER DEFENDANTS, Defendant CITY OF SANTA CLARA, Defendant SANTA CLARA STADIUM AUTHORITY, and the NATIONAL FOOTBALL LEAGUE enabled excessive alcohol consumption despite knowledge of criminal activity at Levi's Stadium and knowledge of the criminal elements who congregate at Levi's Stadium.

31. Under the special relationship doctrine, the DEFENDANTS, and each of them, by serving intoxicating drinks to patrons for consumption on its premises, must exercise reasonable

7

PLAINTIFF'S COMPLAINT FOR DAMAGES

care to protect patrons from injury at the hands of fellow guests. "Businesses, such as shopping centers, restaurants and bars, and stadiums serving alcohol have an affirmative duty to take reasonable steps to secure their premises, as well as adjacent common areas within their control, against reasonably foreseeable criminal acts of third parties" [Delgado v. Trax Bar & Grill (2005) 36 Cal.4th 224; Morris IV v. De La Torre (2005) California Supreme Court No. S119750; Ann M. v. Pacific Plaza Shopping Ctr. (1993) 6 Cal.4th 666].

32.   The DEFENDANTS and each of them had notice that the serving of alcohol at a sporting event could incite violent, criminal behavior.

33.   The 49ers-Raiders game on November 1, 2018 was a nationally televised, high profile game for many reasons; it was a Thursday Night Football game for the San Francisco 49ers, and the game being played would be the last "Battle of the Bay" game played against rivals Oakland Raiders, who recently decided to move their team to Las Vegas, NV.

34.   San Francisco 49ers and the Oakland Raiders games are notoriously sold out events with the stands filled to capacity. Levi's Stadium has capacity for 68,500 spectators. According to Pro Football Reference, there were 69,592 in total attendance on November 1, 2018. Levi's Stadium has the 16th largest of 31 total NFL stadiums seating capacity in the National Football League.

35.   In the weeks prior to San Francisco 49ers and the Oakland Raiders November 1, 2018 game, there were published print and news media reports by FORTY NINER DEFENDANTS, and DEFENDANT CITY OF SANTA CLARA POLICE DEPARTMENT of stepped up security during the game at Levi's Stadium.

36.   On typical game days, according to an October 26, 2017 ESPN video interview with Defendant NFL Chief of Security CATHY LANIER, "Local police are the lead agency for every game throughout the season. A typical game requires at least 10 different agencies, from the FBI to private security."

37.   Defendant SANTA CLARA POLICE DEPARTMENT has stated recently in news media accounts, for a typical NFL game at Levi's Stadium, eighty officers are assigned to work at the stadium.

38.   Defendant SANTA CLARA POLICE DEPARTMENT Captain Tony Parker confirmed during a November 10, 2018 phone conversation with Plaintiff, "there were well in

8

PLAINTIFF'S COMPLAINT FOR DAMAGES

1 excess of 400 (four hundred) Law Enforcement Officers working the game," the night of
2 November 1, 2018.
3   39.   Levi's Stadium is the third newest stadium in football. As a result, the fixtures, and
4 security monitoring equipment of the stadium would be expected to be 'high tech' and 'state of
5 the art'.
6   40.   Plaintiff is informed and believes, and thereon alleges, that one or more of the
   Defendants installed a high-capacity, "high reliability, sequential video surveillance and storage
7 security system." Defendant CITY OF SANTA CLARA POLICE DEPARTMENT officers told
8 Plaintiff in face to face conversation on November 1, 2018, and phone conversation on
9 November 10, 2018, that Levi's Stadium has over 800 network security cameras and that, from
10 the event control room, a dedicated operator works at the direction of law enforcement to
11 monitor all threats. Yet according to Defendant SANTA CLARA POLICE DEPARTMENT
12 during a 2017 Deposition in the Kirin Patel beating case, (*Kirin Patel and Amish Patel v. San*
13 *Francisco Forty Niners, et al.*, Santa Clara County Superior Case no. 115CV286138, (2015),
14 Defendant SANTA CLARA POLICE DEPARTMENT admitted to analyzing social media posts
15 instead of utilizing Levi's Stadium's high technology cameras and security system. And in the
16 police report filed November 1, 2018 by Defendant SANTA CLARA POLICE DEPARTMENT
17 Staff Sergeant Alex Torke, he reports he was working detail at Levi's Stadium as an investigator
18 and relied on a video posted to Instagram involving Victim Crain being severely beaten by
19 Assailant Guardado. The Defendant CITY OF SANTA CLARA POLICE DEPARTMENT admit
20 in multiple court filed depositions and their own police reports of relying on social media rather
21 than the security system or their own eyesight. Defendants' failure to take preventative security
22 measures at Levi's Stadium is alarming. It is even more disturbing that the Defendants do not
23 implement, know how to use or are trained on, or benefit from the installed high technology 'real
   time' cameras and security system, and the Defendant SANTA CLARA POLICE
24 DEPARTMENT defaults to relying on 'unreliable' delayed social media uploads and posts.
25   41.   On November 1, 2018, Plaintiff FRED WEAVER, a 61-year-old real estate
26 developer and general contractor from Mountain View, California, attended the San Francisco
27 49ers nationally televised Thursday Night Football game at Levi's Stadium against longtime
28 rivals Oakland Raiders along with his daughter.

9

PLAINTIFF'S COMPLAINT FOR DAMAGES

42. Plaintiff is a season ticket holding Oakland Raiders fan who travelled to Levi's Stadium for the game. Plaintiff and his daughter were dressed in black and silver Raiders gear for the November 1, 2018 game.

43. The game began at 5:20 p.m. Plaintiff purchased tickets for the San Francisco 49ers game for a considerable amount and was an invitee on the Levi's Stadium premises on the day of the incident. Plaintiff was lawfully seated in upper middle Section 221 on the visitor's side of Levi's Stadium.

44. Before the halftime break, the San Francisco 49ers score was a lead of 17 to 3 over the Oakland Raiders, yet San Francisco 49ers fans were viciously attacking other San Francisco 49ers fans.

45. At approximately two minutes into the start of the third quarter of the game, Plaintiff and his daughter, after returning from the main concourse food court, while seated in upper middle Section 221, noticed a savage and brutal fight starting between two San Francisco 49ers fans in Lower Field Section 119. San Francisco 49ers fan Victim Vincent Crain (hereinafter referred to as either "VICTIM", "Vincent Crain" or "Crain") was brutally attacked by another San Francisco 49ers fan, Assailant Steve Gonzales Guardado (hereinafter referred to as either "ASSAILANT", "Steve Gonzales Guardado " or "Guardado"). During this attack, Plaintiff sitting immediately above in upper middle Section 221, witnessed Assailant Guardado punching Victim Crain with repeated strikes to the head that caused Victim Crain to fall over backwards helpless with both of his feet caught between the seat uprights. Victim Crain struck his head on the ground and the Assailant Guardado continued the brutal attack by punching Victim Crain several more times in the head.

46. Alarmingly, dozens of fans and on-field Defendant NFL security watched this savage attack between two San Francisco 49ers fans for almost two minutes without anyone taking any action against the ASSAILANT or to assist VICTIM. NFL Field Security and Defendant SANTA CLARA POLICE DEPARTMENT and all other law enforcement officers, and security staff failed to respond and or intervene to aid Victim Crain or apprehend Assailant Guardado.

47. Since no law enforcement or security staff were visible in any of the stadium seating area or attempting to diffuse the situation or step in to ensure the safety of other fans attending the game, Plaintiff decided to intervene and rushed down the steps from upper middle Section

PLAINTIFF'S COMPLAINT FOR DAMAGES

Fred Weaver – Plaintiff in Pro Per – www.UnsafeInAnySeat.com

1   221 to intercept the Assailant Guardado as he slowly left the scene of the attack, and ascended

2   the Lower Level seat stairs upwards toward the shared main concourse mezzanine, apparently in

3   an attempt to escape.

4   48.   Despite being only the third quarter of the game, and with such an intense historical

5   rivalry between the San Francisco 49ers and the Oakland Raiders, no law enforcement officers or

6   security were present anywhere near lower Section 119, the main concourse or the outer

     perimeter deck of the entire East side of Levi's Stadium during the brutal attack on Victim Crain.

7   None of those responsible and sworn to 'Protect and Serve' as law enforcement and security

8   were anywhere in the vicinity of where Crain was attacked. In fact, no FORTY NINER

9   DEFENDANTS, Defendants CITY OF SANTA CLARA POLICE DEPARTMENT or any law

10   enforcement officers were present anywhere on the Eastern side of Levi's Stadium to observe or

11   to diffuse the situation or step in for the aggressive behavior towards Crain, and they failed to

12   take any preventative measures to ensure the safety of other fans attending the game. The lack of

13   security presented a perfect opportunity to commit a variety of crimes. Unfortunately, for Victim

14   Crain, this is exactly what happened.

15   49.   Plaintiff worked his way down from his seat in upper Section 221 and intercepted the

16   ASSAILANT at the top of the Section 119 stairs connected to the main concourse. There was a

17   woman on the main concourse, in black 'security' attire, and Plaintiff was yelling very loudly at

     the top of his lungs for the female security member to call police and or backup. The female

18   security member was trying to work some sort of clicking device, as Plaintiff continued

19   screaming for her to get backup or help. As Assailant Guardado in a red shirt and his smaller

20   companion wearing a dark #80 San Francisco 49ers jersey started walking across the main

21   concourse, Plaintiff intercepted and confronted Assailant Guardado and told him to stop. The

22   ASSAILANT continued to walk toward the outer perimeter of the main concourse,

     counterclockwise Northward toward the stairs leading to Levi's Stadium Northeast Exit Gate 'F'.

23   Plaintiff and his daughter continued to closely follow ASSAILANT, and when Plaintiff and

24   ASSAILANT reached the Northeast stairway the smaller companion to the ASSAILANT

25   wearing a dark #80 San Francisco 49ers jersey, grabbed Plaintiff and tried to keep him from

26   following Assailant Guardado. Plaintiff continued following Guardado and his companion down

27   the stairs, while yelling loudly for help, and Plaintiff was finally recognized by a 'visiting' (the

28

Fred Weaver – Plaintiff in Pro Per – www.UnsafeInAnySeat.com

11

PLAINTIFF'S COMPLAINT FOR DAMAGES

1   officer's words) uniformed California Highway Patrol (CHP) officer, who was just outside the

2   Exit Gate 'F' close to the light rail train tracks. The CHP officer grabbed the Assailant Guardado,

3   and a couple of Defendant CITY OF SANTA CLARA POLICE DEPARTMENT officers finally

4   surrounded the ASSAILANT and his companion. Plaintiff first, and then Plaintiff's daughter

5   second, gave individual accounts to one of the arresting Defendant CITY OF SANTA CLARA

6   POLICE DEPARTMENT officers.

     50.   On or about November 1, 2018, Defendant CITY OF SANTA CLARA POLICE

7   DEPARTMENT violated Plaintiff's Constitutional and 14th Amendment Equal Protection

8   Rights protection of the law for Age, Disability, and Color Discrimination.

9   51.   As Plaintiff was closely following Assailant Guardado, on the outer mezzanine and

10   just before descending the Levi's Stadium Northeast Exit Gate 'F' stairs, Plaintiff finally

11   encountered a Defendant CITY OF SANTA CLARA POLICE officer, positioned counter

12   clockwise to the stairs less than 20 yards away. Plaintiff yelled at the top of his lungs, "Give me

13   some help and arrest this guy, he just beat up and severely hurt another 49ers fan!" The

14   Defendant CITY OF SANTA CLARA POLICE officer looked directly at Plaintiff, noticed

15   Plaintiff was limping, and the Defendant CITY OF SANTA CLARA POLICE officer also

16   acknowledged Plaintiff wearing a black Oakland Raiders jersey. The Defendant Santa Clara

17   Police officer literally, and physically turned his back on Plaintiff. Plaintiff was limping due to

18   excruciating pain having to chase the Assailant Guardado three quarters of the length of Levi's

19   Stadium in attempt to keep the Assailant from hurting any other Levi's Stadium patrons. Plaintiff

   underwent surgery exactly fifteen days later for a right hip replacement.

20   52.   It took over five minutes from Plaintiff WEAVER'S initial observation of Assailant

21   Guardado's start of attack on VICTIM until Assailant Guardado escaped the area reaching the

22   main concourse.

23   53.   It took approximately another ten to fifteen minutes while Plaintiff took the actions

   discussed above that finally led to the arrest of Guardado by Defendant CITY OF SANTA

24   CLARA POLICE DEPARTMENT.

25   54.   In total there was a fifteen to twenty-minute period of time when no law enforcement

26   officers or backup security were visible, posted, operating, managing, controlling, maintaining,

27

28

12

PLAINTIFF'S COMPLAINT FOR DAMAGES

1 inspecting or surveilling the East side of the San Francisco 49ers' home stadium, known as

2 "Levi's Stadium."

3   55. However, as documented in a local KNBR news report and video, on-field Defendant

4 NFL field security watched this savage attack between two San Francisco 49ers fans for almost

5 two minutes without anyone from Defendant NFL field security taking any action in any way, or

6 to call ahead for law enforcement or other security backup against the ASSAILANT or to assist

   VICTIM. "Fights break out in stands during 49ers-Raiders game." KNBR 680 - 1050 AM

7 November 1, 2018 http://www.knbr.com/2018/11/01/fights-break-out-in-stands-during-49ers-

8 raiders-game/

9   56. As a result of the lack of security and law enforcement, Plaintiff intervened, acted

10 alone, and restrained, contained and brought Assailant Guardado to custody and arrest by

11 Defendant CITY OF SANTA CLARA POLICE DEPARTMENT.

12   57. On the morning of November 2, 2018, Plaintiff travelled to Defendant CITY OF

13 SANTA CLARA POLICE DEPARTMENT with additional information and backup to assist

14 Defendant CITY OF SANTA CLARA POLICE DEPARTMENT with the previous evening's

15 arrest of Assailant Steve Guardado. Plaintiff was met by Defendant CITY OF SANTA CLARA

16 POLICE DEPARTMENT officers and WEAVER spoke to DEFENDANTS through the glass

17 while standing in the lobby side. Plaintiff provided copies of Plaintiff's and Plaintiff's daughter's

18 seating tickets and marked up Levi's Stadium overall seating diagram from the November 1,

19 2018 game, detailing area of observation by Plaintiff during Assailant Guardado's vicious attack

    on Victim Crain.

20   58. On the morning of November 2, 2018, Plaintiff also travelled to Defendant CITY OF

21 SANTA CLARA's administrative offices with additional information and backup to assist and

22 discuss with Defendant CITY OF SANTA CLARA and Defendant CITY OF SANTA CLARA

23 Attorney BRIAN DOYLE, the events of the previous evening detailed above. Plaintiff was met

24 by Defendant CITY OF SANTA CLARA administrative clerks, and WEAVER spoke to

25 DEFENDANT administrative clerks over the counter. Plaintiff requested meeting with

26 DEFENDANT CITY OF SANTA CLARA Mayor and City Attorney regarding the incident at

27 the November 1, 2018 game. Plaintiff was told by Defendant CITY OF SANTA CLARA's

    clerks that the Mayor and City Attorney were not available.

28

13

PLAINTIFF'S COMPLAINT FOR DAMAGES

59.   Plaintiff is informed and believes and thereon alleges that on or about November 2, 2018, Defendant CITY OF SANTA CLARA POLICE DEPARTMENT violated California Penal Code 118.1 when their officers intentionally filed false police reports regarding the November 1, 2018 incident at Levi's Stadium.

60.   On or about November 5, 2018 Plaintiff initiated email correspondence with DEFENDANTS including Defendant CITY OF SANTA CLARA POLICE DEPARTMENT officers and Defendant Chief of Police MICHAEL SELLERS and Defendant CITY OF SANTA CLARA City Attorney BRIAN DOYLE.

61.   On or about November 8, 2018 Plaintiff WEAVER received a phone call from ex-Oakland Chief of Police Howard Jordan, who informed him that he was calling on behalf of Defendant CITY OF SANTA CLARA City Attorney BRIAN DOYLE. Howard Jordan explained he was a security consultant to the Defendant CITY OF SANTA CLARA.

62.   On or about November 10, 2018, Plaintiff received a phone call from Defendant CITY OF SANTA CLARA POLICE DEPARTMENT Captain Tony Parker. During that phone call, Captain Parker confirmed to Plaintiff that, after reviewing the Levi's Stadium security tapes, WEAVER was positively identified in the tapes and WEAVER was wearing a number 75 Oakland Raider Black Jersey. Captain Parker also informed Plaintiff during that phone conversation that, "there were well in excess of 400 (four hundred) law enforcement officers working the game," the night of November 1, 2018.

63.   On or about November 10, 2018, Defendants CITY OF SANTA CLARA POLICE DEPARTMENT ceased all further communication with Plaintiff.

64.   On or about November 10, 2018, Defendant CITY OF SANTA CLARA City Attorney BRIAN DOYLE ceased all further communication with Plaintiff.

65.   On the morning of November 15, 2018, Plaintiff travelled again to Defendant CITY OF SANTA CLARA's administrative offices with additional information and requested a meeting with its Mayor and City Attorney regarding the incident at the November 1, 2018 game. Plaintiff was told by Defendant CITY OF SANTA CLARA administrative clerks that the Mayor and City Attorney were not available. Plaintiff WEAVER left his business card stapled to hand written note for Defendant CITY OF SANTA CLARA Attorney BRIAN DOYLE.

14

PLAINTIFF'S COMPLAINT FOR DAMAGES

66. On November 26, 2018, Plaintiff sent individual letters via UPS Overnight to Defendant CITY OF SANTA CLARA Mayor Gillmor and copying all Defendant CITY OF SANTA CLARA Councilmembers with extensive narrative and backup including all email correspondence previously sent and received between Plaintiff and the Defendant CITY OF SANTA CLARA City Attorney and Defendant CITY OF SANTA CLARA POLICE DEPARTMENT.

67. On or about November 28, 2018, Plaintiff received a letter from Defendant CITY OF SANTA CLARA Mayor and Council Officers acknowledging receipt of Plaintiff's November 26, 2018 letter stating, "Your letter will be distributed to the Mayor and Councilmembers, as well as the City Manager's Office, for their review."

68. On or about November 28, 2018, Defendant CITY OF SANTA CLARA Mayor Lisa Gillmor and Councilmembers ceased all communication with Plaintiff.

69. On December 16, 2018, Plaintiff returned to Levi's Stadium for the sole purpose of inspecting and reviewing security coverage. That San Francisco 49ers home game at Levi's Stadium was against the Seattle Seahawks. Rather than sit in his assigned seat, Plaintiff walked the entire Levi's Stadium during the first half of the football game and took 630 separate photographs of Defendant CITY OF SANTA CLARA POLICE DEPARTMENT officers, other law enforcement officers and other security personnel mostly standing around, bunched up in groups, tucked away in warm areas, not providing any strategic placement or zone coverage, not observing the crowd fan base. He also saw no law enforcement or security personnel patrolling any of Levi's Stadium fan seating sections or any of Levi's Stadium main entry and exit gates.

70. On or about January 7, 2019, Plaintiff called Defendant NATIONAL FOOTBALL LEAGUE and left a voicemail for Defendant CATHY LANIER, NFL Senior Vice President of Security.

71. On January 8, 2019, Plaintiff received phone call from Defendant BILLY LANGENSTEIN, – Director, Investigations & Security Services – National Football League. During that call Plaintiff discussed with BILLY LANGENSTEIN multiple Levi's Stadium security concerns and other related issues pertaining to Defendant CITY OF SANTA CLARA POLICE DEPARTMENT. Mr. LANGENSTEIN informed Plaintiff both orally and in an email

15

PLAINTIFF'S COMPLAINT FOR DAMAGES

1 later that evening that, "I will follow up with the 49ers on the active investigation that you
2 referenced."

3   72.   On or about January 8, 2018, Defendant NATIONAL FOOTBALL LEAGUE and
4 Defendant NFL Security Representative BILLY LANGENSTEIN ceased all communication
5 with Plaintiff.

6   73.   Plaintiff is informed and believes and thereon alleges that, starting on or about
7 November 1, 2018 through and continuing after January 8, 2019, DEFENDANTS conspired to
8 conceal information, falsify reports, hide, bury, and make any incriminating records disappear.

    74.   Without the implementation of any adequate security measures, inside Levi's
9 Stadium, Plaintiff and the other patrons were inappropriately exposed to the aggressive acts of
10 third parties the night of November 1, 2018. The bottom line is that "with well in excess of 400
11 law enforcement officers working the game that night", the DEFENDANTS failed to provide
12 any security for the entire Eastern side of Levi's Stadium. DEFENDANTS did not have in place
13 or take any reasonable steps to prevent the attack on Victim Crain or any other crimes that might
14 have taken place.

15   75.   These reasonable steps that should have been taken included and should in the future
    include, but are not limited to:

16   a.   The presence of uniformed security (or for any security for that matter) operating,
17   managing, controlling, maintaining, inspecting and surveilling the Eastern side of the
18   San Francisco 49ers' home stadium, known as "Levi's Stadium;

19   b.   Presence of law enforcement officers or security at or near patron seating and main
20   concourse areas;

21   c.   Better communication between all law enforcement officers and security staff during
22   games;

23   d.   Refusing to grant access to the premises (both inside the stadium and in the parking
          lot) to known criminals or gang members;
24
25   e.   Promoting responsible consumption of alcohol; and

26   f.   Ejection from both the stadium and parking lot of those persons exhibiting drunk or
          disorderly conduct, or those persons exhibiting violent conduct.
27
28

16

PLAINTIFF'S COMPLAINT FOR DAMAGES

76.   It is also unfortunate that such a storied and well-respected football team such as the San Francisco 49ers has been made to suffer due to recent turmoil and publicly aired and documented political infighting between the Defendants CITY OF SANTA CLARA POLICE DEPARTMENT, CITY OF SANTA CLARA and CITY OF SANTA CLARA STADIUM AUTHORITY, and FORTY NINER DEFENDANTS. Moreover, Plaintiff is informed and believes and thereon alleges that the toxic environment and relationship between all of the DEFENDANTS has resulted in the deteriorated morale of Defendants CITY OF SANTA CLARA POLICE DEPARTMENT directly leading to chaos in DEFENDANTS' security management exposing sports fans and other patrons of Levi's Stadium to extreme danger and recent near-death experiences by San Francisco season ticket holders. Plaintiff is informed and believes and thereon alleges that, mismanagement by FORTY NINER DEFENDANTS in failing to provide timely security budgets over multiple years to adequately manage security leaves management of adequate security staffing needs only to be guessed at by Defendants CITY OF SANTA CLARA, CITY OF SANTA CLARA STADIUM AUTHORITY and CITY OF SANTA CLARA POLICE DEPARTMENT.

   a.   *An August 24, 2017, City of Santa Clara Agenda Report included a Comprehensive Audit of Stadium Authority Finances, prepared by Harvey M. Rose Associates, LLC. Included in the August 21, 2017 audit Conclusions and Findings, finding 1.D, "The Stadium Lease requires that the Operation and Maintenance Plan Prepared by ManCo (Forty Niners Stadium Management Company) and submitted to the Stadium Authority include an annual Public Safety Budget. At approximately $5.7 million in FY 2015-16, public safety costs are one of the Stadium's largest expenses, but a budget for these costs were not submitted to the Stadium Authority in total or approved by the Board for the two years within the scope of this audit."*

77.   Plaintiff is informed and believes and thereon alleges that an outside audit found that due to the unwillingness of the FORTY NINER DEFENDANTS to provide security budgets for two years, law enforcement officers and security forces headcount at Levi's Stadium were ineffectively managed, endangering the safety of fans attending San Francisco 49ers home games. Plaintiff is informed and believes and thereon alleges that, during this non-budgeted security period on October 4, 2014, due to a lack of security, San Francisco 49ers season ticket

17

PLAINTIFF'S COMPLAINT FOR DAMAGES

holder Kirin Patel was viciously attacked by a drunken gang member, and Kirin Patel suffered a coma, brain damage, and partial paralysis.

78.   Plaintiff is informed and believes and thereon alleges that, as the final decision maker for the Defendant SANTA CLARA POLICE DEPARTMENT and DEFENDANTS, and each of them, Defendant Police Chief MICHAEL SELLERS held the ultimate responsibility for preparation and final review of security budgets, approval of police reports and implementation of security procedures and implementation.

79.   Plaintiff is informed and believes, and thereon alleges, that these and other issues made public as documented in the recent Grand Jury Investigation and City of Santa Clara Meeting Agendas are a direct link to the major deterioration of cooperation affecting morale of all DEFENDANTS. Further, that DEFENDANTS publicly aired political infighting and finger pointing about security budget responsibilities has led to the turmoil and chaos affecting security at Levi's Stadium.

80.   On typical game days, according to an October 26, 2017 ESPN video interview with Defendant NFL Chief of Security CATHY LANIER, "Local police are the lead agency for every game throughout the season. A typical game requires at least 10 different agencies, from the FBI to private security."

81.   As the lead agency for security at Levi's Stadium, the SANTA CLARA POLICE DEPARTMENT itself has been involved in two recent well documented Court Cases involving unconstitutional and illegal activity violating the security and safety of not only Santa Clara residents but also a San Jose resident. (*Moneeb, Ikram and Ikram v City of Santa Clara, Mike Sellers, et al.,* United States District Court (ND CA 2015), Case no. 5:15-cv-01987-NC), (*Danielle Harmon v. City of Santa Clara, City of Santa Clara Police Chief Mike Sellers, et al.,* United Stated District Court (ND CA 2016) Case no. 5:16-cv-04228-EJD).

82.   Plaintiff is informed and believes and thereon alleges that this finding is also directly related to the disturbing, chaotic, and dysfunctional management causing a lack of security and safety at Levi's Stadium.

83.   Plaintiff is also informed and believes, and hereon alleges, that there were various other incidents (including two recent near-death beatings) arising as a result of lack of security since at least 2014 that put the DEFENDANTS and each of them on notice of such a dangerous

18

and unsafe condition both inside the stadium and in the parking lot. Plaintiff is informed and believes and thereon alleges that the DEFENDANTS also had prior knowledge that known members of gangs and other criminals actively used the occasion of San Francisco 49ers games to meet, plan and carry out criminal activity, and that these security and safety issue concerns have been accelerating both prior to and after the 2014 opening of Levi's Stadium.

a. On October 4, 2014, due to a lack of security, San Francisco 49ers season ticket holder Kirin Patel was viciously attacked by a drunken gang member, and Kirin Patel suffered a coma, brain damage, and partial paralysis. (*Kirin Patel and Amish Patel v. San Francisco Forty Niners, et al.*, Santa Clara County Superior Court Case no. 115CV286138, (2015).

b. In September 2015, after a Monday night game, a group of San Francisco 49ers fans punched and kicked a man wearing a Minnesota Vikings jersey.

c. On October 7, 2018 following a San Francisco 49ers vs Arizona Cardinals game, a man punched another fan causing great bodily harm including brain damage and the victim becoming comatose. (*The State of California v Gonzales, David Aguilera,* Santa Clara County Superior Court Case No. C1802883, (2018).

d. Prior to the October 4, 2014 Kirin Patel beating, but later revealed in his subsequent Personal Injury Lawsuit, Court Documents show all of the FORTY NINER DEFENDANT'S, Defendant CITY OF SANTA CLARA and the Defendant CITY OF SANTA CLARA STADIUM AUTHORITY had specific knowledge of reports of more than 500 recent prior assaults and fights at San Francisco 49ers home games. (*Kirin Patel and Amish Patel v. San Francisco Forty Niners, et al.,* Santa Clara County Superior Court Case no. 115CV286138, (2015).

e. During the Personal Injury Trial for the vicious attack and beating of Kirin Patel, FORTY NINER DEFENDANTS, Defendant CITY OF SANTA CLARA and Defendant CITY OF SANTA CLARA STADIUM AUTHORITY defense and contention in court documents was, *"Notifying the public about the lack of security would discourage use of the property and would also serve to invite violent attacks."*

84.   Consequently, Plaintiff is informed and believes and thereon alleges that all the DEFENDANTS had prior notice that Levi's Stadium was unsafe for patrons such as Plaintiff and

19

PLAINTIFF'S COMPLAINT FOR DAMAGES

Victim Crain and could have prevented or at least reduced the severity of the attack on Crain by and through reasonable measures including, but not limited to adequate security.

85. During Plaintiff's January 8, 2019 phone discussion with Defendant NFL Director, Investigations & Security, BILLY LANGENSTEIN, Defendant LANGENSTEIN confirmed the National Football League's knowledge of the Kirin Patel near death beating case at Levi's Stadium. Plaintiff is informed and believes and thereon alleges that this supports the conclusion that the NFL also had specific knowledge of reports of more than 500 recent prior assaults and fights at San Francisco 49ers home games.

86. The FORTY NINER DEFENDANTS, Defendants CITY OF SANTA CLARA POLICE DEPARTMENT, and NATIONAL FOOTBALL LEAGUE personnel did nothing to observe, operate, manage, control, maintain, inspect surveil or stop Crain from being attacked during the game.

87. Plaintiff believed, prior to attending the November 1, 2018 game, that the FORTY NINER DEFENDANTS, Defendant CITY OF SANTA CLARA POLICE DEPARTMENT, and the NATIONAL FOOTBALL LEAGUE personnel were apprised of heightened security needs and the intimidating situation in the stadium and were keeping watch for any signs of violence or retaliation. However, the FORTY NINER DEFENDANTS, Defendant CITY OF SANTA CLARA POLICE DEPARTMENT, and the NATIONAL FOOTBALL LEAGUE were not performing their duty to keep spectators in the stands, and on their property, safe from aggressive acts of third parties.

88. The failure of the DEFENDANTS, and each of them, to provide adequate security allowed Assailant Guardado to brutally attack Crain in a highly visible seating area lower to the field, Levi's Stadium Seating Section 119. Moreover, the failure of the DEFENDANTS, and each of them, to protect Crain, allowed the aggressive act to be perpetrated in the stadium endangering the safety of other fans attending the game seated in the vicinity near to Crain.

89. Plaintiff is informed and believes and thereon alleges that while in or around the Levi's Stadium Seating Section 119 which is owned, operated and controlled by the DEFENDANTS, Victim Crain was brutally attacked by Assailant Guardado punching Victim Crain with repeated strikes to the head.

20

PLAINTIFF'S COMPLAINT FOR DAMAGES

90.   Levi's Stadium Seating Section 119 is located on the DEFENDANTS property and within the control of the DEFENDANTS, and each of them.

91.   Despite the fact that the brutal and vicious attack took place over a prolonged period of time and drew the attention of various other patrons, no law enforcement or security was present or intervened. Moreover, as documented in Defendant SANTA CLARA POLICE DEPARTMENT reports obtained by Plaintiff, it took approximately ten to fifteen minutes for DEFENDANTS SCPD personnel to respond to the scene where Crain was injured. This was ten to fifteen minutes after ASSAILANT Guardado was able to flee the scene of the beating he inflicted.

92.   Furthermore, Plaintiff is informed and believes and thereon alleges that use of non-sworn, non-law enforcement security personnel is not as effective as utilizing law enforcement officers, as non-law enforcement personnel are not as imposing as uniformed officers. The DEFENDANTS' apparent decision to not strategically place uniformed law enforcement officers created a relaxed, unintimidating atmosphere at Levi's Stadium. Plaintiff is informed and believes and thereon alleges that this atmosphere fostered the acts of Assailant Guardado. Plaintiff is informed and believes, and thereon alleges, that FORTY NINER DEFENDANTS, Defendants SANTA CLARA POLICE DEPARTMENT, and Defendant NFL failed to provide adequate security for Levi's Stadium, despite knowledge of gang presence and previous criminal activity on Levi's Stadium property.

93.   Without the Defendants understanding of use and implementation of adequate security measures by the DEFENDANTS, and each of them, along with DEFENDANTS not implementing, not knowing how to use or being trained on, or benefitting from the high technology 'real time' cameras and security system that have been in existence since the opening of Levi's Stadium in 2014, and the Defendant SANTA CLARA POLICE DEPARTMENT default use and relying on 'unreliable' delayed social media uploads and posts, VICTIM, Plaintiff (and his child) and the general public were inappropriately exposed to the aggressive acts of third parties, all to their damage subject to proof at trial.

94.   Moreover, Plaintiff is informed and believes, and thereon alleges, that there should have been heightened security for San Francisco 49ers and the Oakland Raiders game on

21

PLAINTIFF'S COMPLAINT FOR DAMAGES

November 1, 2018. The DEFENDANTS, and each of them, failed to provide heightened security at Levi's Stadium on November 1, 2018.

95.   Plaintiff is informed and believes, and thereon alleges, that there are more instances of criminal activity in Levi's Stadium than in any other National Football League stadium, making Levi's Stadium the most dangerous public venue in North America.

96.   Plaintiff is informed and believes and thereon alleges that the DEFENDANTS, and each of them, with full knowledge of these dangerous conditions carelessly mismanage security forces at Levi's Stadium. This lack of proper security, inability and unwillingness to utilize Levi's Stadium's high technology cameras and security system while relying on social media, knowledge of criminal elements, and the promotion of alcohol in the stadium and surrounding parking lot was the substantial factor that caused injury to Victim Crain and exposed Plaintiff, his child and other fans who attend games to the danger of being victims of crimes. Plaintiff suffered financially because Plaintiff paid a considerable amount for seats and was unable to enjoy the second half of the game. Plaintiff was injured and limping due to excruciating pain having to chase the Assailant Guardado three quarters of the length of Levi's Stadium. Plaintiff was doing the job of law enforcement in attempt to keep the Assailant from hurting any other Levi's Stadium patrons. Plaintiff underwent surgery exactly fifteen days later for a right hip replacement.

97.   The DEFENDANTS were aware that other assaults of a similar nature to the subject incident had occurred on its premises and thus it had reasonable cause to anticipate the misconduct of third persons. Despite their knowledge about numerous prior assaults and fights at its football games, the FORTY NINER DEFENDANTS, the NATIONAL FOOTBALL LEAGUE, the CITY OF SANTA CLARA and the SANTA CLARA STADIUM AUTHORITY failed to provide any warnings whatsoever to its fans about the prior criminal incidents. The FORTY NINER DEFENDANTS, the CITY OF SANTA CLARA, the SANTA CLARA STADIUM AUTHORITY, and the NATIONAL FOOTBALL LEAGUE should have given written notice of the history of violent attacks to its season ticket holders and other paying patrons, so they could make an informed decision about whether to attend games with such an increased risk of harm. The FORTY NINER DEFENDANTS, the CITY OF SANTA CLARA, the SANTA CLARA STADIUM AUTHORITY, and the NATIONAL FOOTBALL LEAGUE

PLAINTIFF'S COMPLAINT FOR DAMAGES

Fred Weaver – Plaintiff in Pro Per – www.UnsafeInAnySeat.com

did not publicize the prior criminal incidents or in any way warn the general public. In fact, the FORTY NINER DEFENDANTS and Defendant NFL actively concealed and have continued to actively conceal the risk of harm to its fan base and have misled its fans into believing that it promotes a safe environment free from intoxication, gang violence and fights or assaults with its highly touted 'Fan Code of Conduct'. The 'Fan Code of Conduct' was a misrepresentation that the environment at Levi's Stadium would be safe.

98.   Plaintiff is informed and believes, and thereon alleges, that Levi's Stadium has the most instances of criminal activity of all stadiums in the National Football League network. Moreover, Levi's Stadium has the 16th largest seating capacity of all stadiums in the National Football League network. Based on the aforesaid, the DEFENDANTS, and each of them, have a duty to protect spectators of known dangers on their property.

99.   The DEFENDANT'S actions and knowing omissions constituted malice, oppression, and/or a willful and conscious disregard of the rights and safety of Plaintiff and the general public pursuant to California Code of Civil Procedure § 3294 entitling Plaintiff to punitive damages. These punitive damages should serve to punish DEFENDANTS for their conscious disregard of safety and to discourage similar conduct in the future.

FIRST CAUSE OF ACTION

NEGLIGENCE

(Against all DEFENDANTS)

100.   Plaintiff hereby realleges and incorporates by reference each and every allegation herein above as if fully set forth in detail therein.

101.   The DEFENDANTS, and each of them, breached their duty of care to Plaintiff, Victim Crain and the general public by failing to take reasonable steps to ensure the safety of the general public, Victim Crain and Plaintiff and prevent them from being exposed to a dangerous condition while they attended a football game at Levi's Stadium on November 1, 2018.

102.   The DEFENDANTS, and each of them, breached their duty of care owed to the Plaintiff because the DEFENDANTS had reason to know of gang and other criminal activity on its premises. As a result of such knowledge, the DEFENDANTS, and each of them, had a duty to take reasonable security precautions for the benefit of the spectators at Levi's Stadium.

103. Plaintiff is informed and believes, and thereon alleges, that the DEFENDANTS, and each of them, had reasonable cause to anticipate criminal acts of third parties and the probability of injury arising from them. DEFENDANTS, and each of them, failed to take affirmative steps to control the wrongful conduct.

104. Plaintiff is informed and believes, and thereon alleges, as described more fully above, the DEFENDANTS, and each of them, had knowledge of prior similar incidents in and around the stadium. However, the DEFENDANTS failed to take appropriate measures to protect patrons on its property and failed to provide proper law enforcement presence on its property exposing at least the entire Eastern (visitor) side to absence of any security whatsoever, all to Plaintiff's damages as described more fully herein.

105. On December 16, 2018, Plaintiff returned to Levi's Stadium for the sole reason to inspect and review security coverage. That San Francisco 49ers home game at Levi's Stadium was against the Seattle Seahawks. Rather than sit in his assigned seat, Plaintiff walked the entire Levi's Stadium during the first half of the football game and took 630 separate photographs of Defendant CITY OF SANTA CLARA POLICE DEPARTMENT law enforcement officers and other security personnel mostly standing around, bunched up in groups, tucked away in warm areas, not providing any strategic placement or zone coverage, not observing the crowd fan base. He also saw no law enforcement or security patrolling any of Levi's Stadium fan seating sections or any of Levi's Stadium main entry and exit gates.

106. Plaintiff is informed and believes, and thereon alleges, that after learning of more than 500 recent prior assaults, fights, and criminal attacks at San Francisco 49ers home games, the DEFENDANTS' installed a "high-technology security and camera system" throughout the new Levi's Stadium.

107. Plaintiff is informed and believes, and thereon alleges, that the DEFENDANTS, and each of them, had actual knowledge of the presence of notorious gangs and affiliated individuals congregating in Levi's Stadium during and after San Francisco 49ers home games.

108. Plaintiff is informed and believes, and thereon alleges, that the DEFENDANTS breached their duty of care to Plaintiff by failing to utilize the alleged installed "high-technology security and camera system" installed in Levi's Stadium. Levi's Stadium is the third newest stadium in the National Football League. Therefore, the newly installed "high-technology

24

PLAINTIFF'S COMPLAINT FOR DAMAGES

security and camera system" should have been a security asset to assist with overall security at Levi's Stadium. Instead, Plaintiff is informed and believes, and thereon alleges, that the non-use by DEFENDANTS and misuse and misunderstanding by DEFENDANTS of the installed security systems features and functionality allowed for known gang and criminal activity to go unnoticed and undetected. Adding "high-technology security and camera system" is a supplemental means of effecting security measures on the premises of Levi's Stadium while the in-person security means by Defendants and visible actively patrolling law enforcement, should have taken first priority.

109. Plaintiff is informed and believes, and thereon alleges, that the installation of the "high-technology security and camera system" in Levi's Stadium shows the feasibility of the safety measure.

110. Moreover, the installation of "high-technology security and camera system" in Levi's Stadium shows that the DEFENDANTS, and each of them, held ownership and control over the security system at Levi's Stadium.

111. Plaintiff is informed and believes, and thereon alleges, at all times the NFL's unique historical vantage point at the apex of the sport of football, paired with its unmatched resources as the most well-funded organization devoted to the business of the game, has afforded it unparalleled access to data relating to trouble at all NFL team stadiums including dangerous and unsafe conditions and prior assaults and fights and made it an institutional repository of accumulated knowledge about security issues at individual stadiums.

112. Plaintiff is informed and believes, and thereon alleges, that in spite of this knowledge, the DEFENDANTS and each of them decided to underutilize the physically installed "high-technology security and camera system" security resources in the stadium, in addition to utilizing unmanaged law enforcement officers as security personnel.

113. This decision was a breach of duty owed to spectators and guests at Levi's Stadium.

114. Plaintiff is informed and believes, and thereon alleges, that despite knowledge of the criminal activity at Levi's Stadium, the DEFENDANTS and each of them initiated alcohol promotion for all games at Levi's Stadium beginning with the 2014 season. Said promotion was initiated despite knowledge of criminal activity at Levi's Stadium and knowledge of the criminal elements who congregate at Levi's Stadium.

PLAINTIFF'S COMPLAINT FOR DAMAGES

115. The DEFENDANTS had and have notice that the serving of alcohol at a sporting event could and did incite violent, criminal behavior.

116. Plaintiff is informed and believes, and thereon alleges, that subsequent to the 2014 opening of Levi's Stadium, the DEFENDANTS, and their promotion of alcohol has enhanced criminal activity at Levi's Stadium directly related to a pair of recent violent and severe beatings of Levi's Stadium fans resulting in comas, brain damage, and in one of the cases partial paralysis, (*Kirin Patel and Amish Patel v. San Francisco Forty Niners, et al.,* Santa Clara County Superior Court Case no. 115CV286138, (2015), (*The State of California v Gonzales, David Aguilera,* Santa Clara County Superior Court Case No. C1802883, (2018).

117. The DEFENDANTS, and each of them, have a duty to protect spectators and those lawfully on their premises. The DEFENDANTS, and each of them, breached this duty by acting below the industry-wide standard in security and below their own standards to guard and protect their guests.

118. The failure of the DEFENDANTS, and each of them, to act according to the standard of care, as explained more fully above, was the proximate and actual cause of Plaintiff's injuries, as well as those that have already been suffered and will be suffered in the future by other members of the general public unless corrective action is taken.

119. Plaintiff is informed and believes, and thereon alleges, that had the DEFENDANTS provided adequate security, adequate use of the installed "high-technology security and camera system," and adequate supervision, as more fully described above, all of which were reasonable measures on the part of the DEFENDANTS, Plaintiff and all other Levi's Stadium patrons would have been adequately protected from third party criminal conduct (or, at least that likelihood and seriousness of incidents would have been substantially reduced).

120. Plaintiff is informed and believes, and thereon alleges, that the DEFENDANTS, and each of them, had law enforcement and security technology available to counter specific conduct of third parties sufficiently in advance of the injury to Plaintiff and injures to other members of the public, giving the DEFENDANTS an opportunity to act to prevent the injury. Based on the foregoing, the causal connection between failure to act and the injury is patent.

121. As explained more fully above, during the first part of the third quarter of the game, a vicious and savage beating of a fan took place with the ASSAILANT able to walk away from the

26

297

injury inflicted upon the other fan, yet the DEFENDANTS and/or security did not take steps to curtail or stop the activity.

122. As explained more fully above, the DEFENDANTS, and each of them, failed to have a security presence in the stadium, despite knowledge that the rowdy behavior was anticipated inside the stadium. In addition to knowledge of the dangerous scene inside the stadium, knowledge that fans were imbibing alcohol for the pendency of the game, and knowledge of the rivalry between the two teams, the DEFENDANTS, and each of them, failed to take any reasonable measures to protect patrons on their property.

123. The DEFENDANTS owe a duty to warn patrons of known dangers and a duty to take other reasonable and appropriate measures to protect patrons from imminent or "ongoing" aggressive conduct. Such measures include protecting patrons or invitees from an imminent and known peril lurking in the stadium by providing trained security personnel.

124. At all times herein mentioned, and prior thereto, DEFENDANTS and each of them had a special relationship with the patrons and invitees present at Levi's Stadium on NFL game days, an environment where guests should be allowed to enjoy their gameday experience in a safe and enjoyable atmosphere free from fighting, overly intoxicated patrons and gang activity; and, thus, had a legal duty to exercise ordinary care to ensure the safety of all persons who were lawfully on the premises of Levi's Stadium

125. Under the special relationship doctrine, the DEFENDANTS, and each of them, by serving intoxicating drinks to patrons for consumption on its premises, must exercise reasonable care to protect patrons from injury at the hands of fellow guests. The law does impose a legal duty to affirmatively act to protect someone else from danger or to control the conduct of a third person if there is a "special relationship" between the defendant and the person in danger or the third person creating the danger. "Businesses, such as shopping centers, restaurants and bars, and stadiums serving alcohol have an affirmative duty to take reasonable steps to secure their premises, as well as adjacent common areas within their control, against reasonably foreseeable criminal acts of third parties" [Delgado v. Trax Bar & Grill (2005) 36 Cal.4th 224; Morris IV v. De La Torre (2005) California Supreme Court No. S119750; Ann M. v. Pacific Plaza Shopping Ctr. (1993) 6 Cal.4th 666]. The DEFENDANTS, and each of them, failed to protect patrons on its property as more fully explained above. Moreover, the DEFENDANTS were warned of potential

27

298

aggressive conduct inside the stadium. However, the DEFENDANTS failed to take suitable measures for the protection of Victim Crain, Plaintiff and his daughter, and all other Levi's stadium patrons including removing dangerous, intoxicated individuals from the property.

126. Moreover, the DEFENDANTS, and each of them, failed to stop the November 1, 2018 fight in the seating area as soon as possible, allowing it to escalate to the point that Victim Crain was exposed to a prolonged attack by another San Francisco 49er fan.

127. As a result of the negligence of the DEFENDANTS, and each of them, Plaintiff has been damaged in an amount to be proven at trial. Further, Plaintiff is informed and believes and thereon alleges that the conditions alleged herein still exist, exposing the general public to likely future injuries unless they are corrected.

128. As a direct and proximate result of the conduct of the DEFENDANTS, and each of them, Plaintiff has experienced damages in an amount to be shown according to proof at trial.

SECOND CAUSE OF ACTION

PREMISES LIABILITY – FAILURE TO PROVIDE SAFE PREMISE – DANGEROUS CONDITION OF PUBLIC PROPERTY

(Against all DEFENDANTS)

129. Plaintiff hereby realleges and incorporates by reference each and every allegation above as if fully set forth in detail herein.

130. The "SUBJECT PROPERTY" refers to Levi's Stadium located in Santa Clara, California, where this incident occurred.

131. At all times herein mentioned the DEFENDANTS, and each of them, and DOES 1 through 40, were the owners and/or operators of the SUBJECT PROPERTY.

132. The DEFENDANTS, and each of them, and DOES 1 through 40, as the owners and/or occupiers of land owe a general duty to exercise ordinary care for the safety of persons who come upon the property.

133. Plaintiff is informed and believes, and thereon alleges, that at all times herein mentioned, the persons acting as the managers, security personnel, and maintainers of Levi's Stadium located in Santa Clara, California, were acting with the knowledge, permission and consent of all the DEFENDANTS, and each of them.

28

PLAINTIFF'S COMPLAINT FOR DAMAGES

134. Plaintiff is informed and believes, and thereon alleges, that at all times herein mentioned, the persons acting as the managers, security personnel, maintainers, and/or lessors of Levi's Stadium located in Santa Clara, California, were the agents, servants and/or employees of and acting within the course and scope of said agency and employed by the DEFENDANTS.

135. Plaintiff is informed and believes, and thereon alleges, that the DEFENDANTS, and each of them, had reasonable cause to anticipate criminal acts of third parties and the probability of injury arising from them. The DEFENDANTS, and each of them, failed to take affirmative steps to control the wrongful conduct on the SUBJECT PROPERTY.

136. Beginning with the 2014 season, the DEFENDANTS initiated alcohol promotion for all football games at Levi's Stadium. Said promotion was initiated despite knowledge of criminal activity at Levi's Stadium and knowledge of the criminal elements who congregate at the Stadium.

137. The DEFENDANTS have and had notice prior to the 2014 opening of Levi's Stadium that the serving of alcohol at a sporting event could and did incite violent, criminal behavior.

138. Plaintiff is informed and believes, and thereon alleges that the DEFENDANTS, and their promotion of alcohol has enhanced criminal activity at Levi's Stadium directly related to a pair of recent violent and severe beatings of Levi's Stadium fans resulting in comas, brain damage, and in one of the cases partial paralysis.

139. Plaintiff is further informed and believes that the precautionary measures that should have been taken by the DEFENDANTS, and each of them, imposed a small burden in relation to the magnitude of harm.

140. Plaintiff is informed and believes, and thereon alleges, that on November 1, 2018 the DEFENDANTS, and each of them, proximately caused damages to said Plaintiff and have endangered the general public since the stadium opened, by negligently, wantonly, recklessly, tortiously and unlawfully:

    a.   Entrusting, permitting, managing, patrolling, maintaining, controlling and operating Levi's Stadium;

    b.   Instructing others regarding patrolling, security, supervision, and operation of the Levi's Stadium;

29

PLAINTIFF'S COMPLAINT FOR DAMAGES

c.   Failing to warn, instruct, advise, protect and guard patrons regarding the Levi's Stadium; and

d.   Conducting themselves with reference to the Levi's Stadium and to Plaintiff, so as to cause the Levi's Stadium to be in a dangerous, and unsafe condition to proximately cause damages to the Plaintiff.

141. Plaintiff is informed and believes, and thereon alleges, that had the DEFENDANTS provided adequate security, adequate use of the installed "high-technology security and camera system", and adequate supervision, as more fully described above, all of which were reasonable measures on the part of the DEFENDANTS, Plaintiff and all other Levi's Stadium patrons would have been adequately protected from third party criminal conduct.

142. As a proximate result thereof, Plaintiff incurred injury, and damages in such amount as will be proven at trial.

143. Furthermore, Plaintiff is informed and believes, and thereon alleges, that the DEFENDANTS, and each of them, acted in conscious disregard of the safety of others, were aware of the probable dangerous consequences of their conduct and misfeasance, and willfully and deliberately failed to avoid those consequences specifically that the DEFENDANTS and each of them were aware of prior incidents where spectators would inflict criminal harm on other spectators.

144. Additionally, Plaintiff is informed and believes, and thereon alleges, that the DEFENDANTS, and each of them, knew that their failure to provide adequate security at the Levi's Stadium would lead to criminal acts on spectators as described more fully above. Therefore, a demand for punitive damages is warranted.

THIRD CAUSE OF ACTION
NEGLIGENT STADIUM SECURITY - NEGLIGENT HIRING, RETENTION, AND SUPERVISION
(Against all DEFENDANTS)

145. Plaintiff hereby realleges and incorporates by reference each and every allegation above as if fully set forth in detail herein.

30

PLAINTIFF'S COMPLAINT FOR DAMAGES

146. The DEFENDANTS, and each of them, had a duty to Plaintiff to hire police, other law enforcement, and other security personnel who were well-trained, restrained in their use of force, and otherwise competent to prevent any injury to spectators and guests on the Levi's Stadium.

147. Plaintiff is informed and believes, and thereon alleges, that the DEFENDANTS, and each of them, failed or refused to properly hire, screen, train, and/or supervise those members of their security team to carry out their duties in a manner that was well-trained, restrained, orderly, and/or competent.

148. Plaintiff is informed and believes, and thereon alleges, that the DEFENDANTS, and each of them, failed to train and/or supervise the security personnel at Levi's Stadium, in proper crowd control procedures. For example, on November 1, 2018, the security personnel at Levi's Stadium did not adequately respond to threats of criminal activity from spectators, nor did they adequately supervise spectators in the stands to provide a safe and enjoyable experience for all guests on the Levi's Stadium.

149. It is common knowledge that violence is deterred by presence of uniformed police officers and security guards. Perpetrators of violent crime thrive in public places where there is no such physical deterrence and the DEFENDANTS and each of them failed to provide such deterrence on November 1, 2018 and December 16, 2018. Plaintiff is informed and believes, and thereon alleges, that this lack of deterrence is common practice at Levi's Stadium.

150. On November 1, 2018, Plaintiff observed that the police officers and security guards at Levi's Stadium did not patrol, manage, control, inspect, surveil, or provide any type of security for the entire East side of Levi's Stadium.

151. On December 16, 2018, Plaintiff returned to Levi's Stadium for the sole reason to inspect and review security coverage. That San Francisco 49ers home game at Levi's Stadium was against the Seattle Seahawks. Rather than sit in his assigned seat, Plaintiff WEAVER walked the entire Levi's Stadium during the first half of the football game and took 630 separate photographs of Defendant CITY OF SANTA CLARA POLICE DEPARTMENT law enforcement officers and other security personnel mostly standing around, bunched up in groups, tucked away in warm areas, not providing any strategic placement or zone coverage, not

31

PLAINTIFF'S COMPLAINT FOR DAMAGES

302

observing the crowd fan base. He also saw no law enforcement or security patrolling any of Levi's Stadium fan seating sections or any of Levi's Stadium main entry and exit gates.

152. As a direct and proximate result of the DEFENDANTS', and each of them, failure to properly hire, screen, train and/or supervise those members of their security team, Plaintiff is injured as explained more fully above.

153. Furthermore, Plaintiff is informed and believes, and thereon alleges, that the DEFENDANTS, and each of them, acted in conscious disregard of the safety of others, were aware of the probable dangerous consequences of their conduct and misfeasance, and willfully and deliberately failed to avoid those consequences. Specifically, Plaintiff is informed and believes, and thereon alleges, that the DEFENDANTS knew of the consequences of failing to staff, train, and hire qualified security personnel.

154. As a direct and proximate result of the conduct of the DEFENDANTS, and each of them, Plaintiff has suffered injury and damage in an amount to be shown according to proof at trial.

FOURTH CAUSE OF ACTION
GROSS NEGLECT OF DUTY – GROSS MISCONDUCT
(Against all DEFENDANTS)

155. Plaintiff refers to, repeats, and re-alleges each and every allegation in the preceding paragraphs of this Complaint and incorporates said allegations into this cause of action as though fully set forth herein.

156. Plaintiff is informed and believes, and thereon alleges, that on or about November 2, 2018 Defendant CITY OF SANTA CLARA POLICE DEPARTMENT violated California Penal Code 118.1 when their officers intentionally filed false police reports regarding the November 1, 2018 incident at Levi's Stadium.

157. Plaintiff is informed and believes, and thereon alleges, that the unconstitutional actions and/or omissions of Defendants, were pursuant to the following customs, policies, practices, and/or procedures of the SANTA CLARA POLICE DEPARTMENT and/or CITY OF SANTA CLARA, which were directed, encouraged, allowed, and/or ratified by DEFENDANT MICHAEL SELLERS and other policy making officers for the CITY OF SANTA CLARA,

32

PLAINTIFF'S COMPLAINT FOR DAMAGES

CITY OF SANTA CLARA STADIUM AUTHORITY, and the CITY OF SANTA CLARA POLICE DEPARTMENT:

    a.   To cover-up violations of constitutional rights by any or all of the following:

           i.   by failing to properly investigate and/or evaluate complaints or incidents;

           ii.   by ignoring and/or failing to properly and adequately investigate and discipline unconstitutional or unlawful police activity; and

           iii.   by allowing, tolerating, and/or encouraging police officers to: fail to file complete and accurate police reports; file false police reports; make false statements; to give false information and/or to attempt to bolster officers' stories; and/or obstruct or interfere with investigations of unconstitutional or unlawful police conduct, by withholding and/or concealing material information;

    b.   To allow, tolerate, and/or encourage a "code of silence" among law enforcement officers and police department personnel, whereby an officer or member of the department does not provide adverse information against a fellow officer or member of the department;

    c.   To fail to institute, require, and enforce necessary, appropriate and lawful policies, procedures, and training programs to prevent or correct the unconstitutional conduct, customs, and practices and procedures described in this Complaint and in sub-paragraphs (a) through (b), with deliberate indifference to the rights and safety of Plaintiff and the public, and in the face of an obvious need for such policies, procedures, and training programs; and

    d.   To use or tolerate inadequate, deficient, and improper procedures for handling, investigating, and reviewing complaints of officer misconduct made under California Government Code§ 910 et seq.

158. Plaintiff is also informed and believes, and hereon alleges, that there were various other similar recent incidents of Gross Neglect of Duty and Gross Misconduct by the Defendant SANTA CLARA POLICE DEPARTMENT including since at least 2016 that put the DEFENDANTS and each of them on notice of such extreme and outrageous behavior

33

PLAINTIFF'S COMPLAINT FOR DAMAGES

Fred Weaver – Plaintiff in Pro Per – www.UnsafeInAnySeat.com

159. Plaintiff is informed and believes, and thereon alleges, that the DEFENDANTS and each of them, including CITY OF SANTA CLARA, CITY OF SANTA CLARA STADIUM AUTHORITY, FORTY NINER DEFENDANTS and the NATIONAL FOOTBALL LEAGUE had prior knowledge that Defendants CITY OF SANTA CLARA POLICE DEPARTMENT have carried out their own recent criminal activity.

a. In April 2016, without a warrant, the City of Santa Clara Police kicked down a door of a San Jose resident injuring and breaking the resident's ankle, who was later paid a $6.7 million-dollar Federal Lawsuit settlement. City of Santa Clara Police Chief Mike Sellers insisted his cops acted responsibly. (*Danielle Harmon v. City of Santa Clara, City of Santa Clara Police Chief Mike Sellers, et al.*, United Stated District Court (ND CA 2016) Case no. 5:16-cv-04228-EJD)

b. Also, in 2016, the City of Santa Clara paid out a $500,000 settlement to a family for multiple illegal searches of their home by the City of Santa Clara Police. (*Moneeb, Ikram and Ikram v City of Santa Clara, Mike Sellers, et al.*, United States District Court (ND CA 2015), Case no. 5:15-cv-01987-NC)

160. Plaintiff is informed and believes, and thereon alleges that not a single Defendant CITY OF SANTA CLARA POLICE DEPARTMENT officer was terminated or disciplined for any of these illegal actions. Further, that there is not one documented resignation, condemnation or taking a stand against these illegal police activities from the Santa Clara Police Officers Association or any of its members.

161. Plaintiff is informed and believes, and thereon alleges, that the lack of consequences for violating policy, or even engaging in criminal misconduct, has fostered a culture of impunity to such behavior. Defendant CITY OF SANTA CLARA POLICE DEPARTMENT officers observe tacit approval of misconduct by supervisors, commanders, and Defendant City of Santa Clara Police Chief MICHAEL SELLERS, so the behavior continues.

162. Plaintiff is informed and believes, and thereon alleges, that policy and practice deficiencies surrounding leadership, accountability, communication and collaboration, technical expertise were not unique to the events set forth in this complaint and are systemic within the Defendant CITY OF SANTA CLARA POLICE DEPARTMENT and are historically and legacy influenced.

34

PLAINTIFF'S COMPLAINT FOR DAMAGES

163. These systematic patterns of violations and practices suggest gross mismanagement, a gross waste of funds, an abuse of authority, and a substantial and specific danger to public health and safety.

164. The willful gross neglect and intentional official wrongdoing by these public officers is a dereliction which, endangers and threatens the public welfare.

165. As per Defendant NFL Chief of Security CATHY LANIER, "Local police are the lead agency for every game throughout the season. A typical game requires at least 10 different agencies, from the FBI to private security." Plaintiff is informed and believes, and thereon alleges, that at all times herein mentioned, the persons acting as the managers, law enforcement or security personnel of Levi's Stadium located in Santa Clara, California, were the agents, servants and/or employees of Defendant SANTA CLARA POLICE DEPARTMENT. As such, the FBI and other law enforcement agencies and private security, accepted and ratified the illegal actions of Defendant SANTA CLARA POLICE DEPARTMENT and Defendant City of Santa Clara Police Chief MICHAEL SELLERS.

166. Plaintiff is informed and believes, and thereon alleges, that the unconstitutional actions and/or omissions of Defendants, as described above, were approved, tolerated and/or ratified by DEFENDANT SELLERS and other policy-making officers for the SCPD. Plaintiff is informed and believes, and thereupon alleges, that the details of these incidents have been revealed to the authorized policy makers within the CITY OF SANTA CLARA, FORTY NINER DEFENDANTS and the NATIONAL FOOTBALL LEAGUE, and Plaintiff is further informed and believes, and thereupon alleges, that such policy makers have direct knowledge of the facts of these illegal incidents. Plaintiff is informed and believes, and thereon alleges, that notwithstanding this knowledge, the authorized policy makers within the CITY OF SANTA CLARA, CITY OF SANTA CLARA STADIUM AUTHORITY, FORTY NINER DEFENDANTS and the NATIONAL FOOTBALL LEAGUE, have approved of the conduct of Defendant CITY OF SANTA CLARA POLICE DEPARTMENT, and have made a deliberate choice to endorse the decisions of those Defendant officers and the basis of those decisions. By doing so, the authorized policy makers of the CITY OF SANTA CLARA, CITY OF SANTA CLARA STADIUM AUTHORITY, FORTY NINER DEFENDANTS and the NATIONAL FOOTBALL LEAGUE, have shown affirmative agreement with each individual Defendant

35

PLAINTIFF'S COMPLAINT FOR DAMAGES

1 police officer's actions, and have ratified the unconstitutional acts of the individual Defendant

2 police officers. Furthermore, Plaintiff is informed and believes, and thereupon alleges, that

3 DEFENDANT SELLERS and other policy-making officers for the SCPD were and are aware of

4 a pattern of conduct and injury caused by SCPD law enforcement officers similar to the conduct

5 of Defendants described herein but failed to discipline culpable law enforcement officers and

6 failed to institute new police procedures and policy within the Defendant SANTA CLARA
   POLICE DEPARTMENT.

7   167. Plaintiff is informed and believes, and thereon alleges, that alarmingly, the FORTY

8 NINER DEFENDANTS, and Defendant NATIONAL FOOTBALL LEAGUE continue to allow

9 Defendant SANTA CLARA POLICE DEPARTMENT to be the lead agency for security at

10 Levi's Stadium.

11   168. Defendant CITY OF SANTA CLARA POLICE DEPARTMENT has refused to

12 produce records and police reports in response to Plaintiff's lawful requests for complete records

13 and information. Plaintiff reserves the right to amend this complaint with further facts and

14 substituting individuals for Doe Defendants after receiving DEFENDANT'S reports and records

15 in this matter.

16   169. DEFENDANTS, and each of them, owed Plaintiff and the general public a duty to

17 conduct their business activities, including monitoring, supervising, managing and controlling

18 the property, in a reasonably safe manner so as not to cause injury to others. Further,

19 DEFENDANTS, and each of them, owed Plaintiff and the general public a duty to train and

20 supervise their employees to conduct themselves in a reasonably safe manner so as not to injure
   others.

21   170. As a direct and proximate result of the negligence of DEFENDANTS, and each of

22 them, as hereinabove alleged, DEFENDANTS created a foreseeable risk of physical injury to

23 Plaintiff and as a result, Plaintiff has suffered injury, in an amount to be determined at trial.

24 ///

25 ///

26 ///

27 ///

///

28

36

PLAINTIFF'S COMPLAINT FOR DAMAGES

FIFTH CAUSE OF ACTION

DISCRIMINATION

(Against DEFENDANTS and DOES 41 through 60)

171. Plaintiff refers to, repeats, and re-alleges each and every allegation in the preceding paragraphs of this Complaint and incorporates said allegations into this cause of action as though fully set forth herein.

172. Plaintiff is informed and believes, and thereon alleges, that on or about November 1, 2018, Defendant CITY OF SANTA CLARA POLICE DEPARTMENT violated Plaintiff's Constitutional and 14th Amendment Equal Protection Rights protection of the law for Age, Disability, and Color Discrimination.

173. As Plaintiff was closely following Assailant Guardado, on the outer mezzanine and just before descending the Levi's Stadium Northeast Exit Gate 'F' stairs, Plaintiff finally encountered a Defendant CITY OF SANTA CLARA POLICE officer, positioned counter clockwise to the stairs less than 20 yards away. Plaintiff yelled at the top of his lungs, "Give me some help and arrest this guy, he just beat up and severely hurt another 49ers fan!" The Defendant Santa Clara Police Officer looked directly at Plaintiff, noticed Plaintiff was limping, and the Defendant CITY OF SANTA CLARA POLICE officer also acknowledged Plaintiff wearing a black Oakland Raiders jersey. The Defendant Santa Clara Police officer literally, and physically turned his back on Plaintiff avoiding any assistance with apprehension of the ASSAILANT and denying protection and security to the Plaintiff who was trying to keep ASSAILANT from harming any other Levi's Stadium patrons.

174. Defendant SANTA CLARA POLICE DEPARTMENT'S unlawful discrimination, unfair and unequal treatment of Plaintiff is based on each characteristic of Age, Disability, and Color. This claim of Discrimination satisfies the three preliminary requirements that apply throughout constitutional law; Court has Jurisdiction, Claim is Justiciable, and Harm was Caused by Government Action of DEFENDANTS.

175. By the actions and omissions described above, Defendants violated 42 U.S.C. §1983, depriving Plaintiff of the following clearly established and well-settled constitutional rights protected by the Fourteenth Amendment to U.S. Constitution.

37

PLAINTIFF'S COMPLAINT FOR DAMAGES

176. Plaintiff is informed and believes, and thereon alleges, that at all material times, each Defendant was jointly engaged in tortious activity, and an integral participant in the conduct described herein including the deprivation of Plaintiff's constitutional rights and other harm.

177. Plaintiff is informed and believes, and thereon alleges, that at all material times, and alternatively, the actions and omissions of each defendant were intentional, wanton and/or willful, conscience shocking, reckless, malicious, deliberately indifferent to Plaintiff's rights, done with actual malice, grossly negligent, negligent, and objectively unreasonable.

178. As a direct and proximate result of the conduct of the DEFENDANTS and each of them, DEFENDANTS have caused damage in an amount to be shown according to proof at trial.

179. The conduct of Defendants entitles Plaintiff to punitive damages and penalties allowable under 42 U.S.C. §1983 and California law.

180. Plaintiff is also entitled to reasonable costs and attorneys' fees under 42 U.S.C. §1988 and applicable California codes and laws.

SIXTH CAUSE OF ACTION
CONSPIRACY
(Against all DEFENDANTS)

181. Plaintiff refers to, repeats, and re-alleges each and every allegation in the preceding paragraphs of this Complaint and incorporates said allegations into this cause of action as though fully set forth herein.

182. Plaintiff is informed and believes and thereon alleges that on or about November 1, 2018 through and after January 8, 2019, DEFENDANTS conspired to conceal information, falsify reports, hide, and cover up any incriminating records.

183. Plaintiff is also informed and believes, and hereon alleges that Defendant City of Santa Clara City Manager DEANNA SANTANA was one of the central figures in orchestrating the laundering and filtering of Plaintiff's documented concerns with other Defendants about the lack of security at Levi's Stadium. Plaintiff is informed and believes, and thereon alleges, that the following recent history from media and court documented sources, show a clear pattern of questionable illegal actions taken during Defendant DEANNA SANTANA's career to suppress evidence and reports of Police Misconduct:

38

PLAINTIFF'S COMPLAINT FOR DAMAGES

Fred Weaver – Plaintiff in Pro Per – www.UnsafeInAnySeat.com

<u>City of San Jose - Deputy City Manager - May 1999 - August 2011</u>

1. In 2006, as Deputy City Manager for the City of San Jose, Deanna Santana attempted to launder reports about police misconduct including illegal searches and excessive force. According to an East Bay Express news article entitled, "*Deanna Santana Tried to Alter Damning Report*," dated September 19, 2012. "There is also evidence that this is not the first time that Santana appears to have attempted to dilute critical analysis of police actions. Deanna Santana was instructed by the San Jose City Council to analyze a report by Independent Police Auditor, Barbara Attard, highlighting San Jose PD's practice of downgrading Internal Affairs complaints against officers. Instead, Santana hired Macias Consulting Group, claiming auditor Attard had used "incorrect units." In response, Attard submitted a sharp rebuttal to the San Jose City Council that all but accused Santana and Macias of going out of the way to deflect attention away from the problem at hand."

2. Subsequently, "None of the twelve cases cited by the police auditor were ever investigated."

<u>City of Oakland - City Administrator - August 2011 - March 2014</u>

1. As the second most powerful city official in Oakland at the time, Deanna Santana as City Administrator of City of Oakland, attempted to launder the 'Frazier Report' about police misconduct and falsifying reports. The Frazier Report was commissioned in response to the aftermath of an October 25, 2011 City of Oakland Police response to Occupy Oakland, the response to which Deanna Santana herself authorized in her capacity as City Administrator. The Frazier Report stated, "In the wake of these events serious concerns were raised by both City Officials and the community at large concerning use of unreasonable force, overall police performance, and OPD's ability to manage future events in an acceptable manner." (Independent Investigation Occupy Oakland Response October 25, 2011 (Frazier Report), Frazier Group LLC - June 14, 2012). In the same East Bay article mentioned above, civil rights attorney Jim Chanin, who helped prepare the Frazier Report, battled with Santana and refused to send a Word copy of the unissued Frazier Report to Santana for her own editing. "A May 11 email from Frazier to Santana's email account at City Hall offered a glimpse into their argument about how much of the Frazier report's damning findings would become public."

39

2. Deanna Santana was also the central figure named in a whistleblower lawsuit after Santana fired Oakland's Director of Employee Relations, Daryelle Preston. The lawsuit stated Deanna Santana pressured Preston to lie on multiple occasions and falsify reports. Plaintiff Preston reported that Fire Chief Teresa Deloach Reed engaged in a violation of Oakland City Ordinance when Reed repeatedly directly negotiated and signed tentative agreements ("TAs") with Firefighters Local 55 without Ms. Preston present as Employee Relations Director or City Council authorization. By law, Ms. Preston must have obtained approval from the City Council for Reed to sign the contract. Santana assisted Reed in attempting to conceal Reed's unlawful negotiation and signature of TAs, and Santana retaliated against Ms. Preston when she reported Reed's acts to Santana and the City Attorney of Oakland. Defendant Santana responded to plaintiff Preston's reports to her regarding these violations of law, and to plaintiff's refusal to obey illegal orders, by (Santana) carrying out a series of adverse actions culminating in plaintiff Preston's termination. A jury agreed with Preston, awarding her $613,302 in damages. (*Daryelle Lawanna Preston v. City of Oakland; Deanna Santana, et al.,* Alameda County Superior Case no. RG14-717585, (2014)

3. It should also be noted, that during Deanna Santana's tenure at the City of Oakland, she had administrative oversight and was the 'boss' of the Building, Police, Fire and Planning Departments. On December 2, 2016, in Oakland, California, a fire broke out in an 'artist collective' warehouse, known as Ghost Ship. A total of 36 people were killed in the fire, the deadliest in the history of Oakland. Multiple factors contributed to these completely preventable deaths, including negligence by the City of Oakland's own Building Inspectors, Police, Fire, and Planning Departments. Police and Fire officials warned that the warehouse was a fire hazard but did not follow through on enforcing the codes already in place. The City of Oakland's Planning Director revealed that the building had not been inspected for three decades. (*IN RE Ghost Ship Fire Litigation,* Alameda County Superior Case no. RG16843631 (2017)

4. Deanna Santana was City Administrator during this period of negligence when Building, Police, Fire and Planning Departments, under Santana's management, were not enforcing

40

311

the codes which, if enforced under Santana's watch, would ultimately have saved 36 innocent lives.

<u>City of Santa Clara - City Manager - October 2017 to Present</u>

1. Defendant DEANNA SANTANA in her current position as City Manager at Santa Clara is again in charge of the Police Department in addition to being Executive Director of the City of Santa Clara Stadium Authority, which involves Santana overseeing contracts related to Levi's Stadium and the San Francisco 49ers.

2. Additionally, in a recent article from The Silicon Valley Voice, "Santa Clara Subject of State Pension Investigation," dated October 12, 2018, Deanna Santana's actions were the reason the City of Santa Clara was the subject of a State Pension Fraud investigation by CalPERS. A letter signed by Deanna Santana was revised and backdated for employment of an Assistant City Manager to Santana.

184. Furthermore, Plaintiff believes Defendant DEANNA SANTANA, based on her career conduct documented above, conspired with Defendant's CITY OF SANTA CLARA POLICE DEPARTMENT, CITY OF SANTA CLARA STADIUM AUTHORITY, FORTY NINER DEFENDANTS, and NATIONAL FOOTBALL LEAGUE Defendant CATHY LANIER and Defendant BILLY LANGENSTEIN to ensure Plaintiff's damning findings about the complete lack of security at Levi's Stadium would not become public.

185. Plaintiff is concerned about the risk of injury to any patron of any future event at Levi's Stadium and all other public venues and Plaintiff has communicated this on multiple occasions both orally and in writing, including certified communication to all DEFENDANTS.

186. Plaintiff acted in good faith as a Good Samaritan, to contain and restrain until his arrest and custody, the ASSAILANT, to keep the ASSAILANT from injuring any additional Levi's Stadium fans, due to the total lack of security on the part of the DEFENDANTS and each of them.

187. Plaintiff is informed and believes and thereon alleges as a drastic and preventative public relations measure starting on or about November 1, 2018, to avoid embarrassment and save face, the DEFENDANTS conspired and assisted Defendant SANTA CLARA POLICE DEPARTMENT Officers in the filing of false police reports regarding the previous day's savage assault at Levi's Stadium and subsequent arrest of the Assailant.

41

PLAINTIFF'S COMPLAINT FOR DAMAGES

188. Plaintiff is informed and believes, and thereon alleges, that on or about November 1, 2018, said DEFENDANTS, intentionally, willfully, wantonly, and maliciously conspired against Plaintiff against Plaintiff's actions taken to prevent any further acts of violence against other patrons at Levi's Stadium. The actions taken by Plaintiff were those that any reasonable person in Plaintiffs situation would have undertaken and were necessitated by DEFENDANTS' failure to perform the duties to the patrons of Levi's Stadium that they were obligated to provide.

189. Plaintiff is informed and believes and thereon alleges, that DOES 1 through 70, inclusive, ceased all communications with Plaintiff in furtherance of conspiring to conceal information, falsify reports, hide, bury, and make any incriminating records disappear, of which information may have posed a detrimental effect to the DEFENDANTS and especially a detrimental effect to the NATIONAL FOOTBALL LEAGUE in its efforts to protect the NFL 'Shield'.

190. The NFL is America's most successful sports organization, generating multi-billion-dollar profits and legions of devoted fans. On average, the NFL generates approximately $9,300,000,000.00 per year. As the organizer, marketer and face of professional football, the NFL zealously protects these profits and the game that produces them.

191. According to a February 1, 2017 Washington Post article, "Former police chief's (Defendant NFL Chief of Security CATHY LANIER) focus in new NFL gig is protecting the league's image," the article states "But there is a fundamental difference between protecting the public and protecting a corporate brand – the NFL or, to insiders, "the Shield." In this context, Lanier's charge isn't simply to keep fans safe. It's also to protect the league's image. For all its popularity, the NFL has an image problem that some believe is cutting into unrivaled hold on U.S. sports fans. The roots of that image problem are complex and lie, in large part, in the league's delayed response to the dangers."

192. Unfortunately, for patrons of Levi's Stadium, and all NFL Stadiums, after Plaintiff communicated the above safety and security concerns with Defendant NATIONAL FOOTBALL LEAGUE NFL Security Representative BILLY LANGENSTEIN on January 8, 2018, the Defendant NATIONAL FOOTBALL LEAGUE ceased all communication with Plaintiff, further evidencing the NFL "delayed response to dangers."

42

PLAINTIFF'S COMPLAINT FOR DAMAGES

193. DOES 1 through 100's extreme and outrageous behavior proximately caused and was a substantial factor in the injury and damages Plaintiff sustained as alleged more fully above.

194. Plaintiff is informed and believes and thereon alleges, that DOES 1 through 100 are those individuals, whose identities are not yet completely known, whose intentional conduct caused the aforesaid injury and damages of Plaintiff in Levi's Stadium on November 1, 2018.

195. As a direct and proximate result of the conduct of the DEFENDANTS, and each of them, and have caused the damages to Plaintiff in an amount to be shown according to proof at trial.

PRAYER FOR RELIEF

WHEREFORE, Plaintiff respectfully requests the following relief against each and every Defendant herein, jointly and severally:

a. compensatory and exemplary damages in an amount according to proof and which is fair, just and reasonable;

b. punitive damages under 42 U.S.C. §1983 and California law in an amount according to proof and which is fair, just, and reasonable;

c. all other damages, penalties, costs, interest, and attorneys' fees as allowed by 42 U.S.C. §§ 1983, and 1988; Cal. Code Civ. Proc.§ 1021.5, Cal. Civil Code § 52 et seq., 52.1, and as otherwise may be allowed by California and/or federal law;

d. Injunctive relief, including but not limited to the following:

1. An order prohibiting DEFENDANT CITY OF SANTA CLARA POLICE DEPARTMENT and its Chief of Police from engaging in the unconstitutional customs, policies, practices, procedures, training and supervision as may be determined and/or adjudged by this case;

2. An order prohibiting DEFENDANT CITY OF SANTA CLARA POLICE DEPARTMENT and their law enforcement officers from engaging in the "code of silence" as may be supported by the evidence in this case;

3. An order of Federal Oversight of DEFENDANT CITY OF SANTA CLARA POLICE DEPARTMENT, similar to recent Federal oversight of Chicago, Oakland, New York, Detroit, and Cincinnati Police Departments.

Fred Weaver – Plaintiff in Pro Per – www.UnsafeInAnySeat.com

43

PLAINTIFF'S COMPLAINT FOR DAMAGES

4. An order of Federal Oversight of DEFENDANT NATIONAL FOOTBALL LEAGUE to ensure all North American NFL Stadiums and Venues benefit from shared and uniform safety and security measures.

5. An order compelling DEFENDANTS to correct the deficiencies in security and failures to protect the public detailed in this complaint.

e. Attorney's fees in accordance with California Code of Civil Procedure Section 1021.5

f. Such other and further relief as this Court may deem appropriate.

DATED: May 1, 2019

_____
Frederick Leo Weaver
Plaintiff In pro per

DEMAND FOR JURY TRIAL

PLAINTIFF hereby requests a jury trial upon the claims so triable.

DATED: May 1, 2019

_____
Frederick Leo Weaver
Plaintiff In pro per

PLAINTIFF'S COMPLAINT FOR DAMAGES

APPENDIX # 6

May 31, 2019 - Ericksen Arbuthnot - Responses to Weaver Complaint

—⚏—

1	Nathaniel R. Lucey, Esq. (SBN 260796) Ian P. Wilson, Esq. (SBN 271075)
2	ERICKSEN ARBUTHNOT
3	San Jose, CA 95112 Tel:
4	Fax:
5	Attorneys for Defendant
6	LANDMARK EVENT STAFFING SERVICES, INC.
7	
8	SUPERIOR COURT OF CALIFORNIA
9	COUNTY OF SANTA CLARA

10	FREDERICK LEO WEAVER,	Case No. 19CV346749
11	Plaintiff,	**DEFENDANT LANDMARK EVENT**
12	v.	**STAFFING SERVICES, INC.'S** **NOTICE OF DEMURRER AND**
13	SAN FRANCISCO FORTY NINERS,	**DEMURRER TO PLAINTIFF'S**
14	LIMITED; SAN FRANCISCO FORTY NINERS II, LLC; FORTY NINERS FOOTBALL	**FIRST AMENDED COMPLAINT**
15	COMPANY, LLC; SAN FRANCSICO FORTY NINERS FOUNDATION; FORTY NINERS	Date: August 29, 2019 Time: 9:00 a.m.
16	STADIUM, LLC; FORTY NINERS STADIUM MANAGEMENT COMPANY, LLC; FORTY	Judicial Officer: Hon Peter H. Kirwan Dept. 19
17	NINERS HOLDINGS LP; FORTY NINERS HOLDINGS LLC; FORTY NINERS SC	Action Filed: May 1, 2019
18	STADIUM COMPANY, LLC; CITY OF	Trial Date: TBD
19	SANTA CLARA; SANTA CLARA STADIUM AUTHORITY; CITY OF SANTA CLARA CITY	
20	MANAGER DEANNA SANTANA; CITY OF SANTA CLARA POLICE DEPARTMENT;	
21	CITY OF SANTA CLARA POLICE CHIEF	
22	MICHAEL SELLERS; NATIONAL FOOTBALL LEAGUE; NATIONAL	
23	FOOTBALL LEAGUE COMMISSIONER ROGER GOODELL; NATIONAL FOOTBALL	
24	LEAGUE SENIOR VICE PRESIDENT OF SECURITY CATHY LANIER; NATIONAL	
25	FOOTBALL LEAGUE DIRECTOR	
26	INVESTIGATIONS & SECURITY SERVICES BILLY LANGENSTEIN; LANDMARK EVENT	
27	STAFFING SERVICES, INC., and DOES 1	
28	through 100, inclusive, Defendants.	

1

Notice of Demurrer and Demurrer to Plaintiff's Complaint

TO ALL PARTIES AND THEIR ATTORNEYS OF RECORD:

    PLEASE TAKE NOTICE that on August 29, 2019, at 9:00 a.m., or as soon thereafter as the matter may be heard, in Department 19 of the above-entitled Court, Defendant LANDMARK EVENT STAFFING SERVICES, INC. ("Defendant") will and hereby does demur to the Complaint of Plaintiff FREDERICK LEO WEAVER ("Plaintiff").

    This Demurrer is made on the grounds that the first, second, third, fourth, fifth and sixth causes of action of the Complaint fail to state facts sufficient to constitute causes of action against Defendant and/or are stated ambiguously and unintelligibly. Code of Civil Procedure section 430.10 (e).

    This Demurrer is based upon this Notice, the attached Demurrer and Memorandum of Points and Authorities, all records, papers and pleadings on file in this action, such oral arguments as the Court may consider at the hearing of this Demurrer, and any matters of which the Court may take judicial notice.

DATED: May 31, 2019

ERICKSEN ARBUTHNOT

NATHANIEL R. LUCEY, Esq.
IAN P. WILSON, Esq.
Attorneys for Defendant LANDMARK
EVENT STAFFING SERVICES, INC.

2

Notice of Demurrer and Demurrer to Plaintiff's Complaint

1	Nathaniel R. Lucey, Esq. (SBN 260796) Ian P. Wilson, Esq. (SBN 271075) ERICKSEN ARBUTHNOT
2	
3	San Jose. CA 95112
4	Tel: Fax:
5	Attorneys for Defendant
6	LANDMARK EVENT STAFFING SERVICES, INC.
7	
8	SUPERIOR COURT OF CALIFORNIA
9	COUNTY OF SANTA CLARA

10	FREDERICK LEO WEAVER, Plaintiff,	Case No. 19CV346749
11	v.	**MEMORANDUM OF POINTS AND AUTHORITIES IN SUPPORT**
12		**DEFENDANT LANDMARK EVENT**
13	SAN FRANCISCO FORTY NINERS, LIMITED; SAN FRANCISCO FORTY NINERS II, LLC; FORTY NINERS FOOTBALL	**STAFFING SERVICES, INC.'S** **DEMURRER TO COMPLAINT**
14	COMPANY, LLC; SAN FRANCSICO FORTY NINERS FOUNDATION; FORTY NINERS	Date: August 29, 2019 Time: 9:00 a.m.
15	STADIUM, LLC; FORTY NINERS STADIUM	Judicial Officer: Hon. Peter H. Kirwan Dept. 19
16	MANAGEMENT COMPANY, LLC; FORTY NINERS HOLDINGS LP; FORTY NINERS	Action Filed: May 1, 2019
17	HOLDINGS LLC; FORTY NINERS SC	Trial Date: TBD
18	STADIUM COMPANY, LLC; CITY OF SANTA CLARA; SANTA CLARA STADIUM	
19	AUTHORITY; CITY OF SANTA CLARA CITY MANAGER DEANNA SANTANA; CITY OF	
20	SANTA CLARA POLICE DEPARTMENT;	
21	CITY OF SANTA CLARA POLICE CHIEF MICHAEL SELLERS; NATIONAL	
22	FOOTBALL LEAGUE; NATIONAL FOOTBALL LEAGUE COMMISSIONER	
23	ROGER GOODELL; NATIONAL FOOTBALL LEAGUE SENIOR VICE PRESIDENT OF	
24	SECURITY CATHY LANIER; NATIONAL	
25	FOOTBALL LEAGUE DIRECTOR INVESTIGATIONS & SECURITY SERVICES	
26	BILLY LANGENSTEIN; LANDMARK EVENT STAFFING SERVICES, INC., and DOES 1	
27	through 100, inclusive,	
28	Defendants.	

0

Memorandum of Points and Authorities in Support of Defendant Landmark Event Staffing Services, Inc.'s Demurrer to Complaint

COMES NOW DEFENDANT LANDMARK EVENT STAFFING SERVICES, INC. (hereinafter "Landmark" or "Defendant") and submits the following memorandum of points and authorities in support of its Demurrer to each of plaintiff FREDERICK LEO WEAVER's (hereinafter the "Plaintiff") causes of action in the Complaint.

I. INTRODUCTION

Plaintiff's Complaint arises out of an assault at a San Francisco Forty-Niner game in November of 2018. Plaintiff was not the victim of the assault. He is one of the 68,000+ fans in attendance at the game. While he witnessed the attack and followed the assailant after the assault ended, he was not injured by the assailant. He brings this law suit as a concerned citizen who is critical of the security measures at Levi's Stadium and who believes that Santa Clara law enforcement and various other agencies are engaged in a cover-up.

Plaintiff pleads six (6) causes of action, including: (1) Negligence; (2) Premises Liability; (3) Negligent Hiring, Retention and Supervision; (4) Gross Misconduct; (5) Discrimination; and (6) Conspiracy. There are multiple flaws in each of Plaintiff's causes of action, but the primary one that dooms them all is that Plaintiff has not identified a duty owed to him that was actually breached. Plaintiff alleges the existence of a special relationship whereby a party owes a duty to protect certain individual from harm caused by third parties. While there is such a duty in the law, it was not breached in this case since Plaintiff was not injured by the assailant. Moreover, Plaintiff has not alleged any injury that can be linked to the breach of this duty, or any other.

II. STATEMENT OF ALLEGED FACTS

Plaintiff's complaint is based on an event which took place during a November 1, 2018 football game between the San Francisco Forty-Niners and the Oakland Raiders at Levi's Stadium in Santa Clara, California. Plaintiff, a Raiders fan, attended the game with his daughter and wore an Oakland Raiders jersey. (See Complaint Page 9-10, Paragraph 41-42.) Plaintiff purchased tickets for himself and his daughter, and both were seated in Section 221, which is located in an upper deck of the stadium. (See Complaint Page 10, Paragraph 43.) Plaintiff alleges he witnessed a fight break out between two Forty-Niner fans, Assailant and Vincent Crain ("Victim") in Lower Field Section 119, which is located at field level. (See Complaint Page 10, Paragraph 45.)

1

321

1   Plaintiff claims that law enforcement and security staff did not intervene as the fight appeared

2   to escalate. (See Complaint Page 9-10, Paragraph 45-47.) Plaintiff, concerned, "acted alone" and

3   "rushed down the steps" from the upper deck to confront Assailant as he escaped. (See Complaint

4   Pages 9-10, Paragraph 47 and Page 13, Paragraph 56.) Once Plaintiff reached the lower deck after

5   working his way down from his assigned seat, it is alleged that he attempted to initially apprehend

6   Assailant, who was still trying to flee. (See Complaint Page 9-10, Paragraphs 47-48.).

7   Plaintiff alleges that he observed no law enforcement officers present on the lower deck, but

8   that a woman in black "security attire" was present. (See Complaint Page 11, Paragraph 49.)

9   Plaintiff then alleges that he screamed "at the top of his lungs" for the security guard to call for

10   backup or further assistance; however, the Complaint does not further allege whether the guard

11   actually called for help or whether the guard attempted to assist Plaintiff, before Plaintiff set off

12   again on his chase. (See Complaint Page 10, Paragraph 49.)

13   Following the alleged experience with the unidentified security guard, Plaintiff then alleges he

14   tried to "intercept" and "confront" Assailant himself, but was thwarted by Assailant's companion.

15   (See Complaint Page 11, Paragraph 49.)   Undeterred, Plaintiff alleges he continued to pursue

16   Assailant and repeatedly called for help until an unnamed California Highway Patrol officer, with

17   the help of the Santa Clara Police Department, apprehended Assailant at or near the Northeast Exit

18   Gate F. (See Complaint Page 11-12, Paragraph 49.) Plaintiff estimates that the entire subject

19   incident, from start to finish, lasted about fifteen to twenty minutes. (See Complaint Page 12-13,

20   Paragraph 54.) During that time, Plaintiff alleges that he observed no police officers or security

21   staff while he travelled roughly three-quarters of the way around Levi's stadium to catch Assailant;

22   Plaintiff also claims that despite the great pain the chase caused him, he was nonetheless

23   determined to apprehend Assailant and continued to walk after him. (See Complaint Page 12-13,

24   Paragraphs 51-54.)

25   Plaintiff is unclear as to the timing of his alleged encounter with an officer, and as to the facts

26   with respect to what actually occurred; however, Plaintiff alleges that at some point during his

27   pursuit of Assailant, he observed a uniformed CITY OF SANTA CLARA POLICE officer

28   ("officer") standing roughly 20 yards away. (See Complaint Page 12, Paragraph 51.) Plaintiff

2

1   claims he again yelled "at the top of lungs" for support. (See Complaint Page 12, Paragraph 51.).

2   It is alleged that the uniformed officer (1) noticed Plaintiff was limping, (2) noticed that Plaintiff

3   was wearing an Oakland Raiders jersey, and (3) turned around, presumably ignoring any further

4   cries for help. (See Complaint Page 12, Paragraph 51.) Officers apprehended Assailant in the

5   stadium. (See Complaint, Page 12, Paragraph 53.)

6   Plaintiff alleges that he underwent right hip replacement surgery approximately 15 days after

7   the subject incident occurred. No further facts are given regarding the procedure or why Plaintiff

8   needed a hip replacement. (See Complaint Page 12, Paragraph 51.).

9   The remainder of Plaintiff's allegations are related to the supposed failure of certain named

10   public entity Defendants to investigate the November 1, 2018 incident and/or allegations of those

11   entities potentially (1) covering up their alleged sub-standard response to the subject incident and

12   (2) stonewalling Plaintiff's own investigation of the event and subsequent investigation. (See

13   Complaint Page 13, Paragraphs 56-195.) Plaintiff makes no specific mention of Landmark with

14   respect to these claims.

15   Plaintiff filed his Complaint on May 1, 2019. Plaintiff mentions Landmark specifically only

16   twice on pages five (5) and six (6): Plaintiff alleges that Landmark does business in Santa Clara

17   County and that it provides "security services" at Levi's Stadium. (See Complaint Page 5-6,

18   Paragraphs 20-22) Plaintiff makes no specific mention of Landmark again for the remaining 39

19   pages of the Complaint, nor does Plaintiff define how Landmark responded to the subject incident

20   or what specific role Landmark played in the incident.

21   **III.   LEGAL STANDARD**

22   A demurrer may be sustained where the pleading does not state facts sufficient to constitute

23   a cause of action or where the person who filed the pleading does not have the legal capacity to

24   sue. Cal. Civ. Code §§430.10(b) & (e). In ruling on a demurrer, the Court looks to the face of the

25   complaint, and upon matters of which the Court may take judicial notice. *Franz v Blackwell* (1987)

26   189 Cal. App. 3d 91, 94. A complaint's material factual allegations are presumed to be true, but

27   this presumption may be rebutted or contradicted by attached documents or facts of which the

28   Court may take judicial notice. Cal. Civ. Code §430.10. Furthermore, the Court may take judicial

3

**Memorandum of Points and Authorities in Support of Defendant Landmark Event Staffing Services, Inc.'s
Demurrer to Complaint**

323

1 notice of facts and propositions that are not reasonably subject to dispute and are capable of
2 immediate and accurate determination by resort to sources of reasonably indisputable accuracy.
3 Cal Evid. Code section 452(h). The Court may take judicial notice of documents that are referred
4 to in the Complaint but are not attached to the Complaint. *Fremont Indemnity Co. v. Fremont*
5 *General Corp.* (2007) 148 Cal.App.4th 97, 133.

6   Additionally, although the allegations are presumed to be true, the Court does not accept
7 bare legal conclusion as true for purposes of ruling on a demurrer. *Serrano v. Priest* (1971) 5 Cal.
8 3d, 584, 591. It is not up to the judge to figure out how the complaint can be amended to state a
9 cause of action. The burden is on the plaintiff to show in what manner he or she can amend the
10 complaint, and how that amendment will change the legal effect of the pleading. *Goodman v.*
11 *Kennedy* (1976) 18 Cal. 3d 349, 354. Furthermore, leave to amend should be denied where the
12 facts are not in dispute and the nature of the claim is clear, but no liability exits under substantive
13 law. *Lawrence v. Bank of America* (1985) 163 Cal. App. 3d 431, 436.

14 **IV.   ARGUMENT**

15   As a preliminary matter, Plaintiff does not properly explain the role that Landmark allegedly
16 played either during the subject incident or the supposed cover-up following the subject incident.
17 Therefore, Landmark cannot determine with reasonable certainty, what specific causes of action
18 are raised against it. Plaintiff's current Complaint simply lumps together each and every named
19 defendant under the phrase "DEFENDANTS" without explaining how each committed the various
20 causes of action in the Complaint. Given this, it is difficult if not impossible for Landmark to
21 address each cause of action without greater factual specificity by Plaintiff. For this reason alone,
22 the Complaint should be dismissed.

23   **A. The First, Second, Third, Fourth, Fifth and Sixth Causes of Action Fail to Establish**
24   **Plaintiff Has Standing to Sue.**

25   Inherent to any lawsuit is the need for a party to be the "real party in interest" with respect to
26 the claim sued upon. Except as otherwise provided by statute, "every action must be prosecuted
27 in the name of the real party in interest." [Cal Code Civ Proc § 367 see *Dino v. Pelayo* (2006) 145
28 CA4th 347, 353, fn. 2 (citing text) 51 CR3d 620, 624; *Cloud v. Northrop Grumman Corp.* (1998)

1   67 CA4th 995, 1004, 79 CR2d 544, 549 (citing text).] Further, and for purposes here, a person

2   invoking judicial process *must* have a real interest in the ultimate adjudication, having suffered (or

3   about to suffer) "an injury of sufficient magnitude reasonably to assure that all the relevant facts

4   and issues will be adequately presented." *Iglesia Evangelica Latina, Inc. v. Southern Pac. Latin*

5   *American Dist. of Assemblies of God* (2009) 173 CA4th 420, 445, 93 CR3d 75, 94. In other words,

6   a party must have suffered a real and *identifiable* injury resulting from the conduct of the

7   defendant. Plaintiff, however, has not established that he suffered an injury sufficient to satisfy the

8   requirements set forth above.

9   In his Complaint, Plaintiff makes clear that he is bringing this lawsuit based upon the duty

10   certain businesses have to protect patrons from the criminal conduct of third parties. (See

11   Complaint Pages 7-8 Paragraph 31) To be the real party in interest to sue for the breach of this

12   duty, one must have been injured by a third party's criminal conduct.

13   Here, the Complaint alleges that Plaintiff witnessed an assault, not that he was a victim of one.

14   The real party in interest here would be the assault victim, Vincent Crain. The Complaint does not

15   explain why Plaintiff, as one of the 68,000 fans who was present during the game in question, can

16   sue in place of, or on behalf of, Mr. Crain.

17   Although it is not entirely clear, Plaintiff appears to claim that the Defendants owed a duty *to*

18   *him* to apprehend the assailant faster than they did. Plaintiff offers no authority for imposing this

19   legal duty. Nor does he offer any authority that the duty to protect patrons from third-party criminal

20   conduct includes apprehending the assailant in a timely manner after the criminal conduct has

21   concluded.

22   In short, if there was a duty owed to protect fans from third party criminal conduct, the real

23   party in interest that may sue in this instance is Mr. Crain.

24   The same standing principle(s) applicable to Plaintiff's four causes of action based on

25   negligence are applicable to his fifth and sixth causes of action, and arguably more so.

26   With respect to the fifth cause of action, Plaintiff fails to allege how he was injured by the

27   discriminatory conduct of public officers. Plaintiff alleges that he was discriminated against and

28   his constitutional rights were violated because an officer did not respond to his request that the

1   officer apprehend the assailant. [Complaint Page 37, Paragraph 173]. However, Plaintiff has not

2   identified a legal right, constitutional or otherwise, to have the assailant arrested. Nor has he

3   explained how the failure of the officer to arrest the assailant harmed him. He also does not manage

4   to specifically allege that Landmark showed any disparate treatment towards him.

5   Regarding the sixth cause of action, Plaintiff does not explain how he, or anyone for that

6   matter, was *specifically* harmed by any alleged conspiracy by Defendants to stymie his

7   independent investigation of the subject incident or to cover up any alleged instance(s) of

8   wrongdoing. Therefore, those claims are also deficient.

9   As a result of Plaintiff's lack of standing to bring suit, and each and every cause of action

10 should fail as a matter of law.

11
12 **B. The First, Second, Third and Fourth Causes of Action Fail to State Causes of Action for Negligence.**

13   Plaintiff has brought four causes of action against Landmark under a negligence theory. In

14 order to establish liability on a negligence theory, a plaintiff must prove duty, breach, causation,

15 and damages. *Conroy v. Regents of University of California*, 45 Cal.4th 1244, 1257 [91 Cal.Rptr.3d

16 532, 203 P.3d 1127] (2009). Plaintiff's negligence claim fails as to each of these elements.

17 *Duty and Breach*

18   "A duty of care is an essential element of a negligence cause of action. 'The determination

19 whether a particular relationship supports a duty of care rests on policy and is a question of law.'"

20 *University of Southern California v. Superior Court*, 30 Cal.App.5th 429, 439 [241 Cal.Rptr.3d

21 616] (2018) [Citations omitted.] Courts have invoked the concept of duty to limit the otherwise

22 potentially infinite liability which would follow from every negligent act. *Ibid.*

23   Plaintiff alleges in his Complaint that the Defendants, including Landmark, owed a "special"

24 or heightened duty "to exercise reasonable care to protect patrons from injury at the hands of fellow

25 guests." (See Complaint Pages 7-8, Paragraphs 30-32.) Plaintiff is correct that, under the special

26 relationship doctrine, some businesses owe a duty to their patrons to protect against foreseeable

27 criminal conduct. *Delgado v. Trax Bar & Grill*, 36 Cal.4th 224, 225 [30 Cal.Rptr.3d 145, 113 P.3d

28 1159] (2005). However, even if Landmark had a special relationship with the Plaintiff that required

1 | it to protect him from the criminal conduct of others, there was no breach of this duty as to Plaintiff.

2 | As pointed out above, Plaintiff was not the victim of a crime, Mr. Crain was.

3 | In reality, Plaintiff contends Defendants owed a duty to him to quickly apprehend a person

4 | who committed a crime against another person. This is a dubious proposition. The existence and

5 | scope of a legal duty is a question of law for the court to determine on a case-by-case basis.

6 | *Thompson v. Sacramento City Unified School Dist.,* 107 Cal.App.4th 1352, 1364 [132 Cal.Rptr.2d

7 | 748] (2003). In determining a duty's existence and scope, courts take into account several factors:

8 | the foreseeability of harm to the plaintiff, the degree of certainty that the plaintiff suffered injury,

9 | the closeness of the connection between the defendant's conduct and the injury suffered, the moral

10 | blame attached to the defendant's conduct, the policy of preventing future harm, the extent of the

11 | burden to the defendant and consequences to the community of imposing a duty to exercise care

12 | with resulting liability for breach, and the availability, cost, and prevalence of insurance for the

13 | risk involved. *Castaneda v. Olsher,* 41 Cal.4th 1205, 1206 [63 Cal.Rptr.3d 99, 162 P.3d 610]

14 | (2007).

15 | The foreseeability factor and certainty of injury factor here are exceedingly low. That the

16 | assailant assaulted Mr. Crain does not make it foreseeable that a spectator that chooses to follow

17 | him will have pain in his leg and later need hip surgery. There is no connection between the injury

18 | suffered and the Defendants' conduct. Moreover, imposing a duty on Defendants would impose

19 | an untenable burden, as it would eliminate law enforcement's and security personnel's discretion

20 | as to how to best address and suppress criminal conduct. Plaintiff is demanding that law

21 | enforcement and security personnel be dutybound to take direction from him and other concerned

22 | citizen vigilantes, regardless of the risk. The police do not have to take orders from an amateur

23 | crimefighter.

24 | Plaintiff also appears to claim that, as an Oakland Raiders season ticket holder, the Defendants

25 | owed him a duty to make sure that no criminal conduct interfered with his enjoyment of the game.

26 | (Complaint Pages 10, 22, Paragraph 42, 96) It is unclear how the Forty-Niners or anyone associated

27 | with Levi's Stadium would owe Plaintiff a legal duty by virtue of him holding season tickets to

28 | another NFL team. In any event, the factors above weigh against finding that Defendants had a

7

Memorandum of Points and Authorities in Support of Defendant Landmark Event Staffing Services, Inc.'s
Demurrer to Complaint

327

1   duty to apprehend the assailant so that Plaintiff could enjoy the game.

2   **Breach**

3   As discussed above, if there is no duty, there can be no breach of that duty. To the extent the

4   Defendants owed Plaintiff a duty to protect him from criminal conduct, they have fulfilled that

5   duty.

6   **Causation**

7   This Court requires that Plaintiff Weaver must prove that the Defendant Landmark owed a

8   specific duty to him and that its failure to perform that duty was the proximate or legal cause of

9   the resulting injury. *Ladd v. County of San Mateo* (1996) 12 Cal.4th 913, 917 [50 Cal.Rptr.2d 309,

10   911 P.2d 496]. Absence of proximate or legal cause, in some circumstances, may be decided as a

11   matter of law. *Weissich v. County of Marin,* 224 Cal.App.3d 1069, 1084 [274 Cal.Rptr. 342]

12   (1990); *Bettencourt v. Hennessy Industries, Inc.,* 205 Cal.App.4th 1103, 1123 [141 Cal.Rptr.3d

13   167] (2012). As pled, Plaintiff has not demonstrated how Defendants' failure to apprehend the

14   assailant caused his leg pain. Plaintiff's leg pain was the result of him walking, something he would

15   have otherwise engaged in regardless of Defendant's conduct. In short, the facts as alleged do not

16   establish either legal or proximate cause as a matter of law.

17   **Injury and Damages**

18   Plaintiff's fourth cause of action for gross negligence focuses on various misdeeds of the Santa

19   Clara Police Department, including falsifying police reports. Plaintiff does not allege how this

20   resulted in any damages to him or anyone else.

21   **C. The Fifth Cause of Action Fails to State a Claim for Which Relief May Be Granted.**

22   Plaintiff's fifth cause of action is based upon the protections afforded to him pursuant to the

23   Equal Protection Clause of the 14th Amendment as enumerated in Article III of the United States

24   Constitution. Plaintiff's allegations include, but are not necessarily limited to the following:

25   "Plaintiff is informed and believes and thereon alleges, that on or about November 1, 2018,

26   Defendant CITY OF SANTA CLARA POLICE DEPARTMENT ("Department") violated

27   Plaintiff's Constitutional and 14th Amendment Equal Protection Rights protection of the law for

28   Age, Disability, and Color Discrimination." (See Complaint Page 37, Paragraph 172-175.) The

8

1   foregoing allegation stems from an alleged incident in which a uniformed officer from the

2   Department supposedly ignored Plaintiff's cries for assistance apprehending Assailant and instead

3   turned his back to Plaintiff. (See Complaint Page 37, Paragraph 172.) This particular cause of

4   action is defective for a number of reasons; however, it is chiefly defective because (1) Landmark

5   is not a state actor or even an alleged actor; (2) no disparate conduct by the officer has been alleged

6   by Plaintiff; 3) Plaintiff had no right to have officer assist him in apprehending criminals; and 4)

7   Plaintiff suffered no damages.

8   *First*, while the alleged act by the officer is arguably a state action, because the officer in

9   question is an employee of the CITY OF SANTA CLARA ("City") and therefore an agent of a

10   public entity or government agency acting on behalf of City while providing security, Plaintiff

11   fails to allege that an agent of Landmark assisted the officer or was even *present* during Plaintiff's

12   alleged encounter with the officer. The foregoing is applicable here, because the Fourteenth

13   Amendment, by its terms, limits discrimination only by governmental entities, not by private

14   parties. The U.S. Supreme Court provides that, absent very exceptional circumstances, the

15   Constitution does not limit private conduct, no matter how discriminatory or wrongful: "It is state

16   action of a particular character that is prohibited. Individual invasion of individual rights is not

17   the subject-matter of the amendment. It has a deeper and broader scope." *Civil Rights Cases,* 109

18   U.S., 3. (1883)

19   Again, Landmark is a private security staffing company which contracts privately with Levi's

20   Stadium, itself a privately controlled entity, to provide *inter alia* protection and/or aid for attendees

21   at public and private sporting events and other events. While it may coordinate events with the

22   help of law enforcement or other government bodies, it does not hold itself out as a public entity,

23   or do business as one.

24   *Secondly*, even assuming Plaintiff could establish that Landmark represents a public entity to

25   any degree, he has not alleged that the officer or a Landmark agent treated him differently on the

26   basis of race, age or disability. The facts merely allege that Plaintiff yelled for help very loudly

27   and that the officer (1) looked "directly" at Plaintiff after turning around, (2) "acknowledged"

28   Plaintiff was wearing an Oakland Raiders jersey and "noticed" his limp and then (3) turned around

9

329

1 | and ignored the Plaintiff. (See Complaint Page 37, Paragraph 173.)

2 | Lastly, Plaintiff has not identified either an underlying right that was violated or an injury that

3 | arose from the alleged discrimination. As discussed above, Plaintiff does not have a right to have

4 | law enforcement and security personnel follow his orders or arrest individuals on his command.

5 | Nor has Plaintiff alleged how he was harmed by this alleged discrimination.

6 | **D. The Sixth Cause of Action Fails to State a Claim for Which Relief May Be Granted.**

7 | Plaintiff's sixth cause of action is based upon the theory of conspiracy in that Plaintiff alleges

8 | Defendants conspired, without specifying exactly which entities conspired or exactly *how* they

9 | conspired, to cover up alleged wrongdoing with respect to so-called lapses in security detail in and

10 | around Levi's Stadium and further conspired to allegedly stall Plaintiff's painstaking efforts to

11 | uncover this apparent wrongdoing. However, for Plaintiff to impose liability upon Landmark

12 | based on conspiracy, he must first allege that there was a common plan that Landmark shared with

13 | other immediate tortfeasors to commit a tort. *Applied Equipment Corp. v. Litton Saudi Arabia*,

14 | (1993) Cal. LEXIS 1529, 93 Cal. Daily Op. Service 1971, 93 Daily Journal DAR 3533. The cause

15 | of action is inapplicable to Landmark for two (2) reasons:

16 | (1) Save for lumping Landmark and the additional parties in interest together as

17 | "DEFENDANTS," Plaintiff fails to mention Landmark specifically during the whole of his

18 | discussion dedicated to conspiracy. Therefore, he does not establish that any shared plan with

19 | respect to Landmark existed. In effect, Plaintiff does not establish that Landmark actually

20 | conspired with anyone else to commit the requisite underlying tort or series of torts.

21 | (2) To the extent the other causes of action are dismissed, so too should this cause of action

22 | be dismissed. "Conspiracy is not an independent tort; it cannot create a duty or abrogate an

23 | immunity." *Id.* at 514. Because Plaintiff has not established any additional claims attributable to

24 | Landmark, then, accordingly, this cause of action should also fail.

25 | **V.   CONCLUSION**

26 | Based on the foregoing, Defendant Landmark respectfully requests that this Court sustain this

27 | //

28 | //

Memorandum of Points and Authorities in Support of Defendant Landmark Event Staffing Services, Inc.'s
Demurrer to Complaint

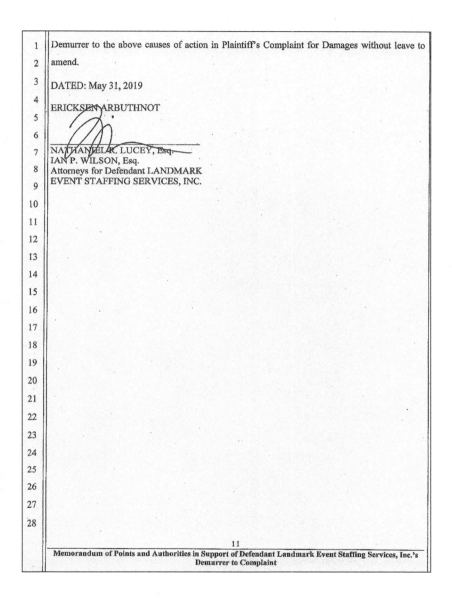

1 Demurrer to the above causes of action in Plaintiff's Complaint for Damages without leave to

2 amend.

3 DATED: May 31, 2019

4 ERICKSEN ARBUTHNOT

5

6

7 NATHANIEL R. LUCEY, Esq.
   IAN P. WILSON, Esq.

8 Attorneys for Defendant LANDMARK
   EVENT STAFFING SERVICES, INC.

9

10

11

12

13

14

15

16

17

18

19

20

21

22

23

24

25

26

27

28

11

Memorandum of Points and Authorities in Support of Defendant Landmark Event Staffing Services, Inc.'s Demurrer to Complaint

APPENDIX # 7

June 3, 2019 - Lombardi, Loper, & Conant, LLP - Responses to Weaver Complaint

—⚭—

<table>
<tr><td>1</td><td>MARIA M. LAMPASONA, State Bar No. 259675</td></tr>
<tr><td>2</td><td>TAYLOR J. POHLE, State Bar No. 299794</td></tr>
<tr><td>3</td><td>LOMBARDI, LOPER & CONANT, LLP</td></tr>
<tr><td>4</td><td>Oakland, CA 94612
Telephone:</td></tr>
<tr><td>5</td><td>Facsimile:</td></tr>
<tr><td>6</td><td>*Attorneys for Defendants*
[SAN FRANCISCO FORTY NINERS</td></tr>
<tr><td>7</td><td>LIMITED, SAN FRANCISCO FORTY
NINERS II, LLC, FORTY NINERS</td></tr>
<tr><td>8</td><td>FOOTBALL COMPANY LLC (erroneously
sued as "FORTY NINERS FOOTBALL</td></tr>
<tr><td>9</td><td>COMPANY, LLC"); and the other
defendants listed on pg. 5.]</td></tr>
</table>

SUPERIOR COURT OF THE STATE OF CALIFORNIA

COUNTY OF SANTA CLARA

FREDERICK LEO WEAVER, Plaintiff, v. SAN FRANCISCO FORTY NINERS LIMITED; SAN FRANCISCO FORTY NINERS II, LLC; FORTY NINERS FOOTBALL COMPANY, LLC; SAN FRANCISCO FORTY NINERS FOUNDATION; FORTY NINERS STADIUM, LLC; FORTY NINERS STADIUM MANAGEMENT COMPANY, LLC; FORTY NINERS HOLDINGS LP; FORTY NINERS HOLDINGS LLC; FORTY NINERS SC STADIUM COMPANY, LLC; CITY OF SANTA CLARA; SANTA CLARA STADIUM AUTHORITY; CITY OF SANTA CLARA CITY MANAGER DEANNA SANTANA; CITY OF SANTA CLARA POLICE DEPARTMENT; CITY OF SANTA CLARA POLICE CHIEF MICHAEL SELLERS; NATIONAL FOOTBALL LEAGUE; NATIONAL FOOTBALL LEAGUE COMMISSIONER ROGER GOODELL; NATIONAL FOOTBALL	Case No. 19CV346749 **DECLARATION OF TAYLOR J. POHLE, PURSUANT TO CODE OF CIVIL PROCEDURE SECTION 430.41(a)(2), REGARDING THE FORTY NINERS DEFENDANTS, THE CITY DEFENDANTS, AND THE NFL DEFENDANTS' INABILITY TO MEET AND CONFER** Action Filed: May 1, 2019 Trial Date: None Set

1

DECLARATION PURSUANT TO CODE OF CIVIL PROCEDURE SECTION 430.41(a)(2)

LOMBARDI, LOPER & CONANT, LLP

1	LEAGUE SENIOR VICE PRESIDENT
	OF SECURITY CATHY LANIER;
2	NATIONAL FOOTBALL LEAGUE
	DIRECTOR INVESTIGATIONS &
3	SECURITY SERVICES BILLY
	LANGSTEIN; LANDMARK EVENT
4	STAFFING SERVICES, INC.; and DOES
	1 through 100, INCLUSIVE,
5	
	Defendants.
6	

7   I, Taylor J. Pohle, declare:

8   I am an attorney licensed to practice before all courts in the State of California and an

9   associate at the law firm of Lombardi, Loper & Conant LLP, attorneys of record for defendants

10 SAN FRANCISCO FORTY NINERS LIMITED; SAN FRANCISCO FORTY NINERS II, LLC;

11 FORTY NINERS FOOTBALL COMPANY LLC (erroneously sued as "FORTY NINERS

12 FOOTBALL COMPANY, LLC); SAN FRANCISCO FORTY NINERS FOUNDATION;

13 FORTY NINERS STADIUM, LLC; FORTY NINERS STADIUM MANAGEMENT

14 COMPANY LLC (erroneously sued as "FORTY NINERS STADIUM MANAGEMENT

15 COMPANY, LLC"); FORTY NINERS HOLDINGS LP; FORTY NINERS HOLDINGS LLC;

16 FORTY NINERS SC STADIUM COMPANY LLC (erroneously sued as "FORTY NINERS SC

17 STADIUM COMPANY, LLC") (collectively, the "Forty Niners Defendants"); CITY OF SANTA

18 CLARA; SANTA CLARA STADIUM AUTHORITY; CITY OF SANTA CLARA CITY

19 MANAGER DEANNA SANTANA; CITY OF SANTA CLARA POLICE DEPARTMENT;

20 CITY OF SANTA CLARA POLICE CHIEF MICHAEL SELLERS (collectively, the "City

21 Defendants") NATIONAL FOOTBALL LEAGUE; NATIONAL FOOTBALL LEAGUE

22 COMMISSIONER ROGER GOODELL; NATIONAL FOOTBALL LEAGUE SENIOR VICE

23 PRESIDENT OF SECURITY CATHY LANIER; NATIONAL FOOTBALL LEAGUE

24 DIRECTOR INVESTIGATIONS & SECURITY SERVICES BILLY LANGSTEIN (collectively,

25 the "NFL Defendants") (and all together collectively, "All Defendants") in the above-referenced

26 matter. I have personal knowledge of the facts contained in this Declaration and if called to

27 testify thereto, I could and would do so competently.

28

2

DECLARATION PURSUANT TO CODE OF CIVIL PROCEDURE SECTION 430.41(a)(2)

(left margin) LOMBARDI, LOPER & CONANT, LLP

LOMBARDI, LOPER & CONANT, LLP

1.   Plaintiff Frederick Leo Weaver, in *propia persona*, filed this action May 1, 2019 and served copies of the Summons and Complaint on All Defendants on May 3, 2019. In this case, my firm was retained to represent the Forty Niners Defendants on or about May 8, 2019, the City Defendants on or about May 14, 2019, and the NFL Defendants on or about May 24, 2019. It is unclear from the Complaint whether City Attorney Brian Doyle is a named defendant because he is omitted from the case caption, but the body of the Complaint references him as a defendant. To the extent Plaintiff intended City Attorney Brian Doyle as a named defendant, and although my firm does not represent Mr. Doyle at this time, I would anticipate that my firm would be called upon to provide Mr. Doyle representation in regards to this matter.

2.   Plaintiff's Complaint for Damages exceeds forty (40) pages. The allegations identify six (6) causes of action against each and every defendant, including: (1) "Negligence"; (2) "Premises Liability – Failure to Provide Safe Premises – Dangerous Condition of Public Property"; (3) "Negligent Stadium Security – Negligent Hiring, Supervision, and Supervision"; (4) "Gross Neglect of Duty – Gross Misconduct"; (5) "Discrimination"; and (6) "Conspiracy." As to All Defendants, the Complaint for Damages seeks compensatory damages, exemplary damages, attorneys' fees, injunctive relief, and further relief as the Court deems appropriate.

3.   My firm's review and analysis of Plaintiff's Complaint for Damages revealed that each cause of action identified in the Complaint for Damages, as to All Defendants, is subject to demurrer for failure to state a viable cause of action under California law, on multiple grounds in some cases. The Complaint for damages is also subject to demurrer for uncertainty. The bases on which demurrer is appropriate are extensively briefed in a fifteen (15) page meet and confer letter addressed to Plaintiff, which is dated June 3, 2019. A true and correct copy of my June 3, 2019 letter to Plaintiff is attached as **Exhibit A**.

4.   Because the Complaint is subject to demurrer on so many grounds as to each of the 19 defendants that my firm represents, because the allegations are lengthy and complex, and because Plaintiff is self-represented, the parties would never have been able to adequately meet and confer 5 days before the responsive pleading deadline. Accordingly, All Defendants will file responsive pleadings by July 3, 2019 pursuant to Code of Civil Procedure section 430.41(a)(2),

3

DECLARATION PURSUANT TO CODE OF CIVIL PROCEDURE SECTION 430.41(a)(2)

1   unless good cause warrants a further extension.

2   I declare under penalty of perjury under the laws of the State of California that the

3   foregoing is true and correct. Executed in Oakland, California on June 3, 2019.

4

5   TAYLOR J. POHLE

6

7

8

9

10

11

12

13

14

15

16

17

18

19

20

21

22

23

24

25

26

27

28

4
DECLARATION PURSUANT TO CODE OF CIVIL PROCEDURE SECTION 430.41(a)(2)

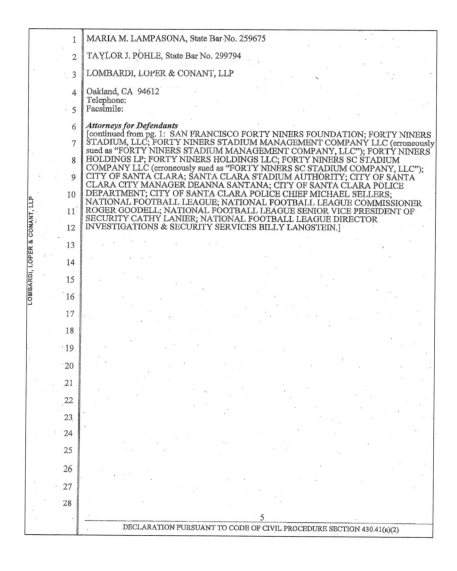

1   MARIA M. LAMPASONA, State Bar No. 259675

2   TAYLOR J. POHLE, State Bar No. 299794

3   LOMBARDI, LOPER & CONANT, LLP

4   Oakland, CA 94612
       Telephone:

5   Facsimile:

6   ***Attorneys for Defendants***
       [continued from pg. 1: SAN FRANCISCO FORTY NINERS FOUNDATION; FORTY NINERS

7   STADIUM, LLC; FORTY NINERS STADIUM MANAGEMENT COMPANY LLC (erroneously
       sued as "FORTY NINERS STADIUM MANAGEMENT COMPANY, LLC"); FORTY NINERS

8   HOLDINGS LP; FORTY NINERS HOLDINGS LLC; FORTY NINERS SC STADIUM
       COMPANY LLC (erroneously sued as "FORTY NINERS SC STADIUM COMPANY, LLC");

9   CITY OF SANTA CLARA; SANTA CLARA STADIUM AUTHORITY; CITY OF SANTA
       CLARA CITY MANAGER DEANNA SANTANA; CITY OF SANTA CLARA POLICE

10   DEPARTMENT; CITY OF SANTA CLARA POLICE CHIEF MICHAEL SELLERS;
       NATIONAL FOOTBALL LEAGUE; NATIONAL FOOTBALL LEAGUE COMMISSIONER

11   ROGER GOODELL; NATIONAL FOOTBALL LEAGUE SENIOR VICE PRESIDENT OF
       SECURITY CATHY LANIER; NATIONAL FOOTBALL LEAGUE DIRECTOR

12   INVESTIGATIONS & SECURITY SERVICES BILLY LANGSTEIN.]

13

14

15

16

17

18

19

20

21

22

23

24

25

26

27

28

LOMBARDI, LOPER & CONANT, LLP

5

DECLARATION PURSUANT TO CODE OF CIVIL PROCEDURE SECTION 430.41(a)(2)

EXHIBIT A

Ralph A. Lombardi (Ret.)
Bruce P. Loper (Ret.)
Matthew S. Conant (Ret.)
John W. Ranucci
Maria M. Lampasona

**LOMBARDI, LOPER
& CONANT, LLP**

Taylor J. Pohle
Sheena B. Patel

Oakland, California 94612

June 3, 2019

<u>VIA FACSIMILE & E-MAIL</u>

Mr. Frederick Leo Weaver
650 Castro Street, Suite 120-211
Mountain View, CA 94041
Fred@UnsafeInAnySeat.com

Re: <u>Frederick Leo Weaver v. San Francisco Forty Niners, Ltd. et al.</u>
Santa Clara County Superior Court, Case No. 19CV346749

Dear Mr. Weaver:

My firm was recently retained to represent the San Francisco Forty Niners, Ltd., San Francisco Forty Niners II, LLC, Forty Niners Football Company LLC, San Francisco Forty Niners Foundation, Forty Niners Stadium, LLC, Forty Niners Stadium Management Company LLC, Forty Niners Holdings LP, Forty Niners Holdings LLC, the Forty Niners SC Stadium Company LLC (collectively, the "Forty Niners Entities"), the City of Santa Clara (the "City"), the Santa Clara Stadium Authority (the "Authority"), the Santa Clara Police Department (the "SCPD"), Chief of Police Michael Sellers, City Manager Deanna Santana, the National Football League (the "NFL"), Commissioner Roger Goodell, Vice President Cathy Lanier, and Billy Langenstein (all collectively, the "Defendants") in the above referenced action that you filed on May 1, 2019. Going forward, direct all communications related to this matter to my office.

This letter identifies many deficiencies and defects that appear of the face of your Complaint for Damages and serves as an attempt to initiate a meet and confer discussion. The Complaint is susceptible to demurrer for failure to state causes of action and for uncertainty. *See* Code Civ. Proc. § 430.10(e), (f). The Complaint is also susceptible to a motion to strike because it contains irrelevant, false, and improper matters. *See* Code Civ. Proc. § 436(a). What follows below is not meant to be an exhaustive list, and Defendants reserve all rights related to all potential defenses.

I. **THE COMPLAINT IS SUSCEPTIBLE TO DEMURRER FOR FAILURE TO STATE CAUSES OF ACTION UNDER CALIFORNIA LAW AND FOR UNCERTAINTY**

Demurrers test the legal sufficiency of the pleadings. *Donabedian v. Mercury Ins. Co.* (2004) 116 Cal.App.4th 968, 994. Demurrers are appropriate where the complaint "does not state facts sufficient to constitute the cause of action." Code Civ. Proc. § 430.10(e). Complaints

June 3, 2019
Page 2

do not state facts sufficient to constitute a cause of action when they do not state any valid cause of action. *Quelimane Co. v. Stewart Title Guaranty Co.* (1998) 19 Cal.4th 26, 38-39.

The Complaint for Damages identifies six causes of actions against each and every defendant, and they are: (1) "Negligence"; (2) "Premises Liability – Failure to Provide Safe Premises – Dangerous Condition of Public Property"; (3) "Negligent Stadium Security – Negligent Hiring, Supervision, and Supervision"; (4) "Gross Neglect of Duty – Gross Misconduct"; (5) "Discrimination"; and (6) "Conspiracy." Each of these causes of action is susceptible to demurrer because they do not state a viable cause of action under California law.

A.   Negligence & Negligent Stadium Security (Causes of Action Nos 1, 3)

The thrust of the "Negligence" (Cause of Action #1) and "Negligent Stadium Security" (Cause of Action #3) claims is Defendants' alleged failure to provide adequate security on or about November 1, 2018. The Complaint alleges, specifically, that the Defendants had a "duty of care to Plaintiff, Victim Crain and the general public," [*see* Complaint at ¶ 101], to "take reasonable security precautions for the benefit of the spectators at Levi's Stadium," [*see* Complaint at ¶ 102], and to "warn patrons of known dangers," [*see* Complaint at ¶ 123], at Levi's Stadium. There is citation to an alleged "special relationship doctrine" at ¶¶ 31, 125.

The California Government Code holds public entities and their employees to a different legal standard as compared to private entities and individuals. *See* Gov't Code § 815 *et seq.* Because of the differences in the applicable legal standards, this letter separates the analysis between the Public Entity defendants (the "Public Entity defendants" includes: the City, the Authority, the SCPD, Mr. Sellers, and Ms. Sellers) and the Non-Public Entity defendants (the "Non-Public Entity defendants" include the Forty Niners entities, the NFL, and the NFL executives), with respect to the negligence and negligent stadium security analyses.

1.   Legal Standing

Before addressing the sufficiency of the negligence and negligent stadium security allegations with respect to the public entity and non-public entity defendants, it is important to consider the legal doctrine called "standing" or, in other words, the right to relief in Court. In California, "every action must be prosecuted in the name of the real party in interest." *See* Code Civ. Proc. § 367. Although it is somewhat unclear from the Complaint's allegations, to the extent that you intend to bring claims on behalf of Mr. Vincent Crain, or any Levi's Stadium spectator other than yourself, you lack standing to assert negligence claims on their behalf. To the extent this is your intent, the Complaint fails to state causes of action as to these individuals.

2.   The Public Entity Defendants

Public entities, and their employees, enjoy an array of immunities codified by the Legislature in the California Government Code, many of which relate directly to law enforcement. *See* Gov. Code §§ 818.2, 820.2, 821, 845, and 846. These immunities provide

341

June 3, 2019
Page 3

affirmative defenses to the negligent security and/or police protection claims presented in the Complaint and act, collectively and in isolation, to immunize the Public Entity defendants from any potential liability for alleged negligent acts related to law enforcement. The two most applicable to the alleged fact pattern are Government Code sections 845 and 846.

California Government Code section 845 immunizes *public entities and their employees* "for failure to provide sufficient police protection service." *See* Gov. Code § 845. The Legislature intended for Section 845 to offer public entities wide protection:

> Whether police protection should be provided at all, and the extent to which it should be provided, are political decisions which are committed to the policy-making officials of government. To permit review of these decisions by judges and juries would remove the ultimate decision-making authority from those politically responsible for making the decisions." (Cal. Law Revision Com. com., 32 West's Ann. Gov. Code (1995 ed.) foll. § 845, p. 452).

Section 845 immunity applies even where a plaintiff creates a question of fact as to the foreseeability of harm associated with lack of security. For example, in *Turner v. State of California* (1991) 232 Cal.App.3d 883, despite evidence of prior gang violence at a state fairgrounds, the Third District Court of Appeal determined that the State was immune from allegedly failing to provide security patrols. Similarly, in *Zelig v. County of Los Angeles* (2002) 27 Cal.4th 1112, the California Supreme Court refused to entertain plaintiff's argument at the demurrer stage that the County could be held liable for improper screening of persons entering a courthouse because "plaintiffs' claim goes to the essence of the county's discretion in determining how much police protection to provide and how to allocate its resources." *Id.* at 1144. Section 845 bars any negligent security claims against the Public Entity defendants.

California Government Code section 846 provides that "Neither a public entity nor a public employee is liable *for injury caused by the failure to make an arrest* or by the failure to retain an arrested person in custody." (Emphasis Added). The allegations set forth in the Complaint implicate this immunity because you allege, in part, that your injuries were caused by Levi's Stadium's security's and police presence's failure to identify and/or apprehend the alleged assailant at Levi's Stadium. The Public Entity defendants therefore are immune, and the Complaint fails to state negligence causes of action for negligence or negligent security.

3. The Non-Public Entity Defendants

The Complaint's allegations portray you, firstly, as a distant bystander to a physical assault, [*see* Complaint at ¶¶ 45, 46], and, secondly, as a good Samaritan in pursuit to apprehend a fleeing assailant, [*see* Complaint at ¶¶ 47-51]. Each portion of the incident deserves a separate

June 3, 2019
Page 4

analysis under California law. Your witnessing of the alleged physical assault requires a bystander analysis under *Dillon v. Legg* (1968) 68 Cal.2d 728 because you were not a party to the physical assault. Your pursuit of the alleged assailment, and the alleged resulting injury, requires a more traditional negligence analysis regarding duty, breach, causation, and damages.

i.   *Dillon v. Legg* Bystander Analysis

The general rule in California is that defendants are not liable in negligence to plaintiffs who merely witness an injury. *Dillon v. Legg* (1968) 68 Cal.2d 728. The exception to the rule is that plaintiffs may recover for negligent infliction of emotional distress for witnessing an injury, but only if they are (a) at the scene and witness the injury *and* (b) the victim is one of their close relatives. *See* California Civil Jury Instruction ("CACI") No. 1621. Close relatives are "relatives residing in the same household, or parents, siblings, children, and grandparents of the victim." *See Thing v. La Chusa* (1989) 48 Cal.3d 644, 668, fn. 10. Here, the Complaint makes no allegation that the alleged victim, Mr. Crain, was your close relative and therefore, under California case law, you may not recover as a matter of law from any alleged injury suffered in witnessing the alleged assault on November 1, 2018.

ii.   General Negligence Pursuit Analysis

The allegations related to your pursuit of the alleged assailant also do not state a cause of action in negligence. The essential elements of negligence are "(a) a legal duty to use due care; (b) a breach of such legal duty; [and] (c) the breach as the proximate or legal cause of the resulting injury." *Ladd v. County of San Mateo* (1996) 12 Cal.4th 913, 917. The existence of a legal duty is a question for the Court. *Kentucky Fried Chicken of Cal. v. Superior Court* (1997) 14 Cal.4th 814, 819. Where reasonable minds can only come to one conclusion, causation is decided by the Court, as a matter of law. *Ash v. North American Title Co.* (2014) 223 Cal.App.4th 1258, 1279. Based on the Complaint's allegations, any alleged breach of the applicable of the standard of care afforded to you as a spectator at Levi's Stadium was not the legal cause of your injuries because the Complaint identifies a superseding legal cause.

The Complaint's allegations show that you allegedly sustained injury because of the physical exertion in chasing the assailant through Levi's Stadium after the physical assault had concluded: "*Plaintiff was limping due to excruciating pain having to chase the Assailant Guardado three quarters of the length of Levi's Stadium in an attempt to keep the Assailant from hurting any other Levi's Stadium patrons,*" [*see* Complaint at ¶ 51]. Based on this allegation, it is clear that any alleged breach of the applicable standard of care was not the proximate or legal cause of your alleged injuries.

/ / /

/ / /

June 3, 2019
Page 5

Quoting from *Ash v. North American Title Co., supra,* 223 Cal.App.4th at 1274:

> The Restatement Second of Torts distinguishes between
> "superseding cause" and "intervening force." The Restatement
> Second of Torts, section 440, provides that "*a superseding cause is
> an act of a third person or other force which by its intervention
> prevents the actor from being liable for harm to another which his
> antecedent negligence is a substantial factor in bringing about.*"
> The Restatement Second of Torts, section 441, subdivision (1)
> states, "An intervening force is one which actively operates in
> producing harm to another after the actor's negligent act or
> omission has been committed." Another authority states, "An
> intervening act is regarded as a superseding cause when it is outside
> the scope of the risk the defendant negligently created. This idea is
> usually expressed in shorthand by saying that if the intervening act
> is itself unforeseeable then it may become a superseding cause." (1
> Dobbs et al., The Law of Torts (2d ed. 2011) § 212, p. 741
> (Dobbs).)
>
> *A superseding cause relieves a defendant from tort liability for a
> plaintiff's injuries, if both the intervening act and the results of
> the act are not foreseeable.* "[W]hat is required to be foreseeable is
> the general character of the event or harm ... not its precise nature or
> manner of occurrence." (*Bigbee v. Pacific Tel. & Tel. Co.* (1983) 34
> Cal.3d 49, 57-58.) "Whether an intervening force is superseding or
> not generally presents a question of fact, but becomes a matter of
> law where only one reasonable conclusion may be reached.
> [Citation.]" (*Chanda v. Federal Home Loans Corp.* (2013) 215
> Cal.App.4th 746, 756; see *Perez v. VAS S.p.A.* (2010) 188
> Cal.App.4th 658, 680-68.) [bold and italicized emphasis added;
> some internal citations omitted].

Even assuming *arguendo* that the Non-Public Entity defendants breached their duty of
care in the context of allowing the physical assault to occur, reasonable minds can only come to
one conclusion regarding causation: the Complaint alleges that a superseding cause is to blame
for your alleged injury. *See* Complaint at ¶¶ 45-51. The intervening act, *i.e.,* your decision to
pursue the alleged assailant and chase him around Levi's Stadium was not a foreseeable response
to the situation. The results of the intervening act, *i.e.,* injuring yourself from physical exertion
in chasing the alleged assailant, was not a foreseeable injury. For this reason, because the

June 3, 2019
Page 6

allegations demonstrate a superseding cause, the Complaint does not state causes of action for negligence and/ negligent stadium security[1] against the Non-Public Entity defendants.

B.   Premises Liability / Dangerous Condition of Property of Public Property (Cause of Action No. 2)

Much like the analysis above with respect to negligence and negligent stadium security, different analyses are required regarding the Complaint's premises liability claim because the California Government Code holds public entities to a different standard than their private counterparts. *See* Gov't Code § 835 *et seq.* The basis for the Complaint's premises liability cause of action appears to be based on the allegations that the combination of alcohol sales and the failure to use "high-technology security and camera system" created an allegedly dangerous condition of criminal activity. *See* Complaint at ¶¶ 129-144.

1.   The Public Entity Defendants

First, as stated above, public entities and their employees have statutory immunity against claims of alleged inadequate security. *See* Gov. Code § 845. Because the Complaint's premises liability cause of action is based primarily on lack of security and the operation of Levi's Stadium (as distinguished from a physical defect in the property), the public entity defendants enjoy absolute immunity from any such claims regardless of whether they are labeled as "negligence" claims, "negligent stadium security" claims, or "premises lability" claims.

Second, public entities are liable only to the extent allowable by statute. *See* Gov. Code § 815. In other words, public entities are not subject to the vague, amorphous negligence and premises liability common law legal doctrines like "ordinary care" or "reasonable care"; instead, we must look to statute to find the appropriate standard of care. Government Code section 835 provides the statutory framework for claims of dangerous condition of property. Plaintiffs must prove that a *physical defect* in the property created a substantial risk of harm to the public:

> "Liability for injury caused by a dangerous condition of property has been imposed when an unreasonable risk of harm is created by a combination of defect in the property and acts of third parties. However, ***courts have consistently refused to characterize harmful third party conduct as a dangerous condition—absent some concurrent contributing defect in the property itself.***" *Hayes v. State of California* (1974) 11 Cal.3d 469, 472. (bold and italicized emphasis added).

---

[1] The claims related to negligent hiring, supervision, or retention is dependent on an underlying negligent act insofar as negligence must be the proximate or legal cause of the injury. *See* CACI No. 426. Therefore, with respect to the Complaint's allegations regarding negligent hiring, supervision, and retention, the causation analysis and the existence of a superseding cause acts to eliminate these claims as well.

June 3, 2019
Page 7

Here, the Complaint does not allege any *physical defect* in the property that combined with or contributed to criminal activity and, therefore, the Complaint is subject to demurrer because it does not state a viable cause of action against the public entities related to premise liability under the Government Code. The dangerous condition claims necessarily fail.

2.   The Non-Public Entity Defendants

The same analysis above, *see* I.A.3., applies here because the allegations within the Complaint's premises liability cause of action are substantially similar to the allegations contained with the Complaint's general negligence and negligent stadium security claims.

C.   Gross Neglect of Duty / Gross Misconduct (Cause of Action No. 4)

The Complaint's "Gross Neglect of Duty – Gross Misconduct" claim is susceptible to demurrer both because it does not state a viable cause of action under California law, and because it is uncertain (not only as to which defendant or defendants to which it is attached, but also the nature and scope of the alleged misconduct). Code Civ. Proc. § 430.10(e), (f).

The allegations in support of this cause of action at first identify an alleged violation of California Penal Code section 118.1 on the part of the SCPD in regards to falsifying police reports related to the November 1, 2018 incident. *See* Complaint at ¶ 156. But, from there, the allegations detail some unrelated misconduct dating back to the 2016, [*see* Complaint at ¶ 159], and a failure to produce documents that you allegedly requested, [*see* Complaint at ¶ 168]. Included within this cause of action is the allegation that "DEFENDANTS, and each of them, owed Plaintiff and the general public a duty to conduct their business activities, including monitoring, supervising, managing and controlling the property, in a reasonably safe manner so as not to cause injury to others. Further, DEFENDANTS, and each of them, owed Plaintiff and the general public a duty to train and supervise their employees to conduct themselves in a reasonably safe manner so as not to injure others." *See* Complaint at ¶ 169.

Gross negligence is an extreme departure from the ordinary standard of conduct that is tantamount to reckless behavior, but *gross negligence is not, by itself, an independent cause of action*. *See Eriksson v. Nunninck* (2011) 192 Cal.App.4th 1072. Gross negligence must be tied to a statute that distinguishes between ordinary negligence and gross negligence. *See Cont'l Ins. Co. v. Am. Prot. Indus.* (1987) 197 Cal.App.3d 322, 329. Here, the Complaint identifies Penal Code section 118.1 as the operative statute. Penal Code section 118.1 is a criminal statute that provides that police officers may not deliberately include false information regarding a material matter in a police report. The statute does not distinguish between ordinary negligence and gross negligence. Furthermore, not every criminal act can be the basis of a civil lawsuit. Penal Code section 118.1 does not provide any basis to bring a civil action in relation to an allegedly falsified police report. For these reasons, the gross neglect claim as alleged in the Complaint for Damages does not state a cause of action and is susceptible to demurrer.

June 3, 2019
Page 8

Also problematic is that the gross neglect claim is uncertain as to which defendant or defendants to which it attaches. The heading states "Against all DEFENDANTS," however, the allegations appear to implicate only the City, the Authority, the SCPD, Police Chief Michael Sellers, and other unidentified "policy making officers." *See* Complaint at ¶ 157. Furthermore, the Complaint also is uncertain because it discusses alleged falsified police reports related to the November 2018 incident, but it also discusses incidents that occurred in 2016, waste of funds, and other vague allegations regarding the City's policies and practices. For these reasons, the Complaint is also susceptible to demurrer because it is uncertain. Code Civ. Proc. § 430.10(f).

D. Discrimination Under 42 U.S.C. § 1983 (Cause of Action No. 5)

The Complaint alleges that all defendants violated, by way of 42 U.S.C. section 1983, the plaintiff's equal protection rights under the 14th Amendment to the United States Constitution on the basis of age, disability and color discrimination. *See* Complaint at ¶ 172. This cause of action is deficient as to all defendants, but for different reasons. As to the Non-Public Entity defendants, the Complaint does not state a cause of action because they are not state actors and there is no allegation they acted under the color of the law. As to the Public-Entity defendants, the Complaint does not state a cause of action for three reasons: (1) there is no allegation you are a member of any protected class of persons; (2) there is no allegation of any causal nexus between the alleged discriminatory conduct and an injury; and (3) most importantly, although 42 U.S.C. section 1983 provides the legal vehicle to bring discrimination claims before the Court, there is no affirmative duty under federal law that requires police to act, restrain, or investigate.

1. The Non-Public Entity Defendants Are Not State Actors

As to the Non-Public Entity defendants, the Complaint's Fifth Cause of Action for discrimination under the 14th Amendment fails because these defendants are not state actors.

Under the Civil Rights Act of 1871, claims arising under 42 U.S.C. § 1983 are actionable when someone acting "under color of" state-level or local law has deprived a person of rights created by the U.S. Constitution or federal statutes. *Brunette v. Humane Society of Ventura County* (9th Cir. 2002) 294 F.3d 1205, 1209, *Gritchen v. Collier* (9th Cir. 2001) 254 F.3d 807, 813; *Lopez v. Dep't of Health Servs.* (9th Cir. 1991) 939 F.2d 881, 883 (per curiam). Generally, private parties are not acting under color of state law. See *Price v. Hawaii* (9th Cir. 1991) 939 F.2d 702, 707-08, *Simmons v. Sacramento* (9th Cir. 2003) 318 F.3d 1156, 1161.

Conclusory allegations that a particular defendant is acting under the color of state law are insufficient. In *Simmons*, cited above, a plaintiff who sustained injuries in an automobile accident filed a suit for civil rights violations under section 1983 naming the other driver's attorney as a defendant. The *Simmons* court explained that plaintiff had no claim under section 1983 against the driver's attorney "because he is a lawyer in private practice who was not acting under color of state law." *Id.* at 1161. The *Simmons* court went on to say that "Plaintiff's conclusory allegations that the lawyer was conspiring with state officers to deprive him of due process are insufficient." *Id.*

Here, the only allegation reasonably related to a "color of the law" arguments appears at paragraph 174 where the Complaint states, *inter alia*: "This claim of Discrimination satisfies the three preliminary requirements that apply throughout constitutional law; Court has Jurisdiction, Claim is Justiciable; *and Harm was Caused by Government Action of DEFENDANTS.*" (Emphasis Added). This conclusory allegation is insufficient and, as a result, the Complaint fails to state of viable claims against the Non-Public Entity defendants for discrimination under 42 USC section 1983.

2. Federal Law Does Not Place an Affirmative Duty on Law Enforcement Officers to Provide Police Protection

The equal protection clause of the Fourteenth Amendment of the United States Constitution provides that no State shall "deny to any person within its jurisdiction the equal protection of the laws." Section 1983 is not a source of substantive rights and *it is only provides a method to vindicate federal rights*. *Graham v. Connor* (1989) 490 U.S. 386, 393-394. State Courts look to federal law to determine what conduct will support a 1983 action. *See Weaver v. State of California* (2015) 242 Cal.App.4th 265, 280.

Here, the Complaint alleges age, disability, and color discrimination in the context a law enforcement officer's failure to assist a citizen's arrest. *See* Complaint at ¶¶ 173, 174. The operative allegation is "The Defendant Santa Clara Police officer literally, and physically turned his back on Plaintiff avoiding assistance with apprehension of the ASSAILANT and denying protection and security to the Plaintiff who trying to keep ASSAILANT from harming any other Levi's Stadium patrons." *See* Complaint at ¶ 173:16-19.

The Complaint's allegations are insufficient to state a cause of action under 42 USC § 1983 for age, disability, and color discrimination for three reasons.

First, there are no allegations in the Complaint that place you within a legally recognized protected class of persons. Under current federal law, the prohibition against age discrimination exists only in the employment context. *See, e.g.,* The Age Discrimination in Employment Act (ADEA). Disabled persons are defined under the Americans with Disabilities Act as individuals with "a physical or mental impairment that substantially limits one or more major life activities of such individual," those individuals with a "record of such an impairment," and those individuals "being regarded as having such an impairment." *See* 42 U.S.C. § 12102(1). Expressly excluded from the definition of "disability" are impairments that are "transitory and minor," *i.e.,* an impairment with an actual or expected duration of 6 months or less. *See* 42 U.S.C. § 12102(3). The Complaint's allegation that you were "limping" after chasing the alleged assailment undoubtedly falls with the category of "transitory and minor" impairments. As to "color" discrimination, there is no allegation as to race or ethnicity, only an allegation as to the

June 3, 2019
Page 10

color of your clothing. *See* Complaint at ¶ 173. There is no legal precedent placing individuals wearing a certain color of clothing within a protected class.

Second, even if you did fall within a protected class of persons, which you do not, there is no allegation linking your protected status to an identifiable injury. By the time the unidentified Santa Clara Police officer "literally, and physically turned his back" on you, your alleged injury (*i.e.,* your alleged hip injury) had already occurred.

Third, and most importantly, well-established Supreme Court case law confirms that police are under no affirmative duty to assist and protect. *See, e.g., DeShaney vs. Winnebago County Department of Social Services* (1989) 489 U.S. 189, 200 ("The affirmative duty to protect arises not from the State's knowledge of the individual's predicament, but from the limitation which it has imposed on his freedom to act on his own behalf..."); *Town of Castle Rick v. Gonzales* (2005) 545 U.S. 748 (police department cannot be sued under 42 USC section 1983 for failure to enforce a restraining order). The Complaint therefore fails to state a cause of action under 42 USC section 1983 for discriminatory action against the Public Entity defendants.

E. Conspiracy (Cause of Action No. 6)

The Complaint alleges that "on or about November 1, 2018 through and after January 8, 2019," the defendants, with Santa Clara City Manager Deanna Santana at the helm, "conspired to conceal information, falsify reports, hide, and cover up any incriminating records." *See* Complaint at ¶¶ 182, 183. The Complaint further includes allegations about "Ms. Santana's career dating back to May 1999, [*see* Complaint at ¶ 183], and further alleges, it appears, that the alleged conspiracy is ongoing, [*see* Complaint at 189]. This claim is susceptible to demurrer with respect to each and every defendant because civil conspiracy is not an independently viable cause of action under California law:

> "Conspiracy is not a cause of action, but a legal doctrine
> that imposes liability on persons who, although not
> actually committing a tort themselves, share with the
> immediate tortfeasors a common plan or design in its
> perpetration." *Applied Equipment Corp. v. Litton Saudi
> Arabia Ltd.* (1994) 7 Cal.4th 503, 510–511.

Because conspiracy is not a cause of action under California law, the allegations in the Complaint related to conspiracy, [*see* Complaint at ¶¶ 181 – 195], do not a cause of action. Furthermore, it is unclear what is the underlying tort related to your conspiracy claim. Withholding, concealing, or hiding information in not a recognized tort. Falsifying reports, although possibly a criminal act, does not give rise to viable civil cause of action. *See* Penal Code § 118.1. To the extent the conspiracy claim is at all linked to claims of negligent security and/or premises liability, the analysis above controls.

June 3, 2019
Page 11

II. THE COMPLAINT IS SUSCEPTIBLE TO A MOTION TO STRIKE BECAUSE IT CONTAINS "IRRELEVANT, FALSE, AND IMPROPER MATTERS" IN VIOLATION OF CCP § 436

California Code of Civil Procedure section 436 states that the Court may, upon a motion made pursuant to Section 435, or at any time in its discretion, strike out any irrelevant, false, or improper matter inserted in any pleading. Irrelevant matters include those matters that are either "not essential to the statement of a claim or defense" and those "neither pertinent to nor supported by an otherwise sufficient claim or defense." *See* Code Civ. Proc § 431.10. There are many allegations and other matters that should be stricken from the Complaint.

A. Improper Case Law Citations

Complaints are pleadings that include "a statement of the facts constituting the cause of action in ordinary and concise language. Code Civ. Proc. § 425.10. Legal conclusions and citations to case law are necessarily irrelevant matters because they are not essential to the statement of a claim or defense and, therefore, are susceptible to a motion to strike. Code Civ. Proc. §§ 431.10, 436. The Complaint includes citations to case law at the following locations: at ¶ 4:25-28 in re *American Needle, Inc. v. NFL* and ¶ 8:1-6 and ¶ 27:22-27in re: *Delgado v. Trax Bar*. These matters are not ultimate facts and must be stricken from the Complaint.

B. Public Entities Are Immune from Punitive Damages

Public entities are not liable for damages awarded under section 3294 of the Civil Code or other damages imposed primarily for the sake of example and by way of punishing the defendant. *See* Gov. Code § 818. Here, Plaintiff prays for the same relief with respect to every Defendant, including "exemplary damages" and "punitive damages under 42 U.S.C. section 1983 and California law." *And see also,* ¶ 99 regarding all defendants owe punitive damages under 3294. Therefore, with respect to the City, the Authority, and the SCPD, these references to punitive damages must be stricken from the Complaint.

C. There are Insufficient Allegations to Support Punitive Damages

It is well-established that allegations for punitive damages must be pled with sufficient specificity such that defendant is provided with adequate notice of the kind of conduct charged against him. *Smith v. Superior Court* (1992) 10 Cal.App.4th 1033, 1041 (citations omitted). Conclusory allegations of oppression, fraud and / or malice[2] do not support a claim for punitive

---

[2] Civil Code section 3294 includes the following definitions

(1) "Malice" means conduct which is intended by the defendant to cause injury to the plaintiff or despicable conduct which is carried on by the defendant with a willful and conscious disregard of the rights or safety of others.

June 3, 2019
Page 12

damages. *Id.* Instead, factual allegations of wrongful motive, intent or purpose must be pled. *Cyrus v. Haveson* (1977) 65 Cal.App.3d 306, 317.

In order to support a claim for punitive damages, the claim must be supported with facts indicating either an intent to injure, or despicable conduct, referring to circumstances that are base, vile or contemptible. *See College Hospital, Inc. v. Superior* Court (1994) 8 Cal.4th 704, 725. The conduct complained of must have "the character of outrage frequently associated with crime." *American Airlines, Inc. v. Sheppard, Mullin, Richter & Hampton* (2002) 96 Cal.App.4th 1017, 1050 (citations omitted). "Mere spite or ill will is not sufficient; and mere negligence, even gross negligence is not sufficient to justify an award of punitive damages." *Ebaugh v. Rabkin* (1972) 22 Cal.App.3d 891, 894 (emphasis in original).

Here, the Complaint asserts general and conclusory allegations related to intentional and/or "willful and conscious disregard" that are directed not any one defendant in particular, but are espoused against all defendants as a group. These allegations include:

> 99.   The DEFENDANT[3]'S actions and knowing omissions
> constituted malice, oppression, and/or a willful and conscious
> disregard of the rights and safety of Plaintiff and the general public
> pursuant to California Code of Civil Procedure § 3294 entitling
> Plaintiff to punitive damages. These punitive damages should
> serve to punish DEFENDANTS for their conscious disregard of
> safety and to discourage similar conduct in the future.
>
> *****
> 144.   Additionally, Plaintiff is informed and believes, and
> thereon alleges, the DEFENDANTS, and each of them, knew that
> their failure to provide adequate security at the Levi's Stadium
> would lead to criminal acts on spectators as described more fully
> above. Therefore, a demand for punitive damages is warranted.
>
> *****

---

(2) "Oppression" means despicable conduct that subjects a person to cruel and unjust hardship in conscious disregard of that person's rights.

(3) "Fraud" means an intentional misrepresentation, deceit, or concealment of a material fact known to the defendant with the intention on the part of the defendant of thereby depriving a person of property or legal rights or otherwise causing injury.

[3] The term "DEFENDANTS" is not defined in your Complaint for Damages.

June 3, 2019
Page 13

> 188.   Plaintiff is informed and believes and thereon alleges, that on or about November 1, 2018, said DEFENDANTS, intentionally, willfully, wantonly, and maliciously conspired against Plaintiff against Plaintiff's actions taken to prevent any further acts of violence against other patrons at Levi's Stadium.

These allegations do not indicate the any of the defendants acted with intent to injure the Plaintiff.   Therefore, according to Civil Code section 3294 the only remaining basis to support allegations of malice or oppression would be allegations demonstrating "despicable conduct." However, the Complaint does not indicate any "despicable conduct" – which is "a powerful term that refers to circumstances that are "base," "vile," or "contemptible" [*see College Hospital, supra,* at 725] against any one defendant.   For that reason, each defendant is not afforded adequate notice of the "despicable conduct" alleged and punitive damages are inappropriate on the Complaint's current allegations.

D.   The Defendants Are Not Liable for Furnishing Alcohol

The Complaint includes a false statement wherein it alleges: "Under the special relationship doctrine, the DEFENDANTS, and each of them by serving intoxicating drinks to patrons for consumption on its premises, must exercise reasonable care to protect patrons from injury at the hand of fellow guests." *See* Complaint at ¶ 31.   First, this is a legal conclusion and not a material fact. Second, this is an incorrect statement of the law.   Civil Code section 1714(c) states that "[N]o social host who furnishes alcoholic beverages to any person may be held legally accountable for damages suffered by that person, or for injury to the person or property of, or death of, any third person, resulting from the consumption of those beverages."   References to incorrect statements of law, such as this one, must be stricken from the Complaint.

E.   The Complaint Includes Several "Immaterial Allegations"

Complaints that contain "immaterial allegations" are susceptible to a motion to strike. *See* Code Civ. Proc. §§ 431.10, 436.   "[T]he complaint need only allege facts sufficient to state a cause of action; each evidentiary fact that might eventually form part of the plaintiff's proof need not be alleged." *See C.A. v. William S. Hart Union High School District* (2012) 53 Cal.4th 861, 872.   Therefore, because evidentiary allegations are unnecessary to the causes of action, evidentiary allegations are "immaterial". *See* Code of Civ. Proc. §§ 431.10 & 436.

The Complaint alleges the following evidentiary facts, which must be stricken from the Complaint because they are either immaterial or irrelevant: ¶ 28 (in re: 49ers Raiders rivalry) ¶ 29 (in re: Joe Montana – "keep families at home") ¶ 33 (in re: a nationally televised game), ¶ 34 (in re: the capacity of Levi's Stadium), ¶ 35-40 (in re: the extent of security), ¶ 55 (in re: KNBR news report and video), ¶ 76a (in re: August 24, 2017 agenda report), ¶ 83(a-e) (in re past violent acts), ¶ 105, (in re: coming back on 12/16/18 -evidentiary pleading), ¶ 116 (in re other cases) ¶

June 3, 2019
Page 14

125 (in re: special relationship doctrine – legal conclusion), ¶ 151 (Plaintiff coming back to Stadium) ¶ 159 (a-b) (in re: other criminal activity), ¶ 183 (in re: Deanna Santana's career).

F. Attorneys' Fees

The Complaint seemingly prays for attorneys' fees in connection with prosecution of this lawsuit under 42 U.S.C. sections 1983, 1988, Code of Civil Procedure section 1021.5, and Civil Code sections 52, 52.1. You are a self-represented litigant. Because you are self-represented, attorneys' fees would be inappropriate because none will be incurred for the duration of this lawsuit. *See, e.g.,* Trope v. Katz (1995) 11 Cal.4th 274 (in re: Civil Code § 1717); *see also* the unpublished opinion *Altmann v. City of Agoura Hills City Council* (2008) Second District, B202996 (in re: Code of Civil Procedure § 1021.5). Regardless of the fact that you are not represented by and attorney, your claim for attorneys' fees under 42 U.S.C. sections 1983, 1988 is inappropriate because you do not state a viable cause of action under 42 U.S.C. section 1983 as described earlier in this letter. Moreover, your claim for attorneys' fees under Civ. Code sections 52, 52.1 (aka the Unruh Civil Rights Act) is inappropriate because the Complaint omits any cause of action or claim for a violation of the Unruh Civil Rights Act, [*see* CACI No. 3060], and this prayer of relief is therefore inappropriate. For these reasons, your prayer for attorneys' fees must be stricken from the Complaint.

G. The Complaint's Requests for Injunctive Relief is Improper

The Complaint prays for injunctive relief, but the types of injunctive relief are improper for one of two reasons: (1) the relief requested is not based on any *imminent harm* and (2) the Superior Court for the County of Santa Clara, a California state court, lacks subject matter jurisdiction to issue "an order of Federal Oversight." For these reasons, each and every request for injunctive relief should be stricken from the Complaint.

The Complaint includes the following injunctive relief requests:

d. Injunctive relief, including but not limited to the following:

1. An order prohibiting [SCPD] and its Chief of Police from engaging in the unconstitutional customs, policies, practices, procedures, training and supervision *as may be determined* and/or adjudged by this case.

2. An order prohibiting [SCPD] and their law enforcement officers from engaging in the "code of silence' as may be supported by the evidence …

3. An order of Federal Oversight of [SCPD], similar to recent Federal oversight in Chicago, Oakland, New York, Detroit, and Cincinnati Police Departments.

353

4. And order of Federal Oversight of [the NFL] to ensure all North American NFL Stadiums and Venues benefit from shared and uniform safety and security measures.

5. An order compelling DEFENDANTS to correct the deficiencies in security and failures to protect the public detailed in this Complaint.

Injunctions may be issued where there is a showing of "irreparable harm." *See* Code Civ. Proc. § 526(a)(2). Irreparable harm is harm that must be imminent, as opposed to a mere possibility of harm in the future. Key language on this issue comes from *Korean Philadelphia Presbyterian Church v. California Presbytery* (2000) 77 Cal.App.4th 1069, 1084:

An injunction cannot issue in a vacuum based on the proponents fears about something that may happen in the future. It must be supported by actual evidence that there is a realistic prospect that the party enjoined intends to engage in the prohibited activity.

All of the requests for injunctive relief fail this test because there are no allegations that any defendant intends to continue any alleged wrongful conduct. Furthermore, there is no allegation that any intended conduct is imminent against you: *e.g.,* there is no allegation you intend to return to Levi's Stadium for any event and that harm to you is imminent.

The requests for injunctive relief for "an order of Federal Oversight" fail because this state court lack the subject matter jurisdiction necessary to award such extraordinary relief because there is the issue of pre-emption. *See* 34 U.S.C. § 12601 (which provides the authority for the Department of Justice to investigate law enforcement agencies that may be violating federal rights). Even a request for State oversight would likely fail. *See, e.g., Alvarado v. Selma Convalescent Hosp.* (2007) 153 Cal.App.4th 205, *Acosta v. Brown* (2012) 213 Cal.App.4th 234.

III.   CONCLUSION

None of the claims contained in the Complaint state a viable cause of action against my clients and there is no reasonable chance to cure the defects based on the allegations. For that reason, the Complaint is susceptible to demurrer and a motion to strike. On behalf of the Forty Niners Entities, the City, the Authority, the SCPD, Mr. Sellers, Ms. Santana, the NFL, Commissioner Goodell, Ms. Lanier, and Mr. Langenstein, I respectfully request that you dismiss your Complaint with prejudice so that we can avoid unnecessary motion practice. To the extent you disagree, please contact me at ‾‾‾‾‾‾‾ ᵘᵛ. or my e-mail ‾‾‾‾‾‾‾ ‾‾‾‾‾‾‾ so that we can set time to meet and confer.

Please be advised that in addition to demurring and moving to strike large segments of your Complaint, we will be filing another special motion to strike pursuant to California's anti-SLAPP statute. If that motion is successful as to any of your causes of action, an award of

June 3, 2019
Page 16

attorney's fees against you is mandatory. In the past, we have typically secured awards of fees on such motions in the range of $20,000. I look forward to your response.

Respectfully,

LOMBARDI, LOPER & CONANT, LLP

By: _____
Taylor J. Pohle

TJP:TJP

355

1	PROOF OF SERVICE
	Frederick Leo Weaver v. San Francisco Forty Niners, Limited, et al.
2	Santa Clara County Superior Court Case No. 19CV346749
3	
	I am a resident of the State of California, over 18 years of age and not a party to the
4	within action. I am employed in the County of Alameda; my business address is:
	Oakland, CA 94612. On June 3, 2019, I served the within:
5	
	DECLARATION OF TAYLOR J. POHLE, PURSUANT TO CODE OF CIVIL
6	**PROCEDURE SECTION 430.41(a)(2), REGARDING THE FORTY NINERS**
	DEFENDANTS, THE CITY DEFENDANTS, AND THE NFL DEFENDANTS'
7	**INABILITY TO MEET AND CONFER**
8	on all parties in this action, as addressed below, by causing a true copy thereof to be distributed
	as follows:
9	
	Frederick Leo Weaver
10	650 Castro Street, Suite 120-211
	Mountain View, CA 94041 Email: Fred@UnsafeInAnySeat.com
11	
	Plaintiff In Pro Per
12	
	☒ By United States Mail: I enclosed the document in a sealed envelope or package addressed to
13	the persons at the addresses listed above and placed the envelope/package for collection and mailing,
	following our ordinary business practices. I am readily familiar with this business's practice for
14	collecting and processing documents for mailing. On the same day that the document is placed for
	collection and mailing, it is deposited in the ordinary course of business with the United States Postal
15	Service, in a sealed envelope with postage fully prepaid. I am aware that on motion of the party served,
	service is presumed invalid if postal cancellation date or postage meter date is more than one day after
16	the date of deposit for mailing an affidavit.
17	I am a resident or employed in the county where the mailing occurred. The envelope or package was
	placed in the mail at Oakland, California.
18	☐ By Fax Transmission: Based on an agreement of the parties to accept service by fax
19	transmission, I faxed the documents to the persons at the fax numbers listed above. No error was
	reported by the fax machine that I used. A copy of the record of the fax transmission, which I printed
20	out, is attached.
21	☐ By Overnight Delivery: I enclosed the document(s) in an envelope or package provided by an
	overnight delivery carrier and addressed to the persons listed above. I placed the envelope or package
22	for collection and overnight delivery at an office or a regularly utilized drop box of the overnight
	delivery carrier.
23	☐ By Personal Service: I personally delivered the documents to the persons at the addresses listed
24	above. (1) For a party represented by an attorney, delivery was made to the attorney or at the attorney's
	office by leaving the documents in an envelope or package clearly labeled to identify the attorney being
25	served with the receptionist or an individual in charge of the office. (2) For a party, delivery was made
	to the party or by leaving the documents at the party's residence with some person not less than 18 years
26	of age between the hours of eight in the morning and six in the evening.
27	☐ By Messenger Service: I served the documents by placing them in an envelope or package
	addressed to the persons at the addresses listed above and providing them to a professional messenger
28	service for service.

LOMBARDI, LOPER & CONANT, LLP

5

DECLARATION PURSUANT TO CODE OF CIVIL PROCEDURE SECTION 430.41(a)(2)

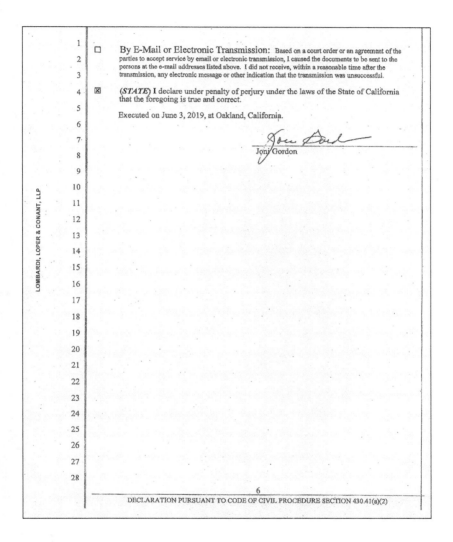

1

2 ☐ **By E-Mail or Electronic Transmission:** Based on a court order or an agreement of the parties to accept service by email or electronic transmission, I caused the documents to be sent to the persons at the e-mail addresses listed above. I did not receive, within a reasonable time after the transmission, any electronic message or other indication that the transmission was unsuccessful.

3

4 ☒ *(STATE)* I declare under penalty of perjury under the laws of the State of California that the foregoing is true and correct.

5

Executed on June 3, 2019, at Oakland, California.

6

7

8 Joni Gordon

9

10

11

12

13

14

15

16

17

18

19

20

21

22

23

24

25

26

27

28

6

DECLARATION PURSUANT TO CODE OF CIVIL PROCEDURE SECTION 430.41(a)(2)

CPSIA information can be obtained
at www.ICGtesting.com
Printed in the USA
FSHW010737260120
66496FS